MACHEL STUDY 10-YEAR STRATEGIC REVIEW

CHILDREN AND CONFLICT
IN A CHANGING WORLD

CONTENTS

FOREWORD

© UNICEF/NYHQ2005-0653/Toutounji

UNICEF was a co-convenor of the 10th anniversary strategic review of the issues raised in the landmark 1996 Machel study on the impacts of conflict on children. UNICEF welcomes the publication of this review, titled *Machel Study 10-Year Strategic Review: Children and Conflict in a Changing World,* which aims to serve as an advocacy and policy tool on children and armed conflict, and as the foundation of a platform for action.

The findings of the report are the results of a wide-ranging, multi-stakeholder process that included participation by young people.

Despite the considerable achievements of the past 10 years, challenges remain. According to 2006 estimates, more than 1 billion children under the age of 18 were living in areas in conflict or emerging from war. Of these, an estimated 300 million were under age five, and more than 18 million children were refugees or internally displaced.

The strategic review notes that there is increased global awareness about deliberate violations against children in armed conflict, such as the recruitment and use of children by armed groups. However, appalling consequences that stem from the complex interplay of conflict, poverty and discrimination are often overlooked. Children living in war-affected contexts are less likely to be in school or have access to clean water and basic sanitation. They are more vulnerable to early mortality as a result of disease and undernutrition, and they have less chance of becoming adults able to play a constructive role in their societies.

In her 2000 critical review, Graça Machel said, "Our collective failure to protect children must be transformed into an opportunity to confront the problems that cause their suffering." UNICEF works collaboratively with governments, multilateral organizations, non-governmental organizations and civil society to improve the quality of basic services that improve the lives of children – including education, water and sanitation, and nutrition – and seeks to strengthen the capacities of families and communities.

This publication is intended to inspire even greater efforts to ensure that children suffering from the consequences of conflict receive the care and support they need grow to productive adulthood and contribute to their communities.

Ann M. Veneman
Executive Director
United Nations Children's Fund

PREFACE

We have come a long way in the decade since Graça Machel first told the world of the horrors being visited upon children in the context of war. "The impact of conflict on children is everyone's responsibility, and it must be everyone's concern," she said.

In response, governments, the United Nations system and non-governmental organizations and other representatives of civil society have moved into action. Collectively, they have helped strengthen inter-national standards and norms. They have advocated to place the plight of war-affected children higher on the agendas of both the General Assembly and the Security Council. And they have raised global awareness of the most effective strategies and programmes to assist and protect children caught up in war. In this regard, I would especially like to acknowledge Olara Otunnu, the Secretary-General's first Special Representative for Children and Armed Conflict, who has worked tirelessly on children's behalf.

That same spirit of collective action has also inspired the immense effort that produced the document you hold in your hands: a 10-year strategic review of the original Machel study. This publication, the first multifaceted global assessment of war-affected children since 1996, details how far we have come – and how much we have yet to do.

As part of my mandate to report on progress, we first presented the findings of this strategic review to the General Assembly in October 2007 as a special section of my annual report. We are encouraged that the Assembly took note of it and agreed to carefully study its recommendations and to continue to discuss the issues raised therein.

The main message we brought to the General Assembly, more fully documented here, is that the situation for millions of children is as dire as ever. Although we have made advances, especially in developing a solid framework of norms and standards, much more must be done to ensure compliance, to fight impunity and to protect children's rights. The changing nature of armed conflict presents new risks and challenges that require our unwavering attention and commitment. Finally, the care and protection of children affected by armed conflict require all stake-holders to devise sensitive programmes that protect all the rights of children living in conflict areas.

I, and my office, will continue to focus on ending impunity, especially for the perpetrators of those crimes determined to be grave violations against children. We will continue to advocate for the rights of children affected by armed conflict. We will also press forward in helping to build the political will and broad-based

© UN Photo/Paulo Filgueiras

partnerships we need if we are to succeed in this most crucial of humanitarian endeavours.

Radhika Coomaraswamy

Radhika Coomaraswamy
United Nations Special Representative of the Secretary-General for Children and Armed Conflict

ACKNOWLEDGEMENTS

This publication would not have been possible without the contributions and guidance provided by the following individuals and groups:

MACHEL STUDY 10-YEAR STRATEGIC REVIEW TEAM

Katey Grusovin, Ann Makome, Baishalee Nayak, Susan Nicolai, Beth Verhey.

INTER-AGENCY ADVISORY GROUP

Agencies. Christian Children's Fund, International Committee of the Red Cross, International Labour Organization, International Rescue Committee, Office for Disarmament Affairs, Office of the Special Representative of the Secretary-General for Children and Armed Conflict, Office of the United Nations High Commissioner for Human Rights, Office of the United Nations High Commissioner for Refugees, Save the Children Alliance, United Nations Children's Fund, United Nations Department of Peacekeeping Operations, United Nations Department of Political Affairs, United Nations Development Fund for Women, United Nations Development Programme, United Nations Office for the Coordination of Humanitarian Affairs, United Nations Office on Drugs and Crime, United Nations Office of Legal Affairs, United Nations Peacebuilding Commission, United Nations Population Fund.

Inter-agency advisory group members. Maja Andrijasevic-Boko, Simon Bagshaw, Amanda Bok, Annalies Borrel, Katharine Burns, Ilaria Carnevali, Jonathan Cauldwell, Maria José Chamorro, Tonderai Chikuhwa, Ilene Cohn, Jane Connors, Pamela Delargy, Christine Evans, Helle Falkman, Kelly Fleck, Manuel Fontaine, Elena Gastaldo, Emanuela-Chiara Gillard, Anne Marie Goetz, Katarina Grenfell, Gillian Holmes, Valeria Izzi, Leanne Kinsella, Corinna Kuhl, Comfort Lamptey, Maura Lynch, Johanna MacVeigh, Ann Makome, Pamela Maponga, Marie-Anne Martin, Louise Maule, Jennifer McAvoy, Silvia Mercogliano, Craig Mokhiber, Simone Monasebian, Christine Muhigana, Sarah Muscroft, Vina Nadjibulla, Djankou Ndjonkou, Yewande Odia, Moses Okello, Ejeviiome Otobo, Carolina Owens, Giorgia Passarelli, Alexandra Pichler, Ron Pouwels, Ana Giudice Saget, Lanre Shasore, Nishkala Suntharalingam, Vanessa Tobin, Carl Triplehorn, Jane Warburton, Mike Wessels, Keith Wright, Fatemeh Ziai.

Expanded inter-agency advisory group. Sarah Sullivan (Amnesty International); Kathleen Hunt (CARE International); Rachel Stohl (Center for Defense Information); Hourig Babikian, Mike Wessells (Christian Children's Fund); Victoria Forbes Adam (Coalition to Stop the Use of Child Soldiers); Jo Becker (Human Rights Watch); Kristin Barstad (International Committee of the Red Cross); Donald K. Steinberg (International Crisis Group); Jane Warburton (International Rescue Committee); Allison Anderson, Jennifer Hofmann, (International Rescue Committee/Inter-Agency Network for Education in Emergencies); Greta Zeender (Norwegian Refugee Council); Michelle Cervantes (Office of the United Nations High Commissioner for Refugees); Nicola Reindorp (Oxfam International); Jessica Huber (Quaker United Nations Office); Michelle Brown (Refugees International); Görel Bogarde (Save the Children Alliance); Monica Lindvall (Save the Children Sweden); Vanessa Farr, Luc Lafreniere, Marc Antoine Morel, Melissa Sabatier (United Nations Development Programme, Bureau for Crisis Prevention and Recovery); Julia Freedson, Sarah Spencer (Watchlist on Children and Armed Conflict); Dale Buscher, Jenny Perlman Robinson, Juliet Young (Women's Commission for Refugee Women and Children); Dr. Laurence Bropleh (World Council of Churches).

EXPERTS AND CONTRIBUTORS

Pilar Aguilar, Eva Ahlen, Priscilla Akwara, Naseem Awl, Anton Baaré, Ishmael Beah, Annalies Borrel, Geert Cappelaere, Tonderai Chikuhwa, Daniel Christensen, Paula Claycomb, Arnaud Conchon, Rosa da Costa, Kimberly Davis, Cooper Dawson, Joanna De Berry, Marie de la Soudiere, Hazel de Wet, Asmaa Donahue, Kendra Dupuy, Anne Edgerton, Vidar Ekehaug, Ben Erwin, Manuel Fontaine, Jim Freedman, Julia Freedson, Richard Garfield, Laurence Gerard, Emanuela-Chiara Gillard, Anne Grandjean, Jason Hart, Alison Holder, Hania Kamel, Greg Keast, Geoffrey Keele, Yvonne Kemper, Sanjiv Kumar, Brooke Lauten, Alexandra Lenton, Jairus Ligoo, Edilberto Loaiza, Elisabeth Lothe,

ACRONYMS

Massimo Lowicki-Zucca, Ann Makome, Julie Ann Marshall, Dudley McArdle, Amanda Melville, Tim Morris, Jeyashree Nadarajah, Robin Nandy, Paulette Nichols, Susan Nicolai, David Nosworthy, Oluwafemi B. C. Odediran, Claire O'Kane, Mima Perisic, Stephane Pichette, David Pitt, Saji Prelis, Gary Risser, Jenny Perlman Robinson, Lara Scott, Susan Shepler, Paul Sherlock, Harry Shier, Pamela Shifman, Flora Sibanda-Mulder, Margaret Sinclair, Marc Sommers, Gary Stahl, Rebecca Symington, Julie Thompson, Ramatou Toure, Polly Truscot, Nurper Ulkuer, Carrie Vandewin, Mark Van Ommeren, Raquel Wexler, Keith Wright, Juliet Young, Louise Zimanyi.

SPECIAL THANKS TO

Radhika Coomaraswamy, Saad Houry, Rima Salah and Dan Toole.

DONORS

Office of the Special Representative of the Secretary-General for Children and Armed Conflict; the Governments of Andorra, Australia, Austria, Belgium, Canada, France, Germany, Luxembourg, Monaco, Norway, Spain and Sweden; the United Nations Children's Fund, Office of the United Nations High Commissioner for Refugees and United Nations Development Programme.

We gratefully appreciate the many people who have contributed to this publication throughout the process.

Edited, designed, translated and produced by UNICEF's Division of Communication. ■

AIDS	acquired immune deficiency syndrome
CERF	Central Emergency Response Fund
CRC	Convention on the Rights of the Child
DDR	disarmament, demobilization and reintegration
ECHA	Executive Committee on Humanitarian Affairs
ECPS	Executive Committee on Peace and Security
GA	General Assembly
HIV	human immunodeficiency virus
IASC	Inter-Agency Standing Committee
ILO	International Labour Organization
INEE	Inter-Agency Network for Education in Emergencies
MDG	Millennium Development Goal
MPLA	Popular Movement for the Liberation of Angola
NGO	non-governmental organization
OECD	Organisation for Economic Co-operation and Development
OPAC	Optional Protocol on the Involvement of Children in Armed Conflict
OSRSG-CAAC	Office of the Special Representative of the Secretary General for children and armed conflict
TB	tuberculosis
UNDP	United Nations Development Programme
UNESCO	United Nations Educational, Scientific and Cultural Organization
UNFPA	United Nations Population Fund
UNHCR	United Nations High Commissioner for Refugees
UNITA	National Union for Total Independence of Angola
WASH	water, sanitation and hygiene
WFP	World Food Programme
WHO	World Health Organization

Angola © UNICEF/NYHQ2002-0440/Pirozzi

1

INTRODUCTION: TOWARDS A COMMON ETHIC

THE STORY BEHIND THIS REPORT

The seeds of this publication were planted in October 1992, in a special discussion on children and armed conflict initiated by the Committee on the Rights of the Child. The following year, the UN General Assembly adopted a resolution calling for the Secretary-General to appoint an independent expert to lead a study on the impact of armed conflict on children. Graça Machel, a Mozambican educator and international advocate for children, was chosen to lead that study. Her groundbreaking report, the 'Impact of Armed Conflict on Children', was presented to the General Assembly in 1996,[1] which led to the creation of the Office of the Special Representative of the Secretary-General for Children and Armed Conflict (OSRSG-CAAC) in September 1997. It was unanimously endorsed and has continued to move the world ever since.

In September 2000, following a recommendation of the Machel report, the Government of Canada hosted the International Conference on War-Affected Children in Winnipeg. The timing of the conference was well planned, coinciding with the 10th anniversary of the World Summit for Children. In preparation for the event, the Governments of Canada and Norway supported a UNICEF team to work with Mrs. Machel on a review of progress since her previous report. The resulting document, 'The Machel Review 1996–2000', was presented to representatives of more than 100 countries at the Winnipeg conference. Several months later the report was circulated to the General Assembly and made into a book, *The Impact of War on Children*.[2]

In 2006, work got under way on a 10-year strategic review of progress since the original Machel study. This ambitious undertaking, financed by the Governments of Australia, Austria, Belgium, Canada, France, Germany, Norway and Sweden, was co-convened by the Office of the Special Representative of the Secretary-General for Children and Armed Conflict and UNICEF. In addition to these two UN bodies, more than 40 UN agencies, non-governmental organizations and academic institutions contributed to the report, along with children from nearly 100 countries. The initial findings were presented to the General Assembly in October 2007, as part of the annual report of the Special Representative of the Secretary-General for Children and Armed Conflict.[3] This publication is a more in-depth look at progress and remaining gaps. It is part of an ongoing advocacy effort to develop a common platform and to keep the cause of children in conflict in the conscience of citizens everywhere.

Central African Republic © UNICEF/ NYHQ2007-0135/Pirozzi

More than a decade after it was presented to the United Nations General Assembly, Graça Machel's report on the agony of children trapped in armed conflict remains the definitive assessment of the issue. It has continuously roused moral outrage and has been a foundation for programming and advocacy.

"I have always believed it is our responsibility as adults to give children futures worth having," she said when releasing the study in 1996. "In the two years spent on this report, I have been shocked and angered to see how shamefully we have failed in this responsibility."

During the intervening years, her challenges have inspired a groundswell of collective action. The Office of the Special Representative of the Secretary-General for Children and Armed Conflict, UNICEF and other UN bodies, Member States, non-governmental organizations and other representatives of civil society have all had a hand in achievements of which we can be proud: the strengthening of international norms and standards, the active involvement of both the General Assembly and the Security Council in making the issue of children in armed conflict a top priority, and the enhancement of strategies and programmes to protect and care for war-affected children.

Although these strides represent significant progress, a great deal remains to be done. There are still gaps in implementation and obstacles

to monitoring the steps already taken. More needs to be done to ensure that the light against impunity is effective and that those who violate children are held accountable. Moreover, the changing nature of contemporary armed conflict cries out for a different approach, one that no longer focuses on particular countries or themes but on the totality of issues affecting children caught in armed conflict, a point captured in Mrs. Machel's study.

That is the central message of this 10-year strategic review, and it grows out of Mrs. Machel's powerful insight that "war violates every right of the

child." We cannot hope to move forcefully on behalf of children in conflict until we turn our attention to all impacts, on all children, in all situations affected by conflict.

The organization of this report aims to heighten our understanding of the myriad ways in which armed conflict affects children – and how children regard their participation not only in war but in programmes aimed at preventing violence against them and in promoting their recovery and reintegration. The report thus frames its findings within three categories: political and diplomatic

actions and responsibilities; system-wide international policies, standards and architectures; and prevention and response.

The challenges before us are steep. As pointed out in chapter 2, inter-state conflicts have declined in number worldwide, but they are being supplanted by smaller-scale, low-intensity intra-state wars. These pose a new category of threats to children because they involve ill-trained combatants armed with readily available small weapons. They fight for economic reasons such as control of natural resources and are often under the sway of transnational organized crime. Terrorism and counterterrorism continue to pose new challenges for the protection of children. All the while, the trend that Mrs. Machel identified in 1996 – the deliberate targeting of civilians, especially children, as a tactic of war – continues to intensify.

The impact on children is more brutal than ever. The decade since the original Machel study has seen increased attention to mitigating the direct consequences of conflict, such as unlawful recruitment, gender-based violence, killing and maiming, separation from families, trafficking and illegal detention. But the indirect

"Children are both our reason to eliminate the worst aspects of armed conflict and our best hope of succeeding in that charge." — Graça Machel, 1996

consequences of war – the severing of basic services, and increased poverty, malnutrition and disease – take a similarly devastating toll on children.

In light of these circumstances, the initial findings of this strategic review, presented to the General Assembly in October 2007, included among its recommendations expanded action in four key areas: securing universal compliance with international norms and standards, with ending impunity the top priority; prioritizing the protection and care of children in armed conflict; strengthening capacity and leadership; and building peace while preventing conflict. These recommendations are outlined in full in chapter 11. And because the focus of this report is on action, the majority of chapters conclude with specific follow-up recommendations.

For all the horrors children face in armed conflict, hope survives, and Mrs. Machel has discerned it in the human heart. "I have learned," she said in 1996, "that despite being targets in contemporary armed conflict, despite the brutality shown towards them and the failure of adults to nurture and protect them, children are both our reason to eliminate the worst aspects of armed conflict and our best hope of succeeding in that charge. In a disparate world, children are a unifying force capable of bringing us all together in support of a common ethic." ∎

LISTENING TO YOUTH

It is Graça Machel's contention that "young people should be seen…as survivors and active participants in creating solutions, not just as victims or problems."[4] With that in mind, a priority throughout this strategic review on children and armed conflict has been incorporating the perspectives of children and young people themselves.

In total, 1,700 youths from 92 countries contributed their thoughts and ideas to this report. As a start, UNICEF, the United Nations Population Fund and non-governmental partners conducted focus group discussions in 18 countries affected by conflict. Although each group concentrated on the same set of questions, the young people chose different methods of response, which allowed them to express their ideas in ways they felt appropriate to their own circumstances. In Somalia, for example, a focus group discussion was held via a radio talk show, which elicited views from 140 children who called in. A compilation of these insights from children around the world was subsequently assembled in *"Will you listen?" Young voices from conflict zones*, launched as a companion piece to the Machel strategic review presented to the General Assembly in 2007. *"Will you listen?"* was produced in four languages and distributed to partner organizations worldwide. Quotes from it appear throughout this publication.

Recognizing that young people are able to both express their concerns and identify ways to address them, a follow-up survey was conducted by youth-led organizations experienced in working with children and young people in conflict zones. Their recommendations for action are outlined in chapter 10.

THE CHANGING NATURE
OF CONFLICT

2

> **"When conflict broke out in the community we fled our homes, and it felt like bullets were chasing us through the woods."** – Young woman, 17, Philippines

The 1996 Machel study noted with deep concern how war tactics had changed, with civilians, including children, increasingly becoming the targets of violence and the victims of atrocities. Regrettably, this trend continues. Armed conflicts today have an even more horrific impact on children, and on civilians generally. In today's wars, the strategies adopted by armed groups "seek to bring the battle more immediately, more systematically, and more massively to the core of the civilian population,"[5] and into the lives of millions of children.

As a result, armed conflict has become more fluid and less easily defined. According to the Stockholm International Peace Research Institute, the trend of armed conflict is towards "further fragmentation of violence." The analysis goes on to say, "This has been accompanied by the diversification of armed groups and the further erosion of the boundaries between different forms of violence. Much of this 'fragmented' violence is difficult to measure and categorize."[6]

The growing involvement of non-state actors and the use of non-traditional forms of warfare add to the difficulty of quantifying the impact of war on children. The 1996 Machel study cited 30 "major armed conflicts" as taking place in 1995, when monitored according to battle deaths. In attempting to assess trends 10 years later, the Machel strategic review found that the number of conflicts in 2005 ranged from 17 to 56 worldwide.[7] The lower figure pertains to conflicts with more than 1,000 battle deaths; the higher derives from a threshold of 25 battle deaths, allowing for the inclusion of lower-intensity conflicts and those in which a State was not a party to the conflict.

The analysis of conflicts in 2005 draws from a recent and much-cited report by the Human Security Centre. It emphasizes that while some analysts see a positive trend – a decline in the number of inter-state conflicts waged around the world since the 1990s and a growing numbers of wars ending with negotiated settlements rather than military resolution[8] – others are not so sure, given the changing nature of warfare. While most countries are no longer engaged in inter-state warfare, they are often host to one or even several armed conflicts involving non-state actors. These can include rebellions or opposition or secessionist movements involving paramilitary groups, anti-government guerrillas or others. Such armed conflicts may yield fewer military battle deaths, but they exact a high human cost: Unarmed civilians are victimized, basic services deteriorate, societal divisions deepen and local economies decline.

It is also important to remember that many of the recognized armed conflict datasets were based on the traditional concept of war, involving inter-state warfare and disciplined military forces. Significantly, some of the lists only include armed conflicts involving a State party. Yet the data from one centre showed that, in 2005, all 56 armed conflicts listed also involved non-state actors, and in 25 of them a State was not a party to the conflict.[9]

Fuelling many of these conflicts is the widespread proliferation and availability of small arms, light weapons and ammunition. Abundant, cheap and easily carried by a child, these weapons are often illegally traded. They are a modern-day scourge. They not only account for the vast majority of direct conflict deaths, they enable wars to continue, sustain a culture of violence and facilitate further conflict.

THE SHIFTING LANDSCAPE OF CONTEMPORARY WARFARE

Haiti provides insight into the challenges on the ground that such trends present. While the United Nations Mission for the Stabilization of Haiti helped quell the conflict that erupted in 2004, many armed groups resisted disarmament and transformed into entities that were primarily criminal in nature. As described in the most recent report of the Secretary-General on children and armed conflict, "Although these groups are currently essentially criminal in nature, their character and motivations may shift between criminal and political depending on the specific time and circumstances and may pose a threat to peace and security."[10]

The majority of children who have been recruited in Haiti remain associated with armed groups, despite their ongoing transformations. In fact, children themselves have found their status changing – once considered victims unlawfully recruited, now they are seen as 'gang members'. In detailing the realities faced by children growing up in such an environment, there are "confirmed reports that children have been used as messengers, spotters, attackers and porters to transfer and hide weapons, as well as for kidnappings."[11] Children have been abducted (in one case, 30 students were abducted while travelling on school buses), gang-raped and become victims of other forms of sexual violence. In some cases, armed entities have used schools as a base of operations.[12]

Recent research and policy analysis on conflict is attempting to document the changing nature of contemporary warfare and the gravity of its impact on civilians.[13] Specific attention to children, however, remains rare, including the delineation of age in data collection. Cross-analysis between such research and expertise on children is therefore urgently needed. In the interim, this report seeks to highlight key issues that require collaborative action.

While each conflict possesses its own unique characteristics, the trends in contemporary conflict that affect

THE DEADLY AND DESTABILIZING EFFECTS OF SMALL ARMS

The poorly regulated and often illicit trade of small arms and light weapons, along with their wide circulation, "increases the intensity and duration of armed conflicts, undermines the sustainability of peace agreements, impedes the success of peacebuilding, frustrates efforts aimed at the prevention of armed conflict, [and] hinders considerably the provision of humanitarian assistance."[14]

Small arms and light weapons are responsible for the majority of direct conflict deaths – between 60 and 90 per cent, depending on the conflict.[15] The ease of handling small arms makes them especially accessible to children. The lightweight Kalashnikov (AK-47) is the most used and available gun in the world. Untold numbers of children living in situations of armed conflict, sometimes as young as seven or eight, learn how to use them.

This familiarity with small arms and their proliferation can sustain a culture of violence in post-conflict societies. At worst it has the potential to reignite conflict. Guatemala, for example, is the most highly armed country in Central America. Only 1,500 weapons were surrendered in the 1996 disarmament and, by 2002, the UN Verification Mission in Guatemala estimated that there were 1.5 million illegal firearms in circulation. The level of violence has reached alarming proportions, with a recent survey showing that 88 per cent of the country's people are worried about becoming victims of armed violence.[16] Southern Sudan is also saturated with small arms and light weapons. Among other factors, persistent insecurity is hobbling attempts to implement the 2005 Comprehensive Peace Agreement between the north and south. A household survey found that almost every household had experienced some form of armed attack since the peace agreement was signed.[17]

The 1996 Machel study stressed the importance for children of shifting resource allocations from arms and military expenditures to human and social development. This shift is still desperately needed. According to the Control Arms Campaign, an average of $22 billion a year is spent on arms by countries in Africa, Asia, the Middle East and Latin America. The campaign points out that this sum "would otherwise enable those same countries to be on track to meet the Millennium Development Goals of achieving universal primary education (estimated at $10 billion a year) as well as targets for reducing infant and maternal mortality (estimated at $12 billion a year)."[18]

Russian Federation © UNICEF/NYHQ2005-1315/Pirozzi

children in particular and demand our attention include the proliferation of armed groups, the emergence of 'resource wars' that incite and sustain conflict, and the internationalization of terrorism.

THE PROLIFERATION OF ARMED GROUPS

While major inter-state armed conflicts are on the decline, there are many prolonged, intractable conflicts within States and across borders involving a variety of non-state actors. In addition, there is an increased use of paramilitary and proxy forces with weak systems of accountability for compliance with international law. The actions and motivations of these armed groups may switch back and forth from armed conflict to criminal violence to other forms of armed political violence.

An array of labels is applied to non-state groups and actors. These range from insurgents and resistance movements to separatists, opposition forces, militias and rebels as well as local defence groups and paramilitary units. In Afghanistan, armed groups include tribal factions, criminal networks and groups ideologically opposed to the Government, including the Taliban and the Hizb-e Islami.[19] Somalia, lacking a central government, presents one of the most complex situations, involving the Transitional Federal Government, the Union of Islamic Courts (a complex union of clan-based sharia courts), various clan militias and Ethiopian government forces (which have the backing of the US Government), along with suspected terrorists with al-Qaida links.[20] Children made up an estimated 35 per cent of 1,200 civilians killed and several thousand injured in Somalia between October 2006 and late 2007.[21] Reports indicate that all parties except Ethiopian government forces have recruited and used children.[22]

In Aceh (Indonesia), where only the Free Aceh Movement (Gerakan Aceh Merdeka) is a party to the 2005 peace agreement, incomplete demobilization has resulted in fluidity among armed groups and an increase in criminal activity and banditry, in which young people still participate.[23] In Nepal, substantial numbers of children were recruited by the Communist Party of Nepal-Maoist prior to the ceasefire agreement. Evolving unrest in the Terai region has led to the emergence of new political and armed groups, whose "actions were criminal as much as they were political in design," and new violations of children's rights, including recruitment.[24]

The miscategorization of certain armed groups – and their exclusion from dialogue concerning conflict resolution or humanitarian access to civilians – has presented major problems. For one, it has restricted child protection workers from reaching children, identifying their needs and highlighting rights violations.

Colombia, for example, has been besieged by armed conflict for almost half a century. A number of highly organized paramilitary groups, private security companies and drug trafficking mafias have emerged over the years. They are financed by kidnapping, extortion, trafficking or other organized criminal activity, in which children have become involved.[25] Between 11,000 and 14,000 children are thought to have served in armed groups in a variety of roles in Colombia,[26] and many of them have remained beyond the reach of child protection workers.

Research suggests that the demobilization process there has been applied inconsistently and is not reaching all armed groups. As reported by the UN Secretary-General, two illegal armed groups outside the demobilization process "have been only partially demobilized, and it is believed that children are still present in those groups."[27] As a result, only 15 per cent of Colombia's former child combatants have access to demobilization and reintegration programmes. Those who remain have little hope of ever resuming a normal life.[28]

The use of paramilitary and proxy forces on the part of States increases the vulnerability of children due to diffuse mechanisms of accountability. Militias allied to the Government of the Sudan, for example, including the Janjaweed, have been among the most egregious violators of children's rights. This includes the recruitment and use of children and the use of rape as a weapon of war.[29]

The Philippines report to the Committee on the Rights of the Child on the Optional Protocol notes that "children are reportedly being recruited into paramilitary structures to provide security and protection against ordinary criminal elements such as cattle rustlers, thieves and other armed bandits" and that these organizations "are also fielded to fight guerrilla insurgents."[30] The Children's Rehabilitation Centre, a national non-governmental organization with three regional centres, has documented 819 incidents of human rights violations involving children in the Philippines from 2001 to April 2005.[31]

A rising trend is the outsourcing of military and police functions to private security companies. Experts have raised concern about the use of force by such companies and the blurring of distinctions between civilians and persons participating in hostilities.[32] Allegations of misconduct by private security staff and of inappropriate links to political parties or paramilitaries are all too frequent. This suggests the need to put greater attention on ensuring that such

companies respect children's rights. Since national law and practice are critical in this area, considerations and recommendations by the Committee on the Rights of the Child will be especially important.

THE EMERGENCE OF RESOURCE WARS

A distinctive feature of contemporary conflict is the emergence of resource wars or 'asset wars', with 'blood' diamonds a particularly notorious example. Increasingly, armed conflicts that may have originated in political grievances are subsequently driven by opportunistic greed. Resource wars are driven by control of assets, illicit trade and exploitation of natural resources – including diamonds, other gems, timber, drugs, gold and other precious metals – intermingled with arms. The Security Council has noted that "the exploitation, trafficking and illicit trade of natural resources have contributed to the outbreak, escalation or continuation of armed conflict."[33]

As parties to armed conflict look for new sources of revenue, children are drawn into additional forms of

"They are not human. They worship guns. They don't have sisters and brothers, they only have a gun." –
Girls and young women, 14–17, Somalia

> "Drugs are the root cause of recent armed conflict. Because of drug trade money, people can acquire arms. These people start using drugs, which makes them act violently, more and more so, until they spur each other on to murder, to rape and to abuse children." –
> Young men, 16–18, Haiti

hazardous labour, in addition to being recruited and used for military objectives. For example, many analysts note that in Angola, the struggle between the Popular Movement for the Liberation of Angola (MPLA) and the National Union for Total Independence of Angola (UNITA) might have ended in 1992 had it not been for UNITA's control over diamond revenues. This was made possible by the seizure of large numbers of children to work as soldiers and as labourers in the diamond mines and by the MPLA's ability to capture revenue from petrodollars. In the Democratic Republic of the Congo, where exploitation of the country's rich mineral resources has been a prominent feature of the conflict, it is common to find large numbers of children working in mines and used in trafficking.

A caring and protective environment for children erodes further as civilians are pillaged, assaulted sexually and forced into labour. Children are at special risk because the groups that control resources typically also control community structures and assume state functions in such areas as health, education, policing and justice. Armed groups cast themselves as officials and extort civilians behind a veneer of legitimacy. They interrupt the delivery of basic services, destroy livelihoods and plunge populations into deep and relentless poverty.

The international community is struggling to respond to resource wars. Sanctions and embargoes can be effective, but they must be carefully targeted to ensure they do not inflict unintended harm. At the time of the 1996 Machel study, sanctions on regimes in a number of countries were having devastating effects on child mortality and the maintenance of basic services. Today, sanction measures by the Security Council are more targeted, and the humanitarian impact is assessed.

Beyond such measures as sanctions, a wider understanding of child rights in situations of armed conflict is required, along with a focus on corporate social responsibility. Some of the most promising measures involve actions and cooperation among UN Member States and multinational enterprises. Certification schemes such as the Kimberley Process are potentially capable of restricting the movement of goods that promote conflict involving children.[34] Such schemes must include strict prohibition of violence against children and exploitation and abuse of them.

To strengthen prevention and sustainable action, children's rights must be integral to measures upholding accountability. The Special Representative of the Secretary-General on human rights and transnational corporations and other business enterprises has stressed that

"no single measure would yield more immediate results in the human rights performance of firms than conducting [human rights impact assessments]."[35] Domestic law and legislation relating to individuals and corporations operating multinationally should complement international treaties by improving provisions regarding labour, disclosure and complicity in situations violating children's rights.

INTERNATIONALIZATION OF TERRORISM

In recent years, terrorism has come to define the security discourse. International terrorist incidents declined during the 1990s and thus did not feature in the 1996 Machel study. But the trend is now reversed: Incidents of international terrorism quadrupled between 2000 and 2004.[36] As recently affirmed by the UN General Assembly, "acts, methods and terrorism in all its forms and manifestations are activities aimed at the destruction of human rights,"[37] including children's rights. As noted in the Machel review presented to the General Assembly in 2007, "such attacks are disproportionately against civilians, often perpetrated in places of worship, market squares and other public places." Children are consequently killed or injured or become indirect victims with the death of their family members, especially parents.

Woefully insufficient attention is being given to children amid the 'war on terror' paradigm. Analyses of terrorism or counterterrorism rarely consider the impact on children. Yet terrorism and counterterrorism measures can have multiple consequences for children, as described below.

Targeting of children as victims. Recent years have witnessed striking instances of terrorism aimed at children. Examples include the 2004 hostage-taking at the Beslan school in the northern Caucasus and the 2007 suicide bomb attack against a delegation of members of parliament and civilians in Pul-i-Khomri district, Baghlan province, Afghanistan. These two attacks alone killed 70 people, including 52 schoolchildren and five teachers. Of the 110 injured, half were students.[38]

Targeting of children as perpetrators. Of great and growing concern is the use of children as perpetrators or accomplices in terrorist acts, including across borders. Reports from Afghanistan note that children are "being used to perpetrate attacks and, in some cases, as human shields by the Taliban and other insurgents."[39] A study by the United Nations Assistance Mission in Afghanistan concluded that at least some of the suicide bombers in that country are children aged 11 to 15 who have been tricked, promised money or otherwise forced. The study also

found that bombers "appear to be young (sometimes children), poor, uneducated, easily influenced by recruiters and drawn heavily from madrasas (Islamic religious schools) across the border in Pakistan."[40]

In Iraq, children have been used as decoys in suicide car bombings "by insurgent group militias, Al-Qaida and Al-Qaida-affiliated groups."[41] In Sulawesi (Indonesia), reports indicate that the young men recruited by the insurgent groups Jemaah Islamiyah and Mujahidin KOMPAK with the help of local leaders were youths who had a "history of violence."[42]

Counterterrorism measures have also posed challenges, especially with regards to the violation of international standards of juvenile justice. Partly because Palestinian children are used in terrorist attacks, they are increasingly under suspicion. Also, more than 1,500 Iraqi children are in detention in Iraq. They are accused of making and planting roadside bombs or caught when acting as lookouts or carrying guns. These children are either under administrative detention by US forces, or in Iraqi detention.[43]

Amnesty International has reported grave abuses against child detainees.[44] Hundreds of children have been detained by Israeli forces, under military provisions that contravene international humanitarian law and standards of juvenile justice. A 2007 report of the Secretary-General notes that "at any given point during the reporting period, between

361 and 416 Palestinian children were being held in Israeli prisons and detention centres, including children as young as 12 years. ... There are reports that some children held in detention undergo physical beatings and psychological torture, including threats of sexual violence. The systematic transfer of Palestinian child prisoners outside the Occupied Palestinian Territory into Israel is in direct violation of the Fourth Geneva Convention."[45] The 2006 report of a children's rights organization operating there showed that 64 per cent of children's sentences were on charges of stone-throwing.[46]

In 2007, UNICEF and other child protection actors worked with the Government of Afghanistan and other rule-of-law actors to advocate for juvenile justice consistent with child rights. They called for the anti-terrorism law under development to explicitly state that, in the case of children, only the Juvenile Justice Code would apply. Other countries face similar legislative challenges. In 2007 in Indonesia, for instance, legislative reform was needed to ensure that the anti-terrorism law complied with domestic and international standards of juvenile justice.

The use of aerial bombardment to deal with terrorism also has consequences for children. In Iraq and Afghanistan, there have been cases of mistaken identity and collateral damage where the victims have been children.

Democratic Republic of the Congo © UNICEF/NYHQ2003-0554/LeMoyne

Restriction of access to basic services. Terrorism and counter-terrorism measures have also multiplied restrictions on children's lives and their access to basic services and protection. Again, the situation in the Occupied Palestinian Territory is especially grave. According to a December 2007 report of the Secretary-General, "The denial of passage or delays at checkpoints has significantly affected the access of civilians, particularly children, to medical care and services, causing serious threat to their physical health."[47] Curfews and checkpoint closures have also disrupted children's access to education. This has contributed to the perpetuation of the crisis, since poor school performance has been a key factor in encouraging young people to join militant factions.[48] In Nepal, contrary to peacebuilding and prevention objectives, donor restrictions prevented some agencies from providing programmes for children associated with the Maoists.[49]

ALTERING OUR RESPONSE

Current methods of counterterrorism may only beget more violence. In November 2007, a report by the UN Special Rapporteur on the promotion and protection of human rights while countering terrorism identified elements in current counterterrorism legislation and strategies that are counterproductive for youth. Other inadvertent effects, the report points out, are marginalization of vulnerable groups, including young people, and the creation of conditions that provide "fertile soil for recruitment to movements that promise prospects for change but resort to unacceptable means of acts of terrorism."[50] Indeed, a more constructive response may be one that echoes the calls made in this report – that is, attention to the multifaceted needs of children and young people in a way that also enlists their active involvement.

Research suggests that urban young people with some education but few job prospects and no opportunity to express dissent or participate constructively in political processes are seen as a pool of potential recruits for those who instigate others to violence.[51] An evaluation of a German anti-terrorism programme provides important insights into approaches that have proved effective with young people. Among them are targeted programmes – such as the participation of youth in the political process in Indonesia, addressing the needs of urban youth in the Maghreb States of north Africa, and promoting dialogue between Muslim and indigenous groups in Mindanao, Philippines – that helped reduce the risk of young people resorting to acts of terrorism. Improving opportunities for political participation and job prospects were identified as key components. The assessment also observed that effective anti-terrorism programming is similar to other peacebuilding programming and should be incorporated into more traditional development activities.[52]

Calls for such multifaceted approaches are being taken up in international reports and guidelines. The *World Development Report 2007* published by the World Bank highlights that increasing the capacity for lasting and productive civic engagement can help to prevent political violence.[53] The OECD-DAC Guidelines for a Development Co-operation Lens on Terrorism Prevention call for "greater attention in donor programming to young people's job opportunities and education to prevent the emergence of fragile, disenfranchised youth." These also cite the need to "deepen analysis of the social changes brought about by development and the multiple causes of disaffection and exclusion among the young."[54]

KEEPING OUR FOCUS ON CHILDREN

As this chapter has attempted to show, the nature of armed conflict is indeed changing. But what has remained constant is the vulnerability of children. The moral outrage galvanized by Mrs. Machel in 1996 is still very much needed today. However, what we also have to draw upon today is a firmer foundation of international humanitarian law that seeks to protect children's rights.

The good news is that States remain committed to the rules that govern and must be applied in armed conflict. The Declaration adopted at the 2002 UN General Assembly Special Session on Children, for example, affirmed the commitment of the international community to protect children from war. The Declaration states, "Children must be protected from the horrors of armed conflict. Children under foreign occupation must also be protected, in accordance with the provisions of international humanitarian law."[55] More recently, at the 2007 International Conference of the Red Cross and Red Crescent, States expressed the fact that they are "convinced that international humanitarian law remains as relevant today as ever before in international and non-international armed conflicts and continues to provide protection for all victims of armed conflict."[56]

In too many spots around the globe, international law and norms appear to be ignored altogether. That may be the case. But the real challenge lies in applying the rules established under international humanitarian law.[57] Children's rights are not subject to derogation. They apply both in peacetime and in war. And even in the shifting landscape of contemporary conflicts, the international community is not absolved from taking action. As Mrs. Machel reminded us in her 1996 report, "The impact of armed conflict on children is an area in which everyone shares responsibility and a degree of blame." ∎

KEY RESOURCES

Stockholm International Peace Research Institute, *SIPRI Yearbook 2008: Armaments, disarmament and international security,* SIPRI, Stockholm, June 2008; and SIPRI website, <www.sipri.org>.

Uppsala Conflict Data Program, 'UCDP Database', Department of Peace and Conflict Research, Uppsala University, Uppsala, Sweden, <www.pcr.uu.se/gpdatabase/search.php>.

Human Security Report Project, *Human Security Report 2005: War and peace in the 21st century* and *Human Security Brief 2006,* School for International Studies at Simon Fraser University, Vancouver, <www.hsrgroup.org/>.

International Crisis Group website, <www.crisisgroup.org/home/index.cfm>.

International Committee of the Red Cross, 'International Humanitarian Law and the Challenges of Contemporary Armed Conflict', ICRC document 30IC/07/8.4, prepared for the 30th International Conference of the Red Cross and Red Crescent, Geneva, 26–30 November 2007.

Lebanon © UNICEF/NYHQ2006-1040/Brooks

3

THE CONSEQUENCES
FOR CHILDREN

"We have all lost a part of our life, and it will never come back." – Young man, 18, Burundi

In many wars, children and young people are not merely bystanders, but targets, as the 1996 Machel study highlighted. "Not only are large numbers of children killed and injured," the study said, "but countless others grow up deprived of their material and emotional needs, including the structures that give meaning to social and cultural life. The entire fabric of their societies – their homes, schools, health systems and religious institutions – is torn to pieces."

The study could only surmise the full extent of the suffering because data collection on the problem was still in its infancy. Although major obstacles remain, the numbers gathered for this strategic review represent a substantial advance over previous quantitative assessments. Yet more than a decade later, the impact of armed conflict on children remains difficult to fully ascertain. The information available is patchy, and it varies in both specificity and accuracy. While efforts to systematically gather details on certain conflict-related violations and their impacts are under way, available data are not sufficient to fully compare or identify trends in the decade since the 1996 Machel study.

"Some children fall victim to a general onslaught against civilians; others die as part of a calculated genocide," the study said. "Still other children suffer the effects of sexual violence or the multiple deprivations of armed conflict that expose them to hunger or disease. Just as shocking, thousands of young people are cynically exploited as combatants."

The study went on to note that both during and after armed conflict, even those children not suffering as a direct result of conflict often suffer equally devastating consequences. It is to the world's shame that more than a decade after this landmark study, these descriptions remain as true as ever. Despite areas of progress, as described in other parts of this report, it is clear that children continue to suffer the extreme effects of war and its aftermath.

THE HUMAN TOLL[58]

In 2005, a set of conflict-related violations against children was identified as part of a periodic report by the UN Secretary-General on children and armed conflict. These six 'grave violations' – killing or maiming children; recruitment or use of child soldiers; attacks against schools or hospitals; rape and other grave sexual violence; abduction of children; and denial of humanitarian access – were chosen for regular monitoring, reporting and response because of their exceptionally brutal and deliberate nature. The overview of the violations presented here only begins to tell the story of the impact of armed conflict on children.

In addition to the violations documented by the UN-led mechanism, a number of other violations are also commonly perpetrated against children during and after war. Torture and other forms of ill-treatment, administrative detention, enforced displacement, sexual exploitation and hazardous work can have equally detrimental effects on the lives of children and young people. Even the briefest analysis of how these violations affect children, outlined below, can deepen our understanding of the consequences of war.

During and after armed conflict, the interruption and disintegration of basic services and sources of social protection also lead to further violations of child rights – with repercussions that could last a lifetime. In an attempt to explore these issues, new analyses conducted for this 10-year review of the Machel study have found that conflict-affected countries and territories have shown less progress towards the Millennium Development Goals (MDGs) than many of their more fortunate counterparts, as described later in this chapter.

This means that children and young people living in those countries are more likely to be poor, malnourished, out of school or in generally poor health than many others around the globe, whether as a cause or a consequence of armed conflict. While overt violations and negative effects may not be solely attributable to war, it is fairly clear that the interplay of armed conflict, poverty and discrimination often compounds the harmful consequences for children.

Populations affected

The scale and scope of armed conflict globally can be measured in different ways. Among these are simply counting the number of conflicts based on a set of defined parameters (as described in chapter 2), estimating the number of people affected or killed, or accounting for other types of human costs. These costs include deaths due to malnutrition and disease, psychological and social harm, damage to property and loss of livelihoods.

Estimates of affected populations. Globally, just over 1 billion children under the age of 18 live in countries or territories affected by armed conflict – almost one sixth of the total world population. Of these, approximately 300 million are under the age of five.[59] In 2006, an estimated 18.1 million children were among populations living with the effects of displacement. Within that group were an estimated 5.8 million refugee children and 8.8 million internally displaced children.[60]

Iraq © UNICEF/NYHQ2003-0493/Noorani

Inaccurate estimates of overall populations, as well as refugees and internally displaced persons, may arise due to ongoing movements of people, deliberate attempts to over-estimate or underestimate numbers, or the fact that available population data may vary in quality. The data are influenced by lack of access to people or communities affected by armed conflict, absence of functioning birth and death registration systems, and populations in hiding.

The Machel study noted that "an estimated two million children have been killed in armed conflict. Three times as many have been seriously injured or permanently disabled." These estimates are repeatedly cited as current, though they refer to the period between 1986 and 1996.[61] It is a concern that such figures, now more than a decade old, are cited without a date or reference.

In attempting to update the statistics on deaths due directly to

"During the war, I lost my 10-year-old brother and 14-year-old sister. Our house was damaged. My father died, and now my older brother works." – Young woman, 15, Afghanistan

Occupied Palestinian Territory
© UNICEF/NYHQ2007-0772/El Baba

conflict, the Machel review presented to the General Assembly in 2007 bypassed the issue altogether. Since conflict-related databases are not disaggregated for children, the review said that it had "found that an attempt to aggregate numbers would give inaccurate results." Instead, it preferred to describe "specific issues and contexts illustrating the impact of conflict on children." Indeed, while there are differing levels of accuracy in quantitative global estimates of populations affected and the number of child deaths, available evidence leaves little doubt about war's horrific consequences.

Further accounting of human costs.
Epidemiological and humanitarian surveys are beginning to quantify the impact of armed conflict on disease, its transmission and the disease burden in a given country. For instance, a series of mortality surveys on

children under five conducted by the International Rescue Committee has documented the humanitarian impact of war in the Democratic Republic of the Congo since 2000. The surveys show that 5.4 million excess deaths occurred between August 1998 and April 2007. The conclusion is that the majority resulted from preventable infectious diseases, malnutrition and neonatal and pregnancy-related conditions. Children were disproportionately affected, accounting for nearly half of the deaths while constituting only one fifth of the population.[62]

A similar survey in northern Uganda found a mortality rate of nearly 1,000 excess deaths per week in the Acholi region in the first half of 2005. Forty per cent were children under five.[63] These cases demonstrate that, globally, the extent of war-related mortality, particularly for children, has yet to be fully measured.

In addition, emotional distress during and after armed conflict is often exacerbated by displacement, life in overcrowded camps, disruption of social institutions or services, loss of livelihoods, tension within communities, and the collapse of political authority and rule of law. The accumulation of stress over time and the long-term consequences of distressing events can have an intensely disturbing and potentially far-reaching impact on children's social, emotional, cognitive and spiritual well-being and development.

While the consequences are difficult to assess, research and programming are beginning to document them. Analysis of global data, for example, has shown "how protective factors such as parental support and moral guidance can help children overcome horrific experiences and help to promote individual healing and community reconciliation."[64]

The effect of armed conflict on communities is often cited in the professional literature, but the extent of disruption to family life is sometimes difficult to capture. It is not uncommon that families cope with the hardships imposed by armed conflict by encouraging children to take on additional responsibilities to provide for the family. This can lead to school dropout, working or living on the streets, engaging in sex work and other activities that carry significant protection risks.

Armed conflict also frays community structures. Research conducted in a number of camps for internally displaced persons in Burundi found a high number of child-headed households. Prior to the conflict, families and neighbours looked out for one another, took care of each other's children and took in orphans. With the ongoing armed conflict, however, families were stretched even to care for their own. This disappearance of informal social networks to look after orphans and other children at risk was shown to have made them even more vulnerable.

"When we were living in the camp [for internally displaced persons] there were people everywhere in a very small place. It was horrible." – Girl, 13, Sri Lanka

Grave violations against children

An examination of the six grave violations against children identified above is an important tool for assessing the consequences of war. The decision by the UN Security Council to focus on these six violations grows out of its determination to fight impunity by delineating specific, targeted crimes committed by persistent violators of child rights.

KILLING OR MAIMING

Killing or maiming includes any action that results in the death or serious injury – such as scarring, disfigurement or mutilation – of one or more children. While often intentional, maiming can also result from wounds caused by bullets in a crossfire or detonation of anti-personnel landmines.

Widespread deliberate targeting of children and other civilians creates a climate of fear that is often effective in destabilizing and scattering civilian populations. Such tactics are a matter of tremendous concern in such countries as Afghanistan, the Democratic Republic of the Congo, Iraq, Somalia, Sri Lanka and the Sudan. The principles of distinction and proportionality require fighters to distinguish between combatants and civilians, and they prohibit civilian damage beyond the scope of military advantage. But this principle is eroding among armed forces and groups. Another worrisome trend is the rise in suicide attacks, and

the manipulation and use of children to carry them out, especially in such places as Afghanistan, Iraq and the Occupied Palestinian Territory.[65]

A positive note is the marked decrease in child casualties from anti-personnel mines, a result of efforts to slow their proliferation. These include adoption of the 1997 Convention on the Prohibition of the Use, Stockpiling, Production and Transfer of Antipersonnel Mines and on their Destruction. Also effective has been the pledge by a number of non-state armed actors to adhere to the 'Deed of Commitment' banning anti-personnel landmines, initiated by the organization Geneva Call.

Yet more than a third of the global casualties from explosive remnants of war are children. Some progress has also been made in this area: Recorded casualties continue to fall, and in 2006 over 450 square kilometres of contaminated land were cleared.[66] Threats remain, however, in as many as 78 countries affected to some degree by landmines and about 85 affected by explosive remnants of war. Around 13 countries continue to produce – or reserve the right to produce – anti-personnel mines, with no decrease in the past two years.[67]

RECRUITMENT OR USE OF CHILDREN BY ARMED FORCES AND ARMED GROUPS

Despite wide condemnation and response over the last decade, girls and boys continue to be recruited or used by the armed forces and armed groups. Recruitment is defined as the

compulsory, forced or voluntary conscription or enlistment of children into any kind of armed forces or organized armed group(s). Once recruited, children might be used as fighters or for non-combat purposes, including sexual ones.

In recent years, concern has increased about the re-recruitment of previously released children. And without specific forms of assistance and support, children recruited into armed forces or groups are often in mortal danger if they try to escape. They also face huge barriers in making the transition from military to civilian life and returning to their families and communities.

In his reports to the Security Council on children and armed conflict, the Secretary-General has listed parties that recruited or used children in situations of armed conflict in 17 countries or territories from 2002 to 2007.[68] These same reports cited a total of 127 different parties involved in such actions during that time. Of these, 16 parties, sometimes referred to as 'persistent violators', have appeared on the list four consecutive times.[69]

The good news, according to the Coalition to Stop the Use of Child Soldiers, is that the number of armed conflicts in which children are involved is down, from 27 in 2004 to 17 by the end of 2007. Still, "tens of thousands of children remain in the ranks of non-state armed groups in at least 24 different countries or territories," according to the Coalition's 2008 Global Report. The report goes on to say, "The record of governments is also little improved – children were deployed in armed conflicts by government forces in nine situations of armed conflict, down only one from the 10 such situations recorded when the last Global Report was published in 2004."[70]

While it is possible to determine where children are associated with armed forces or armed groups, it is much more difficult to determine how many children have been involved. In fact, the Coalition to Stop the Use of Child Soldiers no longer provides estimated figures. However, there is a sense that the numbers have fallen over the past decade, as conflicts in some countries have ended and demobilization agreements have been reached.

The difficulty in assessing the full extent of the problem is partly due to fear about the repercussions of reporting among families and communities, as well as armed forces and groups. Also, formerly recruited children may want to hide their previous association with armed forces or groups to avoid stigma. Field reports often contain scant numbers of recorded cases, and where numbers do exist, they are often not comparable across countries.

ATTACKS AGAINST SCHOOLS OR HOSPITALS

Attacks on schools and hospitals include targeting of educational or medical facilities resulting in their total or partial destruction. They may also involve the occupation, shelling or deliberate targeting of personnel, students or patients. These attacks not only damage property and harm the individuals involved; they also incite fear and limit access to these basic services by other children. Schools and hospitals are often made inaccessible to conflict-affected populations because of military occupation or their use as camps for internally displaced persons.

Attacks on and occupation of education and health-care facilities "have risen dramatically in recent years," according to the Machel strategic review presented to the General Assembly in 2007. The destructive effects of attacks on schools are magnified by the importance of education in sustaining children's well-being in wartime and in helping pave the way to post-conflict recovery.

Incident reporting on education attacks suggests that the worst-affected countries and territories over the past five years are Afghanistan, Colombia, Iraq, Nepal, the Occupied Palestinian Territory, Thailand and Zimbabwe.[71] In Afghanistan between August 2006 and July 2007, 133 incidents of school attacks were documented. A number of deliberate attacks targeted female students and teachers. Of growing concern is the situation in Thailand, where more

"We were mobilized by our clan militia heads to come to the playground. All of us were young people about the same age. They told us to defend our village. We were in the queue with our guns. When the Marehan clan attacked us we defended our village." – Boys and young men, 14–17, Somalia

"For the time being, there are many violent attacks that may happen at any time. Some of us may die in the street or in school or even at home, which means no safety for anyone at any time." – Girl, 12, Occupied Palestinian Territory

than 100 schools were burned down in late 2006 and early 2007.[72] Such attacks are a major factor in keeping children out of school and limiting their ability to concentrate in class.

Similarly, attacks on health facilities and workers continue to hamper access to health care, playing a role in denial of humanitarian access. After the April 2006 attack on a health clinic in Afghanistan and the murder of five of its staff members, Médecins Sans Frontières pulled out of the country – after 24 years of providing health services there. Due to attacks on health centres, along with general insecurity and poor service provision, agencies have estimated that only 40 to 50 per cent of people in Darfur had access to health services in 2007.[73]

RAPE AND OTHER FORMS OF SEXUAL VIOLENCE

The use of rape and sexual violence as a war tactic – and the impunity afforded its perpetrators – poses a particular risk to girls in conflict zones. Attention to rape as a weapon of war began during the conflicts in the Balkans and Africa's Great Lakes region in the early 1990s. Yet limited progress has been made on the ground to end this crime.

From 2000 to 2007, as part of the Secretary-General's reports on children and armed conflict, rape and other forms of sexual violence were cited in 16 countries and territories: Burundi, the Central African Republic, Chad, Colombia, Côte d'Ivoire, the

Democratic Republic of the Congo, Haiti, Israel, Liberia, Nepal, Rwanda, Sierra Leone, Somalia, Sudan, Uganda and the former Yugoslavia.

The risk of sexual violence increases dramatically with the increased presence of fighting forces and the breakdown of law and order. In such cases mechanisms for protection are typically no longer functioning or are not given priority. Moreover, the by-products of armed conflict – poverty and joblessness – can create extremely perilous conditions for young girls, including trafficking for sexual exploitation.

In the Democratic Republic of the Congo, a climate of impunity has resulted in rampant sexual violence:

From October 2006 to July 2007, more than 10,000 survivors of sexual violence, 37 per cent of whom were children, were identified by United Nations partners in the eastern region.[74] It is believed that during the war in Sierra Leone, as many as 10,000 women and girls were abducted, mostly from rural areas, to serve the Revolutionary United Front. Their primary role, according to UNICEF, was to provide domestic and sexual services.

ABDUCTION

The abduction of children by force, either temporarily or permanently, can range in purpose from recruitment by armed forces or groups and

Georgia © UNICEF/NYHQ2008-0683/Volpe

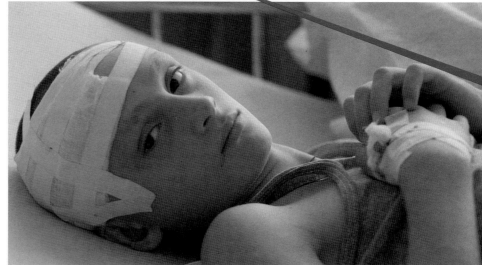

> **"The girls when captured are made wives, and if the girl is not yet of age she gets damaged."** – Young man, 16, Sierra Leone

participation in hostilities to sexual exploitation or abuse, forced labour, hostage-taking, information-gathering and indoctrination. Recruitment of a child by force is considered two separate violations: abduction and recruitment.

The most recent Secretary-General's report on children and armed conflict cited cases of abduction in Colombia, the Democratic Republic of the Congo, Haiti, the Occupied Palestinian Territory, the Sudan and Sri Lanka.[75] Between 2003 and 2006, additional abductions were noted in Angola, Iraq, Liberia, Myanmar, Nepal, Sierra Leone and Uganda.

One of the most notorious situations involving widespread abduction of children over the past 10 years took place in northern Uganda, where the number of abductions since the onset of armed conflict was estimated to have reached 25,000 or more.[76] In fact, the Lord's Resistance Army would likely have been unable to mount a viable fighting force without child abductees.

In the Ugandan districts of Kitgum and Pader, more than one third of all male youths and one sixth of all female youths have been abducted for at least a day.[77] In June 2005, it was estimated that as many as 40,000 children and youth were 'commuting' to city centres each night to escape the possibility of abduction. However, the security situation has improved, and since early 2007 less than 1,000 were continuing to commute.[78]

DENIAL OF HUMANITARIAN ACCESS

'Denial of humanitarian access' entails blocking the free passage or timely delivery of humanitarian assistance to persons in need, including children. There is a pressing need to better define the scope of the term, since it is often used euphemistically.

Humanitarian access may be denied for either security or political reasons. A State or non-state actor may claim it wants to protect humanitarian workers from danger when in reality it has a hidden agenda of limiting witnesses to human rights abuses. Since States are bound to provide access to civilians in need under international humanitarian law, a State's obligation to allow humanitarian access is all the more pressing if the conflict is declared an 'armed conflict'.

The 2007 Secretary-General's report on children and armed conflict highlighted restrictions of humanitarian access affecting children in Colombia, Myanmar, Somalia and Sudan (Darfur).[79] In addition, the Secretary-General's report on protection of civilians cited access restrictions in Afghanistan, the Democratic Republic of the Congo, Iraq, Myanmar, Somalia and the Sudan (Darfur). It specifically highlighted constraints in the Sudanese region of Darfur.[80] Millions of children are denied the humanitarian assistance they need in these and other situations.

Of particular concern is what seems to be an increase in deliberate attacks against humanitarian workers. One report found almost a doubling of major acts of violence against humanitarian workers between 1997 and 2005. National staff were at particular risk.[81] In 2007 in Afghanistan, more than 130 attacks took place against humanitarian programmes, with 40 humanitarian workers killed and 89 abducted.[82]

The most recent report of the Secretary-General on the protection of civilians in armed conflict highlights constraints on humanitarian access as a principal protection concern. The report launched an initiative to better monitor and document access constraints. This includes efforts to better define the concept by developing a typology of access constraints, such as lack of security in the operating environment, blocking of aid shipments and deliberate attacks against humanitarian workers.

OTHER CONFLICT-RELATED VIOLATIONS

Violations against children – including torture, enforced disappearance, administrative detention, forced displacement, sexual exploitation and abuse, and hazardous work – have also been reported during and after armed conflicts.

Torture. Torture and other forms of ill-treatment remain prevalent in armed conflict situations, even though prohibited by the 1984 Convention against Torture and

TABLE 1. ESTIMATED NUMBERS OF PERSONS FORCIBLY DISPLACED IN 2006

	Low estimate, all ages (millions)	High estimate, all ages (millions)	Estimated total, all ages (millions)	Per cent children	Number of children (millions)	Per cent women	Number of women (millions)	Per cent women and children	Number of women and children (millions)
Refugees by origin	11.2	17.2	14.2	41%	5.8	26%	3.7	67%	9.5
Internally displaced persons	15.7	25.2	24.5	36%	8.8	30%	7.3	66%	16.1
Population of humanitarian concern	37.1	52.6	48.9	37%	18.1	28%	13.2	66%	31.3

Sources: Internal Displacement Monitoring Centre of the Norwegian Refugee Council, *Internal Displacement: Global overview of trends and development in 2006,* April 2007; Office of the UN High Commissioner for Refugees, *Global Trends 2006: Refugees, asylum seekers, returnees, internally displaced and stateless persons,* UNHCR, Geneva, June 2007; U.S. Committee for Refugees and Immigrants, *World Refugee Survey 2006,* USCRI, Arlington, Virginia (USA).

Other Cruel, Inhuman or Degrading Treatment or Punishment and other conventions and treaties, including the Convention on the Rights of the Child (CRC). In a 2000 report of the Special Rapporteur of the Commission on Human Rights on torture and other cruel, inhuman or degrading treatment or punishment, particular concern was noted over children's subjugation to extreme forms of torture and other ill-treatment as a result of armed conflict.

Enforced disappearance. The enforced disappearance of children after arrest, detention or abduction with the acquiescence of a government is prohibited by the 1992 Declaration on the Protection of All Persons from Enforced Disappearance. It is considered a crime under international law in the Rome Statute of the International Criminal Court and the recently adopted International Convention for the Protection of All Persons from Enforced Disappearance.

The Watchlist on Children and Armed Conflict identified, among other occurrences, a widespread pattern of enforced disappearances in Nepal, including among those under age 18, as part of the former government's counter-insurgency operations.[83] And in Colombia, para-

military groups were implicated in enforced disappearances of children throughout the late 1990s and the early part of this decade.

Administrative detention. The 2007 Secretary-General's report on children and armed conflict expresses concern over the prevalence of detained children in Burundi, Colombia, the Democratic Republic of the Congo, Iraq, Israel and the Philippines. In the context of armed conflict as well as counter-terrorism activities, an unknown number of children in several parts of the world have been detained on security grounds. They are held through an administrative (non-judicial) process that often denies guarantees of due process, such as the right to legal defence or to challenge the decision with an independent authority. Typical features of administrative detention include undetermined duration, restricted contact with family and limited monitoring.

Forced displacement. A common and visible violation during armed conflict is forced displacement, whether within one's own country or across national borders. Displacement can be both a cause and a consequence of armed conflict, typically increasing children's risk in terms of other

violations. Children's well-being is also in jeopardy if they become separated from their families or caregivers.

As previously mentioned, an estimated 18.1 million children were among displaced populations in 2006 (see table 1). At that time, the estimated total population of internally displaced persons was well over a third higher than the total number of refugees. Despite the somewhat higher percentage of refugees who are children (41 per cent of refugees are children compared to 36 per cent of internally displaced persons), the absolute number of displaced children is a third higher than that of child refugees.

Even when accompanied by parents or caregivers, displaced children often have to take on adult responsibilities or dangerous tasks. Displacement subjects them to precarious living conditions and insecure environments with limited access to education and health care.

Sexual exploitation and abuse. The risk of sexual exploitation and abuse increases dramatically during and after armed conflict. During repatriation and reintegration, for example, children are especially vulnerable to conditions that can exacerbate gender-based violence.

Poverty and lack of livelihood options, limited social services and breakdown in community structures that often accompany conflict can place young girls especially at risk of sexual exploitation and 'transactional' or 'survival' sex. In addition, the preconditions for and causes of sex trafficking are compounded in armed conflict and post-conflict settings. They can lead to enslavement, forced prostitution and rape.

Finally, the visibility and persistence of allegations of sexual exploitation and abuse by peacekeepers has been striking in recent years. The Under-Secretary-General for Peacekeeping Operations has acknowledged the endemic nature and exploitative dimensions of the problem.

Hazardous work. As described in chapter 2, children have increasingly been pulled into hazardous forms of work as parties to armed conflict seek new sources of revenue to sustain military campaigns. Children work because their survival and that of their families depend on it – a situation that often worsens in an environment of armed conflict. However, such work can put them at risk. International Labour Organization Convention 182 identifies child slavery, trafficking, debt bondage, forced recruitment of children for use in armed conflict, prostitution, pornography and the production or trafficking of drugs as the worst forms of child labour. It calls on these to be immediately eliminated.

THE HARMFUL EFFECTS OF CONFLICT ON DEVELOPMENT

It is readily apparent that armed conflict not only leads to violations of children's rights but in many contexts hampers development progress, and thus children's opportunities. There are many ways to explore this issue, and discussion of specific consequences follows throughout this report. A comparison of progress towards the MDGs in conflict-affected countries and elsewhere provides a more global understanding of how conflict interrupts and delays development.[84]

The MDGs have become a universal framework for reducing poverty and promoting development since adoption of the Millennium Declaration by UN Member States in 2000. Six of the eight goals include specific commitments to promote child rights; the remainder address problems of the communities around them. Given the goals' emphasis on children, progress towards achieving them – or lack thereof – can be an important indicator in understanding the situation of children affected by armed conflict.

The Machel review presented to the General Assembly in 2007 noted that, "whether as a cause or as a consequence, conflict is a significant obstacle to achievement of the MDGs." Despite this assertion, halfway to the 2015 target date for achievement of the MDGs, limited analysis has been

made of progress in conflict-affected countries. Most research on these countries has concentrated on sectors, such as education, rather than the full set of goals.

The impact of conflict as measured by the MDGs

Identifying conflict-affected countries. As highlighted earlier, the number of armed conflicts said to be taking place at any one time across the globe varies widely depending on the criteria used. To analyse MDG progress, it was first necessary to identify a recognized set of conflict-affected countries. Through comparison of three reliable conflict databases, 33 countries were found to have experienced at least one armed conflict on their own soil between 2002 and 2006 (see table 2).[85]

The 33 countries and territories identified are Afghanistan, Algeria, Angola, Burundi, Central African Republic, Chad, Colombia, Congo, Côte d'Ivoire, Democratic Republic of the Congo, Ethiopia, Haiti, India, Indonesia, Iraq, Israel, Lebanon, Liberia, Myanmar, Nepal, Nigeria, the Occupied Palestinian Territory, Pakistan, Philippines, Russian Federation, Rwanda, Senegal, Somalia, Sri Lanka, Sudan, Thailand, Turkey and Uganda. From this list it is clear that armed conflict is a global phenomenon, although Africa and Asia are affected disproportionately: Among the 33 countries and territories, 16 are in Africa and 9 are in Asia. The remaining

TABLE 2. COUNTRIES AND TERRITORIES AFFECTED BY CONFLICT, 2002–2006

For each database, countries were included if they were considered affected by conflict at any time during the 2002–2006 period.

Countries and territories	Uppsala Conflict Database	Institute of Heidelberg	Project Ploughshares
Afghanistan	X	X	X
Algeria	X	X	X
Angola	X	X	X
Burundi	X	X	X
Central African Republic	X	X	
Chad	X	X	X
Colombia	X	X	X
Congo	X	X	X
Côte d'Ivoire	X	X	X
Democratic Republic of the Congo		X	X
Ethiopia	X	X	X
Haiti		X	X
India	X	X	X
Indonesia	X	X	X
Iraq	X	X	X
Israel	X	X	X
Lebanon	X	X	X
Liberia	X	X	X
Myanmar	X	X	X
Nepal	X	X	X
Nigeria	X	X	X
Occupied Palestinian Territory	X	X	X
Pakistan	X	X	X
Philippines	X	X	X
Russian Federation	X	X	X
Rwanda	X	X	
Senegal		X	X
Somalia	X	X	X
Sri Lanka	X	X	X
Sudan	X	X	X
Thailand	X	X	X
Turkey	X	X	
Uganda	X	X	X

Total conflict-affected countries and territories, 2002–2006: 33

Notes: 'X' indicates at least one violent conflict (minor conflict or war, as per the Uppsala Conflict Database; severe crisis or war, as per the Institute of Heidelberg) in a given year. Data from the Uppsala Conflict Database includes both 'wars' and 'minor conflicts'. 'War' is defined as a conflict with at least 1,000 battle-related deaths in a year. 'Minor conflict' is defined as having at least 25 but less than 1,000 battle-related deaths in a year. Institute of Heidelberg data include 'violent conflicts of high intensity', referring to conflicts scoring 4 or 5 ('severe crisis' or 'war') on the 0–5 range of the databases. Project Ploughshares defines an armed conflict as having at least 1,000 battle-related deaths in a year. For the purposes of this analysis, minor conflicts were also included, based on the Uppsala Conflict Database criterion of at least 25 but less than 1,000 battle-related deaths.

Sources: Uppsala Conflict Database; Institute of Heidelberg; Project Ploughshares.

8 are in the Middle East, Central and Eastern Europe and Latin America. It is also noteworthy that armed conflict occurs in countries with widely varying levels of economic development. Roughly half the 33 countries or territories have been designated as 'least developed', while the other half represent a fairly broad range, including some middle-income countries.

Analysing specific MDG indicators. This analysis compared the 33 conflict-affected countries that have global and regional estimates for each MDG indicator. This includes selected indicators, such as underweight prevalence for children under five, primary school enrolment and under-five mortality rates. For each MDG indicator reviewed, 196 countries were ranked, regardless of whether they were affected by conflict, to identify those countries appearing among the worst 20 performers. In addition, a review was made to determine whether conflict-affected countries were considered on track for each MDG target. While this initial analysis has not determined any degree of causality, a number of interesting findings emerged that reinforce a special concern for children in conflict-affected countries.

Globally, more than two thirds of children under five who are undernourished live in countries affected by conflict. Children out of primary school in these countries constitute as many as two thirds of that group

> **"Most of the children in Afghanistan work on the streets. At the age when they should just study, they are forced to work and earn a living for their families."** – Girl, 14, Afghanistan

worldwide. And two thirds of conflict-affected countries have shown insufficient or no progress in reducing under-five mortality rates. Of populations without improved sanitation and safe drinking water globally, approximately half live in countries affected by conflict. And such countries have higher debt service costs and lower overseas development aid per capita than non-conflict countries. This limits state budgets and other support for children.

Furthermore, countries in conflict generally show slow progress towards the MDGs. Of the 20 lowest achievers across all the goals, typically half were affected by armed conflict (see table 3). The countries that appeared most frequently among the 20 lowest achievers in each of the MDGs are conflict-affected least-developed countries: Afghanistan, Chad, Ethiopia, Somalia and the Sudan.

MDG 1: Eradicate extreme poverty and hunger. Levels of poverty and hunger are a critical factor in children's health and development. A target for this MDG is, between 1990 and 2015, to reduce by half the proportion of people who suffer from hunger.

In reviewing the MDG indicator of underweight prevalence for children under five, this analysis has found that there are 98.5 million under-nourished children below the age of five living in conflict-affected countries. This is more than two thirds of the 143 million children

under five globally who suffer from undernutrition.

The average underweight prevalence for children under five is 32 per cent in these conflict-affected countries, compared to an average of 25 per cent for the world as a whole. In addition, 19 of the 33 conflict-affected countries have shown either insufficient or no progress towards the target of halving the proportion of people suffering from hunger by 2015.

MDG 2: Achieve universal primary education. Achieving the education-related MDGs is recognized as pivotal in meeting many of the other goals. MDG 2 targets the completion of a full course of primary schooling for boys and girls everywhere by 2015.

This analysis reviewed the number of children out of primary school as well as the net enrolment/attendance rates in countries affected by conflict. In 2006, nearly 60 million children were not in school in the 33 conflict-affected countries,[86] out of approximately 93 million children of the same age group out of school globally in 2005–2006.[87]

In these conflict-affected countries, the average primary school net enrolment/attendance ratio (essentially the percentage of children of the appropriate age group enrolled/attending classes) is 81 per cent. While 10 of these countries are on track to reach universal primary education by 2015, another 19 have shown no progress at all.

MDG 3: Promote gender equality and empower women. As a starting point for women's equality and empowerment, a target was set of eliminating gender disparity in primary and secondary education by 2005 and at all levels by 2015.

In reviewing the primary school net enrolment/attendance ratio and gender parity index, this analysis found that in conflict-affected countries, just over half of those not attending primary school, 31.3 million, are girls. Girls clearly fall behind on this indicator in 13 of the 33 conflict-affected countries where the gender parity index is below 0.96.[88]

While an impressive 21 conflict-affected countries are on track towards eliminating gender disparity in primary education by 2015, another 12 have made insufficient progress.

MDG 4: Reduce child mortality. Addressing child survival is literally a matter of life or death. This MDG targets a two-thirds reduction in under-five mortality between 1990 and 2015.

This analysis found an average under-five mortality rate of 81 per 1,000 live births in conflict-affected countries.[89] This compares to a world average of 72 deaths per 1,000 live births. Among the 33 countries affected by conflict, 20 have shown either insufficient or no progress towards achieving the target.

MDG 5: Improve maternal health. A mother's health is an important factor in a child's survival and

**TABLE 3. DISTRIBUTION OF CONFLICT-AFFECTED COUNTRIES,
NON-CONFLICT COUNTRIES AND THOSE WITH LOWEST MDG PERFORMANCE**

On average, 29 per cent of all conflict-affected countries rank among the 20 lowest achievers in terms of the MDGs,
compared to only 8 per cent of all non-conflict countries.

MDG	Indicator	Conflict-affected countries		Non-conflict countries	
		Among 20 lowest achievers	As a proportion of all conflict-affected countries (N=33) (%)	Among 20 lowest achievers	As a proportion of all non-conflict countries (N=163) (%)
1	Underweight prevalence in children	9	27	11	8
2	Primary school net enrolment/attendance ratio	10	30	10	8
3	Gender parity in primary school	10	30	10	8
4	Under-five mortality rate	9	27	11	8
5	Maternal mortality	11	33	9	7
7	Use of improved sanitation	9	27	11	8
7	Use of improved drinking water source	8	24	12	9
	Average number of countries	9	29	11	8

development. This MDG aims to reduce the maternal mortality ratio by three quarters between 1990 and 2015.

This analysis found that, on average, women in conflict-affected countries face a lifetime risk of dying from the complications of pregnancy or childbirth of 1 in 276. This is less than the world average of 1 in 92 but far higher than the average for industrialized countries of 1 in 8,000. (The average risk in conflict-affected countries is heavily skewed by Israel [1 in 7,800] and the Russian Federation [1 in 2,700]).[90]

The average maternal mortality ratio for the 33 conflict-affected countries is considered high at 477 per 100,000 live births, compared to a world average of 400 per 100,000 live births. In fact, about half of the 33 conflict-affected countries have maternal mortality rates of 550 or more, considered very high.

MDG 6: Combat HIV/AIDS, malaria and other diseases. As data for these indicators were consistently available only for conflict-affected countries

from sub-Saharan Africa, a comparative analysis was not possible.

MDG 7: Ensure environmental sustainability – basic sanitation and safe drinking water. Use of basic sanitation and safe drinking water is a key strategy for child survival. This MDG aims to halve, by 2015, the proportion of people without sustainable access to safe drinking water and basic sanitation.

This analysis, based on 2004 data, found that just over half a billion people (529 million) lack access to improved drinking water sources in the 33 conflict-affected countries. This represents about half of the 1.1 billion people without safe drinking water globally. That said, 21 of the 33 conflict-affected countries are on track to reach the MDG target.

In terms of sanitation, a staggering 1.4 billion people living in conflict-affected countries do not have access to improved sanitation facilities. This represents about half of the 2.6 billion people globally without toilets or other forms of improved sanitation. Fewer countries have made progress

in sanitation than in water: 16 of the 33 countries affected by conflict have made no progress at all towards halving the proportion of people without sustainable access to basic sanitation.

MDG 8: Develop a global partnership for development. This MDG calls for comprehensive action to deal with the debt problems of developing countries and to address the special needs of the least-developed countries. Such initiatives are especially important for children because of their impact on national budgets and the provision of services.

A review of debt servicing found that the 33 conflict-affected countries had overall higher debt service payments than countries not affected by conflict (8.5 per cent versus 5.9 per cent).[91] Moreover, the 33 conflict-affected countries received less aid per capita – $28.20 compared to $43.70 – than non-conflict countries. This means that, on average, less aid is available for each child in a conflict-affected country than for children in other developing countries (see table 4, page 31).

DEVELOPMENT IS SLOWED IN WAR-TORN AREAS OF UGANDA

The situation in Uganda offers insights into the disparities in development that may be linked to armed conflict. Data from a number of indicators in the northern region of the country, which has suffered more than two decades of war, show outcomes that are clearly worse than national estimates.

By comparing national estimates with 2006 data compiled by Demographic and Health Surveys for regions that included the North and West Nile and Karamoja, along with a sampling of camps for internally displaced persons, this analysis found that:

- **Levels of poverty are greater in conflict-affected regions; 58 per cent of the poorest households in the North fall within the poorest quintile nationally.**

- **While the prevalence of malnutrition among children under five (as measured by weight for age) was 16 per cent for the whole of Uganda, this rose to 22 per cent in the North and 36 per cent in Karamoja.**

- **School attendance is lower in some conflict areas. For instance, 43 per cent of children in the Karamoja area attend primary school versus 82 per cent at the national level.**

- **The conflict-affected areas of Uganda have a higher under-five mortality rate, with a rate of 185 in West Nile versus 134 nationally.**

- **In general, a lower percentage of births are assisted by a skilled birth attendant in areas affected by conflict – 42 per cent at the national level compared to just 18 per cent in the Karamoja area and 31 per cent in the North.**

Limitations and further analysis

Certain aspects of the impact of armed conflict on development were not explored in this analysis. These include the geographic location of an armed conflict and how that might relate to certain development disparities, the influence of armed conflict as opposed to poverty or discrimination on development outcomes, and the continuing legacy of armed conflict once a conflict is considered over.

Geographical disparities. Armed conflicts in certain countries are confined to particular areas, such as the northern region of Uganda, Darfur in the Sudan, eastern portions of Turkey, certain parts of India, southern regions of Thailand and Chechnya in the Russian Federation. Only a small percentage of the entire population in those countries is directly affected. It can be argued, however, that in some cases, the presence of armed conflict in a country drains state resources from other activities and can impede foreign investment, thus affecting children's development opportunities. Because comparable region/state/provincial-level data are not currently available for many of the 33 countries being considered, this analysis was not able to differentiate findings within a country. Unfortunately this means that large-population countries with armed conflicts confined to portions of their territory skew certain figures.

The socio-economic situation before a conflict. Countries also differ in their ability to deal with the effects of armed conflict because of pre-existing socio-economic conditions. For instance, despite having been devastated by three wars since 1980, Iraq is a middle-income country. Far more Iraqis have access to improved sources of drinking water and sanitation facilities than Afghans, who live in a least developed country and have experienced several decades of conflict. While inequality and poverty can lead to or result from

**TABLE 4. DEBT SERVICE AND AID PER CAPITA
FOR CONFLICT AND NON-CONFLICT STATES, 2005**

	All countries	Conflict-affected countries	Non-conflict countries
Debt service as a per cent of exports of goods and services, 2005*	6.5%	8.5%	5.9%
Aid per capita (current US dollars), 2005	$40.70	$28.20	$43.70

* Long-term public and publicly guaranteed debt and repayments to the International Monetary Fund only; excludes workers' remittances.

Source: 'Millennium Development Goals: Data – Query', World Bank Group website, <http://ddp-ext.worldbank.org/ext/GMIS/gdmis.do?siteId=2&menuId=LNAV01HOME3>.

armed conflict, it is not possible to establish any causality or clear correlation based on data.

The continuing legacy of armed conflict. This analysis has taken into account only countries in which active conflicts were under way over the period 2002–2006; post-conflict environments were not considered. Nevertheless, the time it takes from the end of a conflict to achieve demonstrable improvement in MDG indicators can be critical. Data from Rwanda, for example, show that it can take more than a decade for child mortality indicators to improve after fighting has ended. It takes time to rebuild in all areas, underlining the importance of sustained funding and support.

Building on this analysis. In further expanding this analysis, it would be useful to develop a more detailed assessment and explore specific challenges for children in countries affected by conflict. For example, what unique factors are present in conflict-affected countries that are making progress and are on track to meet the MDG targets versus those that are not? What are the key differences between conflict-affected countries and other low achievers? How do disparities in development progress play out in areas of the country where armed conflict is present versus areas where it is not? Data on progress made before the outbreak

of and during armed conflict could likewise be compared in order to assess the extent to which armed conflict slows or halts development.

GAPS AND RECOMMENDATIONS

A major gap in monitoring the situation of children in armed conflict remains the availability of accurate and reliable data. This is true in terms of both specific violations and progress towards a full range of rights.

In the coming years, greater emphasis must be placed on the enhanced coordination needed to analyse gaps in knowledge, conduct research, strengthen capacity, address programme needs and establish realistic goals and plans to respond to violations of children's rights and interruptions or delays to development during and after armed conflict. Interventions aimed at preventing armed conflict and building peace should be prioritized. A strong focus is needed on human rights, conflict resolution and the involvement of children and young people in framing solutions.

The following chapters will explore in more detail many of the consequences highlighted here and suggest specific recommendations to further address the situation of children caught in the crossfire of war. ■

KEY RESOURCES

K. Eck, 'A Beginner's Guide to Conflict Data: Finding and using the right dataset – UCDP Paper #1', Uppsala Conflict Data Program, Department of Peace and Conflict Research, Uppsala University, Uppsala (Sweden), December 2005.

Human Security Centre, *Human Security Brief 2006,* University of British Colombia, Vancouver, 2006.

Internal Displacement Monitoring Centre–Norwegian Refugee Council, *Internal Displacement: Global overview of trends and development in 2006,* IDMC, Geneva, April 2007.

United Nations Children's Fund, *Progress for Children: A World Fit for Children tatistical review,* Number 6, UNICEF, New York, December 2007.

World Bank, *Global Monitoring Report 2007: Millennium Development Goals – Confronting the challenges of gender equality and fragile states,* International Bank for Reconstruction and Development/World Bank, Washington, D.C., 2007.

Sudan © UNICEF/NYHQ2006-0461/Furrer

4

CHILDREN AS PEACEMAKERS

"We feel and understand what's happening, so we want to do something to change it." – Age and sex not specified, Indonesia

Children's participation is itself a human right as well as a means to secure other rights, including survival, protection and development. These rights apply to all children in all contexts, including situations of armed conflict. When girls and boys, especially the most marginalized, have the opportunity to express themselves, to access information and to participate in decisions that affect their lives, they are better able to claim their rights and to hold adults accountable.

At the time of the 1996 Machel study, child participation was emerging as an important aspect of development practice among child-focused agencies.

But uncertainty existed about the participation of children in humanitarian endeavours, specifically in settings affected by conflict.

In the intervening years, the nature and scope of participatory programming has expanded, though its application in conflict situations remains limited. Greater emphasis is being placed on the involvement of younger children as well as adolescents, taking into account their evolving capacities. At the same time, there is growing recognition of the need to engage with children and youth as participants within specific projects and programmes as well as in the various dimensions of their everyday lives – domestic, educational, economic, cultural and political.

The value of understanding and responding to the political and social reality of children's lives has been highlighted by a growing number of practitioners and academics in the years since the 1996 study.[92]

WHAT THE MACHEL STUDY SAID

While the Machel study did not focus at length on children's participation, the potential of such an approach to programming was indicated in various sections of the study. In paragraph 182, for example, the study says that "young people should themselves be involved in community-based relief, recovery and reconstruction programmes. This can be achieved through vocational and skills training that not only helps to augment their income, but also increases their sense of identity and self-worth in ways that enhance healing." It goes on to say that "developing and implementing programmes for younger children" has been successful in "giving adolescents a sense of meaning and purpose."

PROGRESS IN POLICY AND PRACTICE

At the global level. A number of important global developments in the past decade have supported children's participation, including involvement in two major international events: the UN General Assembly Special Session on

Sudan © UNICEF/NYHQ2006-2173/Cranston

Children in 2002 and the 2006 *World Report on Violence against Children*.

For both of these undertakings, children's participation was encouraged at the local, district, national, regional and global levels. Drawing upon lessons learned, standards in children's participation have been established, adapted, adjusted and applied in various contexts to ensure more ethical and meaningful engagement on the part of children.

In 2006, for example, the Committee on the Rights of the Child held a 'Day of General Discussion on the Child's Right to be Heard'. The event was part of the process of preparing a 'General Comment' to be adopted by the Committee in 2008 that would provide guidance to States parties in realizing children's right to participate. The importance of ensuring implementation of article 12 of the CRC,[93] even in situations of conflict and their aftermath, was raised in the course of this discussion.

Participants acknowledged the contributions that children can make in situations of conflict, post-conflict resolution and reconstruction following emergencies. It was also noted that participation can enhance children's psychosocial well-being and benefit the wider community. The importance of protecting children from exposure to situations that may cause them harm was also reiterated.

As noted in the introduction, this 10-year strategic review of the original Machel study also involved extensive consultations with and engagement of children and young people affected by armed conflict.

At the field level. A growing number of initiatives in conflict situations have been undertaken by local agencies and government institutions with the support of such organizations as UNICEF, the Women's Commission for Refugee Women and Children, Save the Children, Christian Children's Fund and Plan.[94] For example, efforts have been increasing to involve children – including children associated with armed forces – in research, monitoring and evaluation to understand and strengthen the impact of humanitarian responses.[95]

The Women's Commission for Refugee Women and Children, for instance, has undertaken programme and policy reviews and has supported participatory research with adolescents in Kosovo, northern Uganda and Sierra Leone, aiming to highlight adolescents' distinct experiences and their potential as active members of society.[96]

Save the Children Norway launched a thematic evaluation of children's participation in armed conflict, post-conflict transition and peacebuilding in Bosnia and Herzegovina, Guatemala, Nepal and Uganda. Throughout this effort, which lasted from 2006 to 2008, children aged 10 to 18 were recruited as advisers, researchers, reporters and advocates.[97]

Children's involvement in peacebuilding is not an isolated activity; it is part of a larger process of transition and reconciliation. While still not commonplace or consistently carried out, children's participation in peacebuilding has contributed to formal mechanisms, such as peace talks and truth and reconciliation commissions. The Sierra Leone Truth and Reconciliation Commission is widely considered a milestone in having created the first 'child-friendly' forum to enable children to participate in the search for closure to the violence that tore their country apart.

Overcoming constraints to children's participation. One constraint on the development of participatory activities has been the concern for children's protection, an especially urgent issue in situations of

"We agree that we have destroyed this country. And it is us – the young people – that should be empowered to rebuild our communities. We need basic training to make this country good again. It can't be the NGOs that do all the work for us. It has to be us." – Young man, 18, Liberia

CHILDREN MAKE THEIR VIEWS KNOWN DURING PEACE TALKS IN UGANDA

The situation in Uganda offers insights into the disparities in development that may be linked to armed conflict. Data from a number of indicators in the northern region of the country, which has suffered more than two decades of war, show outcomes that are clearly worse than national estimates.

By comparing national estimates with 2006 data compiled by Demographic and Health Surveys for regions that included the North and West Nile and Karamoja, along with a sampling of camps for internally displaced persons, this analysis found that:

- "Recognize and consider the experiences, views and concerns of children."

- "Protect the dignity, privacy and security of children in any accountability and reconciliation proceedings."

- "Ensure that children are not subjected to criminal justice proceedings, but may participate in reconciliation processes."

- "Encourage and facilitate the participation of children in the processes for implementing this agreement."

Source: Concerned Parents Association, 2007, pp. 4-9, 31-35; and http://northernuganda.usvpp.gov/downloads.html.

mechanisms are needed to allow young people to bring emerging issues to light with confidence that child-rights violations will be dealt with swiftly and appropriately.

As with all participatory endeavours, the involvement of children in protection efforts is not only a means to improve interventions but may also be a beneficial process for participants. As experience is starting to show, participation can enhance the competencies, confidence and networks that enable boys and girls to better protect themselves and others.[100]

As illustrated in the boxes on pages 36 and 37, participation spearheaded by children themselves has taken many diverse forms. These examples illustrate the potential of such efforts to enhance not only children's lives but those of others.

REMAINING GAPS

In many countries afflicted by armed conflict, engagement in public decision-making is largely denied to citizens regardless of their age. Such exclusion can give rise to frustration, including among the young, that can ignite or further fuel conflict. The challenge is thus twofold: first, to address the systems and structures that inhibit the full functioning of civil society, and second, to transform relationships between adults and children and among children and youth to open up avenues for all to participate in civil society processes.

armed conflict. Participation has been seen by some as an unnecessary risk to children that could compromise their protection or as a time-consuming luxury. Certainly, safety should always be the primary concern of organizations responsible for such activities, with careful attention paid to issues such as timing, location and the nature

and content of activities.[98] However, failure to include children in protection strategies may also put them at risk.

An important lesson along these lines has emerged from recent cases of abuse that took place under the noses or even with the complicity of humanitarian agency staff in west Africa and Nepal.[99] Bodies and

Given the relative newness of participatory approaches to working with children in armed conflict, much remains to be done. Gaps are evident in various dimensions of programming, including understanding children's involvement in political violence and confrontational politics; addressing diversity and disparities in participation; and promoting the ethos of participation, even in institutional hierarchies.

Understanding children's involvement in political violence and confrontational politics. The 1996 Machel study observed that it is misleading to describe any military recruitment of boys and girls as voluntary. Rather than exercising free choice, these children are more likely responding to a variety of pressures – economic, cultural, social and political.

The study recognizes, however, that young people may engage in political struggles for ideological reasons: "It is important to note that children may also identify with and fight for social causes, religious expression, self-determination or national liberation," the study said. "As happened in South Africa or in the Occupied Palestinian Territory, they may join the struggle in pursuit of political freedom."

It is important to understand more thoroughly the motivation behind some children's use of violence – or support for it – while avoiding judgements arising from

KOSOVAR YOUTH BECOME A FORCE FOR PEACE

During the 1999 Kosovo crisis, around 20,000 young Kosovars in six Albanian refugee camps came together to form their own Youth Councils. The councils took action to improve safety and living conditions in the camps, organized sports and music events, distributed landmine-awareness information and provided psychosocial counselling for younger children. When the young activists subsequently returned to their home villages, many continued their community development work, setting up a network that promotes local peacebuilding efforts.

AFGHAN CHILDREN SEEK SOLUTIONS TO THE PROBLEM OF INSECURITY

In north-eastern Afghanistan, children were ask to map what they perceived to be safety risks in their communities, providing poignant evidence of the different realities faced by girls and boys. The exercise, supported by the Afghan arm of the Christian Children's Fund, led to the formation of local Child Well-Being Committees – one for girls and women, the other for men and boys – in individual villages. The committees are monitoring the risks identified by local children and taking action to mitigate them. The committees are also facilitating the use of small grants to conduct civic works projects that will improve children's quality of life.

Source: M. Wessells, *Child Soldiers: From violence to protection*, Harvard University Press, Cambridge, MA, 2006, pp. 228–249.

SIERRA LEONE'S TRUTH AND RECONCILIATION COMMISSION BREAKS NEW GROUND

The involvement of children in Sierra Leone's Truth and Reconciliation Commission in 2002–2003 has been hailed as a significant shift that placed children's participation in truth-seeking bodies firmly on the international agenda. Although children's issues were addressed in other truth commissions – in Argentina, El Salvador, Guatemala and Peru – the process in Sierra Leone set a new precedent by:

■ Soliciting confidential statements from children in all districts of the country

■ Inviting children to testify in district hearings (with support from child protection agencies)

■ Organizing a two-day thematic hearing on children in Freetown

■ Allowing official submissions from children to the Commission

■ Supporting children's contributions to a child-friendly version of a Truth Commission study

■ Using a 'Voices of Children' radio programme to disseminate information during the truth and reconciliation process

■ Creating opportunities for children's representatives from a Children's Forum Network to meet with the Special Representative of the Secretary-General for Children and Armed Conflict and the President of Sierra Leone

Source: United Nations Children's Fund, *Adolescent Programming Experiences during Conflict and Post-Conflict: Case Studies*, UNICEF, New York, 2004, p. 59; 'Children and Adolescents in Transitional Justice Processes in Sierra Leone', Contribution of the Women's Commission for Refugee Women and Children to the Machel study 10-year strategic review, June 2007.

stereotypical views of the young as either innocent victims or wayward villains. Approaching children's participation in political violence or confrontational politics, at times as a consequence of some degree of choice, is important for programming efforts for the following reasons:

■ Addressing the experiences, frustrations, needs and aspirations that move children to participate in violence is vital in transitioning away from conflict.[101]

■ The knowledge, skills, strengths and identities that children acquire through participation in political violence or confrontational politics can be put to beneficial use in peacetime.

■ Inclusive and appropriate processes of transitional justice and peacebuilding are part of reintegrating war-affected children.

Indications suggest that participatory programming can actually strengthen the ability of children to resist efforts by armed groups to recruit them. For example, some members of village-based children's clubs in Nepal targeted for recruitment have said that their participation in these clubs helped them assert themselves, negotiate and avoid being lured into dangerous situations.[102] On the other hand, organized participatory activities can also be a stepping stone towards involvement in violence.[103] When such activities fail to lead to meaningful change, children whose consciousness and confidence have been raised through such activities may be susceptible to groups promising change, including through political or criminal violence. This has been evident in such settings as Kosovo.[104]

Addressing diversity and disparities in participation. Factors such as gender, age, class, caste, ethnicity, religion, language, birth order, residence, level of education, and disability and HIV status all affect the influence of conflict on children. They also affect the evolving roles, responsibilities, needs and aspirations of children. Moreover, conflict invariably creates new roles and responsibilities for them. These include the full-time care of younger siblings because of the death, injury or disappearance of parents. If programming fails to take into account the realities of girls' and boys' daily lives and their diverse needs – assuming instead a singular 'ideal' of childhood – it is "unlikely to prove sustainable and may be counterproductive, contributing to a sense of disempowerment and alienation amongst participants," according to a report by the Refugee Studies Centre.[105]

Community-based organizations for children and youth – such as clubs, committees and other groups – provide a regular space for expression, analysis, collective action and election

Cambodia © UNICEF/NYHQ2004-0763/Thomas

of representatives. However, it is important to recognize the tendency for certain children to be over-represented. Urban children typically enjoy greater opportunities than those in rural areas, for example, and boys tend to participate more than girls in many settings. Moreover, educational level, class or caste, along with the force of one's personality or physical ability, can create unequal power relations among children and youth. Participatory activities are not immune to the consequences, with the result that some children may dominate others or cause their exclusion.

As a recent experience in youth programming in Afghanistan has suggested, such inequalities may reflect and reinforce relations of power within wider society.[106] This raises particular concerns where patterns of domination or exclusion follow entrenched lines of difference in such categories as class, ethnicity, religious affiliation and gender, thereby echoing and reinforcing the dynamics of conflict.

Promoting the ethos of participation, even in institutional hierarchies. In recent years, great strides have been made in developing standards

Syrian Arab Republic © UNICEF/NYHQ2007-0737/Noorani

that is sustained throughout the conflict and post-conflict phases and from emergency to development programming.

Promoting and strengthening child-led organizations can be an effective way to bring about sustainable and democratic participation. However, for this to happen, participants may need support in challenging established patterns of discrimination and exclusion based on such factors as gender, class, religion and ethnicity.

Collaboration with governments and community leaders is also required to ensure that spaces for children's participation are incorporated in local governance structures. This includes in schools, local government and child-protection systems – as well as in policy-formation processes, including formal peace talks. In working with boys and girls as partners in this endeavour, it is vital to take into account not only the suffering they may have experienced but the skills, insights and knowledge they have acquired.

RECOMMENDATIONS

While participation received limited attention in the original Machel study, it was highlighted as an important issue in the 10-year strategic review presented to the UN General Assembly in 2007. The review encouraged Member States to make a greater commitment to

and guidelines for participatory programming with children. These include the practice standards of Save the Children Alliance outlined in the box on page 35. Nevertheless, participation as an applied approach remains marginal or even antithetical to much of the work of UN and international organizations in settings of armed conflict. In such circumstances, the expertise of outsiders is commonly valued more than the views, knowledge and experience of local people. In emergency settings especially, organizational hierarchies are commonly reinforced – to the detriment of consultative ways of working. Much thought needs to be

given to developing the skills, knowledge and dispositions of humanitarian workers, as well as to creating organizational structures and cultures in keeping with the ethos of participation.[107]

Humanitarian programming is usually short-lived. Once a perceived period of 'emergency' is over, agencies often withdraw or refocus their efforts.

Children's participation, however, is inherently development oriented and long term in nature. It offers opportunities for both the personal and collective development of children. The specific challenge of engaging children in the transition away from conflict requires support addressing obstacles to the participation of young people in decision-making and to actively promote their engagement in national and local-level governance, peace processes and justice, and truth and reconciliation processes. The review also urged an increase in technical and financial investment, including focused support for youth activities, secondary and tertiary education, and livelihood projects.

With the aim of further mainstreaming children's participation in the coming years, the following are recommended as priorities for action:

1. **Mainstream children's participation.** Member States, humanitarian actors and communities should promote the safe and meaningful engagement of children and young people in decisions that affect their lives. To achieve this involves (1) institutionalizing mechanisms for participation; (2) adapting and using global standards and guidelines with careful consideration of the local context; (3) promoting an egalitarian, democratic organizational culture that is consistent with the philosophy and aims of children's participation; and (4) building the capacity of adults and staff to work with children and youth in conflict and post-conflict situations.

2. **Facilitate participation in political processes by children and young people.** Member States should facilitate the input and views of children and young people in political processes, including the development and monitoring of peace agreements. Children's participation is required to identify, address and monitor structural factors that inhibit peace and/or the fulfilment of child rights.

3. **Support organizations led by children and youth.** Member States, UN and international and local non-governmental organizations should increase support for the development of inclusive child-led and youth-led organizations, networks and partnerships by increasing children's access to information, helping them build their skills and sensitizing adults to the importance of children's participation in civil society.

4. **Pursue sustainability of participation.** Donors, Member States, UN and international and local non-governmental organizations should seek to make participatory processes sustainable, ensuring continuation of donor support and integration into local and national systems.

5. **Develop research initiatives.** Member States, humanitarian agencies and research institutes should develop participatory research initiatives with the aim of involving a greater number and range of children in collaborative and sustained efforts to analyse the causes and consequences of political violence in each specific context. ■

KEY RESOURCES

Hart, J., *Children's Participation in Humanitarian Action: Learning from zones of armed conflict*, Refugee Studies Centre, University of Oxford, Oxford, February 2004, <www.rsc.ox.ac.uk/PDFs/Childrens%20Participation%20Synthesis%20Feb%202004.pdf>.

Save the Children Norway, Child Participation Web Group at <www.reddbarna.no/chp> for information, participatory toolkit, ethical guidelines, findings and recommendations, child-led documentation and advocacy initiatives relating to their two-year global thematic evaluation on children's participation in armed conflict, post-conflict transitions and peacebuilding.

It included subsequent action on the part of the Security Council to progressively incorporate the protection of children in conflict in its work, as described below.

Action on the recruitment of children and other rights violations. Since 1999, the Council's resolutions, statements and debates have generated significant momentum and pressure to hold parties accountable for violations of child rights, to galvanize work by diverse entities to protect and assist children in conflict, and to begin to redress impunity.

A turning point in efforts to address the behaviour and responsibilities of parties to conflict came in 2001, with Security Council Resolution 1379. It recommended that the Secretary-General attach to his annual report a list of parties to armed conflict that have recruited or used children in violation of international obligations applicable to them. It also called for the list to include a description of country situations that were on the Council's agenda or that could be brought to the Council's attention under article 99 of the UN Charter, which allows the Secretary-General to bring to the Council's attention anything that he or she believes may threaten international peace.

The first list, presented as an annex to the 2002 Report of the Secretary-General on children and armed conflict, concentrated on situations on the Council's agenda.

It listed 23 parties, including governments. One of the challenges in preparing it was the lack of information on the specific ages of children involved in armed conflict, which was necessary in determining whether a party was in violation of its particular obligations.

The next year's report of the Secretary-General was expanded to include parties in country situations outside the Council's agenda that recruited or used children in armed conflict. These were listed in a separate annex. All subsequent reports have included country situations both under consideration by the Council and outside its formal agenda. As discussed in chapter 2, 127 parties in 17 country situations were cited on lists covering the years 2002 through 2007.

The 'name and shame' initiative provided the Security Council with a valuable tool to press for accountability among parties recruiting children. Nevertheless, Council consideration of situations outside its agenda has required regular advocacy efforts.

The lists also offered child protection actors a useful instrument for negotiating with parties to conflict. This has resulted in the subsequent release of children. In its Resolution 1539 of 2004, the Security Council turned up the heat even more by calling on parties listed by the Secretary-General to prepare and implement concrete, time-bound action plans to halt the recruitment and use of children.

Entry on the list is limited to parties that recruit and use children, even though five other 'grave violations against children' are now monitored by the Security Council. This is a point of ongoing discussion. It is therefore important to consider the list in conjunction with the Secretary-General's full reports, in which the recruitment and use of children is put into context with progress and shortfalls in releasing children and other violations committed by a party. For example, the situation of Haiti has not been cited in the Secretary-General's lists. But reporting on other grave violations of children's rights in Haiti, outlined in the body of the Secretary-General's reports, has contributed to a more coordinated response by the peace-keeping mission there and by other actors. Most recently, Security Council Resolution 1780 condemned the grave violations against children in Haiti, including "widespread rape and other sexual abuse of girls."[112] A constructive development in 2005 was the notation of other grave violations committed by a party in the annexes of the Secretary-General's report.

Another recent advance has been the 'delisting' of certain armed groups that have come into verified compliance. The situation of Côte d'Ivoire is one example. Following the 2003 listing of certain parties to the conflict there and subsequent efforts of child protection organizations on the ground, the Forces armés des forces nouvelles released approximately 1,200 children to UNICEF in 2005. In 2006, four militia groups submitted an action plan and also began to release children who had been recruited for combat or non-combat purposes. In 2007, it was determined that some parties had fulfilled their action plans and could be 'delisted'. It is clear that the listing process is an incentive for parties to halt the recruitment of children and ensure their release.

Monitoring and reporting on grave violations of children's rights. In Resolution 1539, the Security Council also called on the Secretary-General for urgent development of a mechanism to systematically monitor and report on the situation of children affected by armed conflict. The aim was to provide the Council with accurate, reliable, objective and timely information on the recruitment and use of children by parties to armed conflict as well as on other violations of children's rights. Based on discussions with relevant organizations inside and outside the UN system, the Secretary-General determined that the monitoring mechanism would focus on six grave violations against children: killing or maiming; recruiting or using child soldiers; attacks against schools or hospitals; rape or other grave sexual violence; abduction; and denial of humanitarian access.

Following extensive discussions among Council members, led by

Occupied Palestinian Territory © UNICEF/NYHQ2007-0773/El Baba

Benin and France, the Security Council advanced the drive for compliance by establishing the proposed monitoring and reporting mechanism in its Resolution 1612 (2005). The resolution created both a monitoring and reporting mechanism at the country level and a Security Council Working Group on children and armed conflict – essentially bridging the gap between political action at the highest levels and action in the field.

In a relatively short period of time, the monitoring and reporting mechanism has expanded from a pilot project in seven countries – Burundi, Côte d'Ivoire, Democratic Republic of the Congo, Nepal, Somalia, Sri Lanka and Sudan – to implementation in 11 countries by the end of 2007.[113] It is especially significant that the mechanism has been adopted by countries outside

the agenda of the Security Council, including Chad, Nepal, the Philippines, Sri Lanka and Uganda. The engagement of these countries is a clear sign of the persuasive effect of both dialogue and the threat of action against violators of child rights. In Myanmar in 2007, two non-state groups agreed to halt and prevent the recruitment and use of children after being cited in the Secretary-General's list and following a series of discussions with UN personnel.

The monitoring and reporting mechanism is clearly a milestone in progress for children affected by armed conflict. Nevertheless, it still has shortcomings, including the fact that it is only triggered by the citing of situations and parties for which recruiting and using children is an issue, not the five other grave violations. The mechanism is based on the listing process established in

Afghanistan © UNICEF/NYHQ2007-1137/Noorani

of Resolutions 1261 and 1612, and the demonstrated impact of the mechanism as a deterrent and tool to fight impunity, the Machel strategic review suggests expansion of the mechanism to include all situations in which grave violations against conflict-affected children have occurred.

Resolution 1612 also reaffirmed the Council's resolve to impose targeted measures against parties that continue to violate their obligations to children. Translating this into concrete action remains a central issue, one that will challenge the credibility of the international community in terms of its commitment to children in the decade to come.

Advances made by the Security Council Working Group. The Working Group established by Resolution 1612 reviews reports of the monitoring mechanism, assesses progress on action plans for the release of children, reviews information on the other five grave violations against children and makes recommendations to the Council as well as other bodies in the UN system on measures to promote the protection of children affected by armed conflict. The Working Group has adopted terms of reference and a programme of work for bimonthly meetings and consideration of scheduled country reports.

The leadership of France as chair of the Working Group and that

Resolution 1379, despite the broader efforts of the Secretary-General to report on all six grave violations of children's rights and other issues of concern. To date, the action plans called for also focus exclusively on child recruitment and use. To be sure, this emphasis has been strategically helpful in calling attention to the threats to peace and security posed by child recruitment. It has also contributed to a degree of success on that issue since the 1996 study. But it has been at the expense of other equally grave violations of children's rights.

Recent discussions among Member States, experts and advocates have considered an incremental approach to addressing the problem. For example, adding incidents of rape

against children and other forms of sexual violence as a 'trigger' for citation in the Secretary-General's lists would mean that such situations would be included in the monitoring and reporting mechanism and in the work programme of the Security Council Working Group. The Machel strategic review recognizes the practicality of an incremental approach in view of the workload generated by the mechanism and challenges in preparing verified reports on perpetrators in conflict-affected contexts. However, in keeping with the original vision of the mechanism, it strongly recommends that all six grave violations be included, as expressed by the Secretary-General in reports S/2006/826 and S/2007/757. Furthermore, in view

country's overall commitment to the issue of children and armed conflict have been a vital source of the progress since 2005. Part of the Working Group's success is due to its innovative nature among sub-organs of the Security Council. For example, in addition to its regular work programme, the Working Group also considers what is called a Horizontal Note, which helps to monitor – in the most up-to-date way possible – key developments in all situations covered in the annual report of the Secretary-General and in other emerging crises. The Working Group also invites other Member States to relevant discussions on situations of concern and has adopted a 'toolkit' of 26 possible actions in response to violations. These include various diplomatic actions, field visits, public statements and targeted measures.

The Working Group has taken a firm stand in dealing with egregious violations against children. For example, it has drawn attention to cooperation with the International Criminal Court (ICC) in reviewing the situation of the Democratic Republic of the Congo and Uganda and has issued letters to relevant parties in response to all reports reviewed by the end of 2007.

While this is an impressive amount of work in a relatively short time, the effectiveness and credibility of the Working Group will hinge on addressing a number of key challenges. Among them is the need

to take serious action against persistent perpetrators, including the imposition of targeted measures as detailed in Resolutions 1539 and 1612. To date, 16 parties have repeatedly been cited in the Secretary-General's annual annexes, as mentioned in chapter 3.

The situation in the Democratic Republic of the Congo is a case in point. Parties and individuals operating in that country have been referred to the Council's sanctions committee since 2006, but no further action has been taken. Where a sanctions committee exists, and where sanctions are recognized, more must be done to curb abuses.

The adoption of targeted measures by the Council is not only a matter of political will. It also requires an organizational infrastructure. Towards that end, the Security Council should seriously consider establishing a sanctions committee exclusively for grave violations against children in situations of armed conflict.

Contrary to a number of specific calls in its resolutions on children and armed conflict, there has been weak overall integration of child protection into the peacekeeping and peace agreement work of the Council, as discussed below. In fact, some observers worry that the Working Group is emerging as the body primarily responsible for ensuring implementation of Council resolutions related to children and armed conflict.

For field-level results for children, it is essential that protection of their rights is given priority in all of the Council's work.

Mainstreaming action for children in peacekeeping mandates. Successive Security Council resolutions, the Secretary-General's reports on children and armed conflict, and even Graça Machel herself have all requested that country-specific reports to the Council include issues on the protection of children and their integration into peacekeeping operations and peace processes. Advancements in this area over the past decade have shown distinct progress, but the track record is insufficient to make a real difference in children's lives.

For example, in 2004 the Watchlist on Children and Armed Conflict analysed the integration of child protection concerns in relevant Security Council resolutions. It found that fewer than 10 of more than 80 country-specific resolutions in the previous three years included any references to children. Those that did were limited to three countries: Angola, the Democratic Republic of the Congo and Sierra Leone.[114] As noted above, progress for children has accelerated with establishment of the Security Council Working Group. Still, even in 2007, only 15 of 38 relevant resolutions included specific references to children.[115]

At present, the Council's attention in deliberating a situation is determined by quarterly reports of the Secretary-General. Yet even here, insufficient progress has been demonstrated. In 2006 and 2007, 38 per cent of relevant reports of the Secretary-General to the Council included specific references to child protection in situations of armed conflict. This is a decline from 43 per cent in 2005, but an improvement from 2003, when only 18 per cent of such reports included references to children.[116]

A key point of success since the 1996 Machel study is the integration of issues related to children and armed conflict in establishing peace-keeping and political missions. Where there was previously no reference to children, some aspect of children protection is included in the mandates of 12 of the 13 peacekeeping missions established between 2000 and 2007.

While this demonstrates progress, greater attention must be devoted to the ongoing implementation and reporting of a mission over time. Child protection was featured in the establishment of the UN Mission in Liberia in 2003, for example. But specific attention to children proved to be problematic on the ground. Provisions for children were at first overlooked in a disarmament, demobilization and reintegration initiative in that country. And throughout the process it was difficult for child

protection actors to influence the mission's approaches and actions related to children, including in regard to sexual exploitation and violence.[117]

Nevertheless, there appears to be growing recognition that peacekeeping can play a major role in advancing the political dimensions of child protection. This includes more systematic monitoring and reporting, and dialogue with parties to achieve action for conflict-affected children.

A key development facilitating the role of peacekeeping operations in the protection of children is the deployment of child protection advisers. They assist the head of a mission in devising a comprehensive approach to the problem, which may include monitoring and reporting; dialogue with perpetrators; assisting the UN Country Team in developing action plans; and ensuring that all civilian, military and police personnel attached to peacekeeping operations receive comprehensive training in how to protect and promote child rights. The first peacekeeping mandate to include a child protection adviser was the United Nations Assistance Mission in Sierra Leone in 2000; over subsequent years, 60 posts have been established in 10 different missions.

The issue of children and armed conflict is firmly on the peace and security agenda. Now the Security Council, UN entities and advocates should further explore how peace-keepers could play a more active

role in protecting children's rights. Drawing on the prevention and protection goals of the 'responsibility to protect', as set out in the 2005 World Summit outcome document, advocates note greater scope for peacekeeping in places where there is a need to protect populations, including children, from grave human rights violations. Inputs to the strategic review suggested that more robust peacekeeping includes more forceful means of intervention to protect children and bring perpetrators to justice.

Bringing children into peace negotiations and agreements.
The 1996 Machel study noted that "children are rarely mentioned in reconstruction plans or peace agreements, yet children must be at the centre of rebuilding." In the ensuing years, the importance of bringing children into peace processes has been recognized, but the actual inclusion of relevant provisions has been random and uneven.

For example, in one analysis of 30 peace agreements from 1999 to 2007, only six made reference to child protection imperatives. Another, wider analysis of 103 publicly accessible peace agreements between 1989 and 2005 found that just over half addressed education in some way. Children's issues that are less frequently found in such agreements include general commitments to uphold international legal obligations, such as the Convention on the Rights of the Child; ending the use of children by armed groups and their release and reintegration; attention to refugee and displaced children; and attention to rehabilitation programmes and health care for children.[118]

While engagement by the Security Council on such issues is crucial, many peace processes and agreements are forged outside the auspices of the United Nations. The Security Council's collaboration with regional organizations and other mediators on child protection priorities therefore needs to be promoted and integrated. In this regard, greater collaboration is needed between political leaders, child protection organizations and experts to ensure timely advice to peace mediators (both inside and outside the United Nations), as well as training in child protection for their support teams.

Though it has not been entirely successful, the 2006 Darfur Peace Agreement did a good job of incorporating child protection issues. The agreement gave extensive coverage to the release of children associated with armed forces and groups, compensation for war victims, the role of the African Union Mission in protecting children from gender-based violence and the prosecution of perpetrators. As an important follow-up action, the Security Council adopted Resolution 1769 in 2007, requesting that child protection be addressed in the imple-

Sudan © UNICEF/NYHQ2005-0370/Parker

mentation of the Darfur Peace Agreement. The resolution also requested that monitoring of and reporting on grave violations against children continue, as well as dialogue on protection with parties to conflict for the development of action plans.

Child protection was also highlighted in the 1999 Lome Peace Accord on Sierra Leone, which addressed the special needs of children in the disarmament, demobilization and reintegration process. It also established the Special Court for Sierra Leone, reconciliation processes and a national commission for war-affected children. The 2005 Comprehensive Peace Agreement on Sudan stipulated a six-month timeframe for the demobilization of children and registration of separated children. And the 2006 peace agreement in Nepal included provisions to cease all types of violence against children, including child labour and sexual exploitation and

abuse, and the use of children less than 18 years of age in the armed forces and armed groups.

It is crucial that the concerns of children be integrated at the earliest phases of the negotiation process and followed through in agreements and implementation. Furthermore, child-specific provisions should be viewed as opportunities, rather than as potential areas of discord.

Human Rights Council

The Human Rights Council, which includes the protection of children affected by armed conflict within its mandate and responsibilities, is also a crucial destination for action. The Council meets annually to examine issues concerning the rights and protection of children and adopts an omnibus resolution on the rights of the child every four years. The Special Representative for Children and Armed Conflict submits a report to the Council on this basis, as mandated by the General Assembly.

The Human Rights Council has also indicated its strong commitment to ending grave violations against children, pursuant to Security Council Resolution 1612 (2005). The Council's recently launched Universal Periodic Review (UPR) process enables issues of child protection in general, and children impacted by armed conflict in particular, to be scrutinized by its members as part of Council efforts to ensure the application and enforcement of international norms and standards to protect children's rights and end the impunity of violating parties. The work between the UPR and treaty body mechanisms, in particular the Committee on the Rights of the Child, could be enhanced through coordinated and complementary efforts, which could ensure a more systematic main-streaming of the rights of children affected by armed conflict throughout the work of the council. For example, the Human Rights Council could ensure that concluding observations and recommendations made by the Committee on the Rights of the Child on reports submitted by States parties in compliance with article 8 of the Optional Protocol to the Convention on the Rights of the Child on the involvement of children in armed conflict also form the basis of the UPR process.

ENGAGEMENT BY REGIONAL BODIES

In view of the changing nature of conflict and its increasingly trans-national dimensions, regional political and diplomatic engagement has an increasingly important role to play in responding to such concerns as grave violations, trafficking and displacement. The 1996 Machel study called on regional and subregional bodies to "formulate plans of action to protect children." While there are important examples of regional action, this dimension of political and diplomatic engagement has lagged over the past decade. It requires more concerted commitment from political leaders and other key actors to move from declarations to more structured mechanisms and follow-up.

Constructive action by the Security Council would include integration of child protection into its thematic work on cooperation with regional and subregional organizations. This would help ensure that child protection receives the high-level political attention it deserves and is integrated into established structures. These should include secretariats, coordination mechanisms, mediation teams and partnerships for maintaining peace and security.

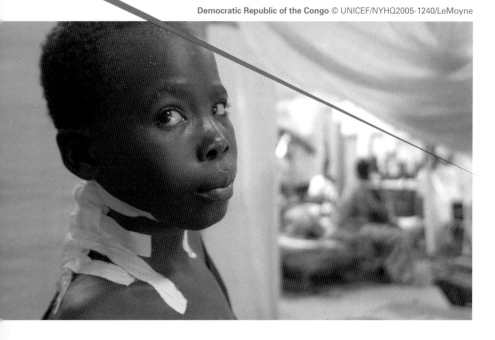

Democratic Republic of the Congo © UNICEF/NYHQ2005-1240/LeMoyne

Among regional organizations, the European Union stands out in terms of integrating issues related to children and armed conflict in a progressive and systematic way. Guidelines on the subject were adopted by the European Union in 2003 – including a commitment to influence third countries and non-state actors to address the impact of armed conflict on children, to put a stop to the recruitment and use of children, and to end impunity. An implementation strategy for the guidelines was adopted in 2006. The experience of the European Union suggests that persistent advocacy is needed to succeed in these objectives and that regional engagement is important. Working across the European Community and European Union system, and in partnerships with other regional bodies, is complementary to approaching governments directly. It also tends to form synergies that strengthen implementation and thus the success of programmes.

Re-energizing Mrs. Machel's call for regional action plans featured in the strategic review's consultations with regional groupings. It led to promising developments – including pledges for follow-up within the Commonwealth Ministerial Action Group and by the League of Arab States, which agreed to action on children's rights in armed conflicts among the priorities resulting from the Third Regional Conference for the Middle East and North Africa on violence against children. Particularly welcome is the African Union's 2007 'Call for Accelerated Action', which notes that progress on the issue has been "grossly inadequate." It goes on to commit States parties to "protect children from the impact of armed conflict and include children in post-conflict reconstruction and rehabilitation activities." It also promises to implement the recommendations of the 10-year strategic review of the Machel study.[119]

Other channels of political engagement

Beyond the United Nations and regional organs, political and diplomatic engagement on children and armed conflict must include the full spectrum of channels, mechanisms and even direct bilateral action.

A number of direct initiatives on the part of governments feature as highlights of progress since 1996. These include the efforts of Norway along with those of Austria, Ireland, Peru, New Zealand and the Holy See in achieving the recent Convention on Cluster Munitions. France played a key role in achieving the 2007 Paris Commitments to protect children from unlawful recruitment or use by armed forces or armed groups, which have been endorsed by 66 governments. Likewise, Canada's leadership was invaluable in pushing through the 1997 Mine Ban Treaty. Partnerships that developed since

Central African Republic
© UNICEF/NYHQ2007-2444/Holtz

the Mine Ban Treaty have led to an especially innovative mechanism to include non-state armed groups in its goals. By signing the Geneva 'Deed of Commitment', non-state armed groups commit to comply with the spirit and intentions of the Mine Ban Treaty and other international instruments. Indeed, the success of the achievements highlighted here is due to multifaceted collaboration among States, UN agencies and civil society.

In view of the changing nature of armed conflict, such engagement with non-state armed groups is vital in realizing the rights and protection of children. While international humanitarian law establishes the foundation for holding non-state armed groups accountable for protecting children, other tools and instruments, such as the Secretary-General's lists and action plans, are needed to bring about tangible results. At the same time, it is vital to maintain the political and diplomatic involvement that is necessary to

Iraq © UNICEF/NYHQ2007-2305/Kamber

support the United Nations and other agencies in engaging armed groups directly.

For the purpose of protecting children, it is critical that the United Nations has the option to engage in dialogue with all parties to the conflict, whether they are States parties or non-state actors. Such engagement, particularly with non-States parties, should not prejudge the legal status of any party. Even though non-state actors are not signatories to international legal standards, it is necessary to develop systems that hold such actors accountable. In the Security Council's framework for engagement on Children and Armed Conflict, the emphasis has been on fostering dialogue towards the preparation of concrete and time-bound action

plans – with all parties to conflict – to address the recruitment and use of children and to address all other grave violations against children. This has been a collaborative process led by OSRSG-CAAC and UNICEF, to work closely with the UN Country Task Force for the Monitoring and Reporting Mechanism on grave child rights violations.

Finally, in view of resounding calls for a focus on implementation, action at the national level is crucial. In this regard, parliamentarians are essential stakeholders and should be engaged more actively in promoting political action for children affected by armed conflict. A useful resource is a handbook prepared by UNICEF and the Inter-Parliamentary Union on child protection, which highlights key actions for parliamentarians in

advocacy, legislation, policy development, monitoring and reporting, and allocation of resources to priorities for children.[120]

All of these initiatives demonstrate the power of political and diplomatic engagement and what can be achieved. They expand our vision of what is possible in the next decade – if the political will is there.

RECOMMENDATIONS

Benchmarks for future action come from the commitments adopted by Member States over the past decade through the General Assembly, the Security Council, regional bodies and other mechanisms. In view of this sound body of guidance, the 10-year strategic review presented to the General Assembly in October 2007 included a platform of recommendations. It focused on achieving universal implementation of international norms, ending impunity and integrating priorities for children in peacemaking, peacekeeping and peacebuilding. Key political and diplomatic actions needed to fulfil those recommendations and previous commitments include the following:

1. **Promote wider engagement on the issue of children and armed conflict in regional bodies.** In order to more specifically translate commitments and declarations into action, regional bodies should: review previous commitments, including through peer review

mechanisms; include an agenda item dedicated to children affected by armed conflict in annual summit meetings; seize opportunities for action through, for example, regional follow-up to A World Fit for Children; and establish a high-level advocate and develop child-rights expertise in their peace and security structures.

2. **Encourage timely action on Security Council recommendations.** The Security Council Working Group on Children and Armed Conflict, established pursuant to Security Council Resolution 1612, should ensure timely follow-up to its conclusions and recommendations.

3. **Ensure that children's concerns and child protection issues are systematically incorporated into every peace process.** This needs to take place at the earliest stages, regardless of the mediating parties, whether United Nations political departments, regional bodies or a country-led initiative. To facilitate fulfilment of child protection obligations, the UN Secretariat should adopt a mechanism to ensure that peacemaking, peace-keeping and peacebuilding take into account the needs and problems of children affected by armed conflict.

4. **Protect children from grave violations of their rights through provisions in peace negotiations.** Such provisions should also ensure accountability for such violations, including through truth and reconciliation commissions and the establishment of institutional and legal reforms that protect children from exploitation and ensure their full and successful reintegration in post-conflict structures.

5. **Seek mechanisms to impose sanctions when required.** The Security Council should establish mechanisms enabling it to impose sanctions in all situations of concern on the children and armed conflict agenda. This includes exploring the possibility of establishing a sanctions committee for children and armed conflict. The Security Council should give equal priority to all categories of grave violations and all relevant situations of concern.

6. **Facilitate dialogue with non-state actors.** The United Nations should, when possible, engage in dialogue and support the development of concrete and time-bound action plans with all parties to conflict to halt recruitment and use of children in violation of applicable international law, and to address all other grave violations and abuses against children in close cooperation with the Office of the Special Representative of the Secretary-General, with UNICEF and with the UN country task forces on monitoring and reporting. Continuous monitoring and verification of action plans should be ensured. ■

KEY RESOURCES

The following websites provide regular updates and links to information regarding advocacy and political action on children and armed conflict:

Security Council Report, <www.securitycouncilreport.org>.

United Nations Office of the Special Representative of the Secretary-General for Children and Armed Conflict, <www.un.org/children/conflict>.

United Nations Children's Fund (UNICEF), <www.unicef.org/emerg>.

Watchlist on Children and Armed Conflict, Women's Commission for Refugee Women and Children, <www.watchlist.org>.

Haiti © UNICEF/NYHQ2004-0129/Kamber

6

UPHOLDING JUSTICE

Russian Federation © UNICEF/NYHQ2004-0622/Pirozzi

6.1 ADVANCING INTERNATIONAL LEGAL STANDARDS AND NORMS

The 1996 Machel study highlighted that we must frame the protection of children in armed conflict by using the standards and norms embodied in international law, national legislation and local custom and practice. The 2001 review went further, stating, "International standards and their enforcement are the strongest defence against impunity for child rights violations in armed conflict. Yet they will only be effective if and when they are widely known, understood and implemented by everyone."

In many ways, international attention on children in armed conflict, galvanized by Graça Machel's original study, has been a catalyst in the fight to end impunity. In fact, the first case of the newly established International Criminal Court (in 2006) concerned the illegal recruitment and use of children in hostilities, which constitutes a war crime.

A decade later, significant achievements have been made in improving the legal protections provided to children and ending impunity for perpetrators. But it is obvious from the situation on the ground that much remains to be done.

PROGRESS TO DATE

Building a global framework for justice

Children benefit from a comprehensive framework of international law that protects their rights, including in times of war. Under the broad scope of international human rights, refugee law and humanitarian law in particular provide the basic international legal framework for protecting children caught in situations of armed conflict.[121]

The Convention on the Rights of the Child (CRC) provides the most comprehensive code of rights as well as the highest standards of protection and assistance specific to children of any international instrument. In addition to protections derived from this and other treaties, gains are also being made in customary international law, which is derived from common acceptance and consistent practice by States with respect to the rule of law.

A wide range of other international instruments and guidelines have emerged to complement, elaborate upon or operationalize many of these standards. Among them are instruments providing special measures and protections for children interacting with justice systems, as described in the second half of this chapter, on ending impunity and securing justice.

In addition to this international framework for protection, regional and national instruments are critical to securing children's rights and protection. Action at the national level is of the greatest importance in providing timely and concrete measures to both prevent and respond to violations of children's rights.

Advancing international human rights

The Convention on the Rights of the Child. As noted above, the CRC, together with its Optional Protocol

"It is one thing making resolutions and another enforcing and monitoring their progress." – Young man, 24, Ghana

on the Involvement of Children in Armed Conflict (OPAC), provides the most comprehensive legal foundation for the protection of children's rights, including in situations of armed conflict. At the time of the 1996 Machel study, the CRC had already been ratified by 179 States. Today, all but two countries are States parties to it.

While particular provisions address armed conflict specifically, the CRC provides protection to all children affected more generally by situations of armed conflict and displacement.[122] For example, as stated in its provision on non-discrimination (article 2), the CRC applies to all children within the jurisdiction of States parties, not only to nationals. Moreover, the CRC defines a 'child' as anyone under 18 years of age,[123] meaning that its provisions apply to adolescents as well as younger children.

The Committee on the Rights of the Child, established in 1991 to monitor States' implementation of the CRC, has adopted various General Comments in recent years illustrating how different provisions can be interpreted in relation to armed conflict.[124] The Comments have highlighted, for example, the critical role of education in peaceful conflict resolution. They have noted that specific attention must be paid to the relationship between HIV and the abuse suffered by children in the context of war. They have also drawn

attention to the obligation of States to protect children from the dangers posed by small arms, light weapons and landmines both during war and its aftermath and to ensure the rights of children with disabilities resulting from armed conflict.[125]

Indeed, the Committee has repeatedly emphasized that "the effects of armed conflict on children should be considered in the framework of all the articles of the Convention; that States should take measures to ensure the realization of the rights of all children in their jurisdiction in times of armed conflict; and that the principles of the Convention are not subject to derogation in times of armed conflict."[126]

The CRC also provides for measures to be taken by States parties to assist child victims recovering from armed conflict. Article 39 broadly encourages the development of comprehensive programmes to alleviate mental distress, promote reintegration into society and the education system, and bolster the delivery of basic resources.[127] Its focus on the well-being, recovery and reintegration of children affected by armed conflict applies to children involved in justice or reconciliation mechanisms, release and social reintegration programmes, and to refugee and internally displaced children.

Legal and normative advances have been especially remarkable on the issue of the recruitment and

use of children by armed forces or groups. A key provision in the CRC, article 38, maintains that States parties are required to respect and ensure respect for rules of international humanitarian law that apply to conflict situations and are relevant to the child.

The protection of children was strengthened even more by OPAC, which was promoted by the 1996 Machel study and entered into force in February 2002. Among other things, it requires States parties to "take all feasible measures" to ensure that persons under the age of 18 are neither compulsorily recruited into their armed forces (article 2) nor take a direct part in hostilities (article 1).

As of March 2008, OPAC had been ratified or acceded to by 119 States parties, the majority of which had made declarations indicating that 18 years or older should be the minimum age for voluntary recruitment. It is noteworthy that under OPAC, armed groups (as distinct from the armed forces of a State) are themselves directly prohibited from recruiting persons under age 18 or using them in hostilities. States retain the obligation to take all feasible measures to prevent such practices by armed groups, including the use of legal means to prohibit and criminalize these practices.

States parties to OPAC are required to submit a report to the Committee on the Rights of the

STRENGTHENING THE OPTIONAL PROTOCOL THROUGH STRICTER REPORTING REQUIREMENTS

The revised reporting guidelines recently issued for the Optional Protocol on the Involvement of Children in Armed Conflict are an important step in protecting children's rights.[128] The guidelines, which describe in detail the information necessary to assess progress made by States parties, will enable the Committee on the Rights of the Child to provide appropriate recommendations.

For example, in order to ensure that recruitment is voluntary, the guidelines ask for information on incentives used by the national armed forces to encourage volunteers (such as financial incentives, scholarships and advertising). Countries are also asked to report on measures put in place to prevent attacks on civilians and civilian 'objects', including places where children are usually present, such as schools and hospitals. Other requirements include information on all criminal legislation in force covering relevant offences in the Optional Protocol and whether such provisions have been included in transitional justice measures, such as war crimes tribunals or truth commissions.

Reflecting the changing nature of warfare, the guidelines also request a description of laws concerning the criminal liability of 'legal persons', such as private military and security companies, and of legal provisions allowing extraterritorial jurisdiction over serious violations of international humanitarian law. It is hoped that such detailed provisions will result in more comprehensive monitoring and will guide States parties and civil society in instituting concrete measures they can take to protect children.

Child within two years and follow-up reports every five years thereafter. In October 2007, new reporting guidelines were adopted that aim to strengthen its implementation (see box above). As of 17 March 2008, the Committee had reviewed the reports of 34 countries (out of a total of 49 received) on their implementation of OPAC.[129]

ILO Convention 182. Other positive developments since the Machel study include the elaboration of the International Labour Organization Convention 182 (1999). It obliges States parties to take immediate and effective measures to prohibit and eliminate the worst forms of child labour, including the forced or compulsory recruitment of children

(under the age of 18) for use in armed conflict.

African Charter on the Rights and Welfare of the Child. Progress at the global level was brought one step further with the entry into force of the African Charter on the Rights and Welfare of the Child (1999). It is the first regional treaty establishing 18 as a minimum age for military recruitment and participation in hostilities.

Paris Commitments and Principles. Mindful of the need for more detailed operational guidance in addressing the unlawful recruitment and use of children in combat, UNICEF spearheaded a process that resulted in the 2007 'Paris Commitments' and 'Paris Principles'.[130] Although non-binding, these two documents lay out legal and operational principles as well as guidelines to protect children from recruitment and use in armed conflict. The documents include advice pertinent to specific groups of children, such as girls, refugees and those internally displaced, and on issues related to prevention, family reunification and reintegration.

Ending impunity before the law. Critical developments since 1996 in the fight to end impunity include a number of Security Council resolutions, which are binding, and formation of the International Criminal Court (ICC). The importance of the ICC cannot be overstated. The 1998 Rome

> **"The UN should also take strict action against a battling nation which violates the rights of the children in a country it is attacking. Areas harbouring civilians must not be attacked at any cost, [and] this rule should be implemented on a more permanent basis."** – Young woman, 15, Pakistan

Statute, out of which the ICC emerged, classified as war crimes the enlistment or use of children under the age of 15 to take an active part in hostilities. Other acts cited as war crimes include deliberate attacks on hospitals and schools, along with rape and other grave acts of sexual violence, including against children.[131]

Security Council resolutions. Certain Security Council resolutions have highlighted specific areas of concern, such as underage recruitment and the special vulnerabilities of girls.[132] They also make detailed recommendations for action by all parties to armed conflicts. These include requests to States parties to submit concrete action plans and establish structures such as working groups and monitoring and reporting mechanisms to address specific aspects of the protection of children in armed conflict.

Cross-fertilization with other treaty bodies. The momentum generated by the Machel study over a decade ago, together with efforts by the Committee on the Rights of the Child, has resulted in greater awareness and cross-fertilization with the work undertaken by other treaty bodies and mechanisms. For example, treaty bodies including the Committee on the Elimination of Discrimination against Women and the Committee against Torture have repeatedly raised concerns related to children affected by armed conflict.[133]

Looking ahead, it is equally important to capitalize on the synergies between the work of the Committee on the Rights of the Child (especially its monitoring role under OPAC) and other mechanisms, such as the monitoring and reporting mechanism on the use of child soldiers established under Security Council Resolution 1612.

Promoting international humanitarian law

The Geneva Conventions. International humanitarian law, which is intended to regulate the means and methods for conducting military operations, has its primary basis in the four Geneva Conventions of 1949 and three Additional Protocols.[134] In 2006, the Geneva Conventions achieved universal acceptance when all Member States of the United Nations had either ratified or acceded to them.

The Fourth Geneva Convention, which addresses the protection of civilians in armed conflict, offers general protection to children as civilians. Together with Protocols I and II, added in 1977, it contains over 20 provisions specifically focused on safeguarding children affected by armed conflict.

While primarily concerned with international armed conflicts, the four Geneva Conventions contain a common article 3 that covers "armed conflicts not of an international character." It obliges parties to the conflict to respect certain minimum humanitarian rules with regard to persons not (or no longer) taking an active part in hostilities. Such persons, including children, are to be treated humanely and protected from "violence to life and person," which includes murder, mutilation, torture and hostage-taking.

Significantly, both Protocols stipulate that respect and additional protections should be accorded to children. This includes both protection against any form of indecent assault and the obligation to provide them with care and aid. Provisions in Protocol I include the right to be kept separate from adults in situations of detention or internment. Article 4 of Protocol II details aspects of the care and aid that children in armed conflict require, including receiving an education and family reunification services.

Customary international law. Specific provisions applicable to children are also to be found in customary international humanitarian law. A study conducted by the International Committee of the Red Cross has shown that such provisions include the obligation to provide special respect and protection to children affected by armed conflict (Rule 135) and the prohibition against recruiting children into armed forces or armed groups and allowing them to take part in hostilities (Rules 136, 137).[135] Such rules are applicable both in international and non-international armed conflicts and are binding for State armed forces and non-state armed groups.

Protecting the rights of refugees and those internally displaced

Armed conflicts typically result in mass population movements, forcing persons to become refugees in an asylum country or displacing them from their homes within their own country. In addition to the dangers they are fleeing, children who are either refugees or internally displaced are vulnerable to a host of other threats, including separation from family, trafficking, abduction by military groups, lack of food and basic services, and exploitation and abuse.

Convention Relating to the Status of Refugees. The legal framework providing protection to refugees includes the 1951 Convention Relating to the Status of Refugees and its 1967 Protocol, as well as regional refugee instruments.[136] Executive Committee Conclusions by the United Nations High Commissioner for Refugees (UNHCR), along with various policies and guidelines, also provide important normative guidance. In particular, Executive Committee Conclusion No. 105, on Women and Girls at Risk (2006), and No. 107, on Children at Risk (2007), provide detailed guidance on issues and standards relating to children who are either

refugees or internally displaced.[137] The Conclusion on Children and Risk (2007) specifically identifies wider environmental and individual risks and recommends that measures be taken to address such factors as capacity building, access to resources, unaccompanied and separated children, and integration and resettlement. Special considerations must be taken into account in determining refugee status for children, as spelled out in a number of UNHCR policy documents and guidelines.[138]

The Committee on the Rights of the Child. The Committee on the Rights of the Child has also referred to the situation of refugee children in various General Comments. For example, General Comment No. 6 (2005) states that determination of national refugee status must take into account gender-based violence and child-specific forms of persecution, including persecution of kin, under-age recruitment and trafficking.

No matter what country refugee children are in, States parties are obliged to extend the full range of rights inscribed in the CRC to them, including children who are unaccompanied by parents or other caregivers. Provisions such as article 2, on the principle of non-discrimination, and article 22, on the rights of refugee and asylum-seeking children to protection and assistance, confirm that the rights in the CRC apply to children even in States that have not

ratified the 1951 Convention and its 1967 Protocol.

Guiding Principles on Internal Displacement and the humanitarian reform process. Perhaps the most important development in this sector during the past 10 years has been the emergence of new international standards and practice relating to internally displaced persons. Both the Guiding Principles on Internal Displacement, issued in 1998,[139] and the humanitarian reform process, which has established an international response mechanism through the 'cluster' approach (described in chapter 7), have stepped in to fill important gaps for those displaced within the borders of their own country. In addition to describing a comprehensive set of rights, the Guiding Principles emphasize the particular needs of internally displaced children and their rights to basic services, education and civil liberties. They also prohibit the recruitment or participation of these children in hostilities.

Alleviating the threat from landmines, weapons and other instruments of war

The 1996 Machel study exposed the lethal threat to children posed by landmines and explosive remnants of war and the illicit flow of small arms and light weapons. In addition to calling for assistance to children victimized by these weapons, it called

on States to mitigate the impact of
armed conflict on children by adopting
legislation to ban the development,
production, use, trade, transfer and
stockpiling of anti-personnel mines.

The Mine Ban Treaty. In 1996,
Canada initiated the 'Ottawa process',
which culminated in the Convention on
the Prohibition of the Use, Stockpiling,
Production and Transfer of Anti-
Personnel Mines and on their
Destruction. The Convention, which
became known as the Mine Ban
Treaty, came into force in 1999 and
was a major step forward in reducing
the threat of anti-personnel landmines.
In addition to the 156 States parties
that have ratified the Convention,[140]
34 non-state armed groups have also
committed to uphold its objectives
by signing the Geneva 'Deed of
Commitment' banning anti-personnel
mines.[141] Many States that are not parties
to the treaty abide by its provisions,
undertaking mine clearance, stockpile
destruction, mine-risk education and
assistance to victims.

As a result, activity related to the
production and sale of anti-personnel
mines, once a large component of
the global arms industry, has almost
ceased.[142] Still, States that have not
become parties to the Mine Ban Treaty
continue to stockpile more than 160
million anti-personnel mines, with
the vast majority held by five States.[143]
In 2005 and 2006, non-state armed
groups used anti-personnel mines or
similar improvised explosive devices
in at least 13 countries.[144]

Syrian Arab Republic © UNICEF/NYHQ2007-0742/Noorani

**Protocol on Explosive Remnants
of War.** The additional Protocol on
Explosive Remnants of War (Protocol V
to the International Convention
on Certain Conventional Weapons)
came into force in 2006, obliging the
parties to a conflict to clear explosive
remnants of war, share information
and provide warnings to civilians and
assistance to survivors of accidents.[145]

Banning cluster munitions. Cluster
munitions and other explosive
remnants of war continue to pose a
serious threat to children in conflict
and post-conflict zones.[146] In May
2008, a global initiative by 46 States,
led by Norway, resulted in the
adoption of an international treaty
banning cluster munitions. The treaty
is expected to be ratified and enter
into force.

**Prohibiting trade in small arms
and light weapons.** In April 2008,
the UN Secretary-General's report
on small arms and light weapons was
presented to the Security Council.
The report noted that "small arms
facilitate a vast spectrum of human
rights violations, including killing

and maiming, rape and other forms
of sexual violence, enforced disappearance, torture, and forced
recruitment or use of children by
armed groups or armed forces.
More human rights abuses are
committed with them than with
any other weapon." During the past
10 years, the Committee on the
Rights of the Child has repeatedly
expressed its concern over the
proliferation of small arms and light
weapons and the proportion of
children both carrying them and
who have become their victims.
Most notably, it has recommended
that States parties ensure that their
domestic law and practice prohibit
trade in small arms and light weapons
to countries where children take part
in armed conflict.[147]

REMAINING GAPS

Translating international
standards into national action

Despite the broad and rapid
acceptance of international legal
standards to protect children in
armed conflict, a significant gap
remains between these standards and

> **"So many people break the Convention on the Rights of the Child and nothing happens."** – Young woman, 18, Sri Lanka

their implementation at the national level. The most important challenge today is translating international standards into action that can make a tangible difference on the ground.

States generally incorporate or adopt international instruments in two ways: either directly by virtue of a provision in the national constitution, or by incorporating the specific provisions of international treaties into national legislation. However, adoption of relevant national legislation is not sufficient. To give the legislation 'teeth' requires administrative and other implementation mechanisms, such as the establishment of relevant institutions or bodies with corresponding powers and training. While vitally important, these mechanisms require more resources than the simple adoption of legislative provisions. International cooperation and support are often critical to help countries emerging from armed conflict meet their obligations.

That said, the onus of responsibility remains clearly with the State. "Governments have the most direct formal, legal and political responsibility to ensure the protection of all children exposed to armed conflict within their countries," wrote the Special Representative of the Secretary-General for Children and Armed Conflict in a 2005 report. "Any actions by United Nations entities and international NGOs at the country level should always be designed to support and complement

the protection and rehabilitation roles of national authorities, never to supplant them."[148]

Ensuring consistency between international standards and national legislation and practice.
An important first step is for countries to ensure that international humanitarian law is reflected in relevant national legislation and practice. For instance, international humanitarian law obliges States parties to take legislative measures to prohibit the use of the death sentence against anyone under the age of 18 at the time of the offence. In addition, they have an obligation to undertake activities at the national level to disseminate knowledge of and compliance with international humanitarian law,[149] including through training programmes.

Ensuring that national implementation is consistent with international standards and, more particularly, the Rome Statute, is also important in enabling national authorities to cooperate with the ICC. National provisions relating to genocide, crimes against humanity and war crimes should ensure that these crimes are punishable under national law and have the same scope as the definitions contained in the Statute. Many States are already taking steps in this direction.[150] In addition, criminal provisions relating to such areas as defence, statutes of limitation

and rules of evidence should not create obstacles to the investigation and prosecution of international crimes, including against children.[151]

Promoting implementation of national laws. The treaty-body monitoring process, especially that of the Committee on the Rights of the Child, is another important mechanism for bridging the gap between the standards States have accepted and their implementation.[152] States parties to the CRC commit to undertake "all appropriate legislative, administrative and other measures for the implementation of the rights recognized in the Convention" (article 4). States must report to the Committee on the Rights of Child on the measures they have adopted to this effect.

National implementation can also be encouraged by regional bodies and initiatives. For example, a key objective of the 2003 European Union Guidelines on Children in Armed Conflict is to "influence third countries and non-state actors to implement international [and regional] human rights norms and standards and humanitarian law."[153]

One positive note in this regard is the progress made in securing commitments from armed groups to comply with international humanitarian law. For example, a number of armed groups have agreed to participate in action plans to cease the recruitment and use of children and ensure their reintegration, rather than face the possibility of sanctions. In June 2007 in the Central African Republic, for example, the Government, the Assembly of the Union of Democratic Forces rebel group and UNICEF signed an agreement for the release and reintegration of 400 children associated with armed groups.

RECOMMENDATIONS

The 10-year strategic review of the Machel study presented to the UN General Assembly in 2007 made four principal recommendations that concern this chapter. The first appears below and is followed by additional suggestions that seek to complement it. The remaining three recommendations, along with key resources, appear on pages 78 and 79.

GA RECOMMENDATION 1

Achieving universal implementation of international norms and ending impunity.

1. **Contribute to treaty reporting.** Civil society actors, such as national human rights institutions and NGOs, should be encouraged to submit independent reports on the implementation of treaties, including the CRC and OPAC, to relevant treaty bodies.

2. **Provide follow-up to the recommendations of treaty bodies.**

BRINGING TANGIBLE GAINS TO WAR-AFFECTED CHILDREN: IMPLEMENTING THE OPTIONAL PROTOCOL

A recent analysis by the Office of the High Commissioner for Human Rights (OHCHR) of 16 country reports to the Committee on the Rights of the Child identified several areas in which national implementation of OPAC must be strengthened.[154] Most countries, for instance, still lack an adequate legislative framework to protect children in armed conflict. Many lack provisions in their penal code prohibiting child recruitment, and many lag in exercising their jurisdiction (including extraterritorial jurisdiction) over this crime. The absence of adequate birth registration systems is another obstacle to preventing recruitment of children under the age of 18. For example, in reports to the Security Council Working Group on Children and Armed Conflict, many countries have cited the lack of birth registration as a reason for the failure to prevent underage recruitment.[155]

Asylum countries must also do more to assist the physical and psychological recovery of victims in their territory, especially refugee and asylum-seeking children who have fled conflict in their countries of origin. Also key is better dissemination of information on the provisions under OPAC, including to children, the public at large and professionals, such as members of the judiciary, police, immigration authorities and the military. States parties also have an obligation to stop arms trade with countries that use child soldiers and provide support and assistance to other States in implementing the provisions under OPAC. In the case of state practices that allow voluntary recruitment of children, the Committee has consistently encouraged raising the age of recruitment to 18.

Civil society actors should be supported in providing sustained national follow-up (including monitoring) to the recommendations of relevant treaty bodies, as benchmarks for measuring further implementation.

3. **Promote and disseminate information on the rights of the child.** States, UN agencies and civil society should facilitate strategic dissemination of information on the rights of children in armed conflict and the corresponding obligations in international law to groups including children, the public, non-state armed actors and professionals working in related areas, such as members of the police, judiciary and military, as well as medical, immigration and refugee authorities. The international community should support international cooperation and assistance programmes towards this end.

"[Resolutions and treaties] are pretty ineffective, as it seems they try to affect issues at the top of the tree. Children are at the bottom of the tree and seem to be forgotten." – Young man, 16, United Kingdom

6.2 ENDING IMPUNITY AND SECURING JUSTICE

The past decade has seen major advances towards justice for children. This culminated in the first prosecutions of perpetrators of violations against children in special courts and the newly established International Criminal Court. However, as noted in the 2007 review of the Machel study presented to the General Assembly, "much more remains to be done." The review goes on to say that "greater will and commitment are needed to accelerate accountability and to operationalize legislation, policy and action at the national and field levels."

Children, and disadvantaged children in particular, face over-whelming obstacles in accessing justice. In time of war, these include fear of reprisal and inadequate protection. Children may also lack knowledge of or trust in formal institutions or simply be unable to access them, especially if they are economically disadvantaged. Even if they manage to do so, children often face justice systems that do not take them into account, in terms of either the law or legal processes, a situation that is tantamount to legal and institutional discrimination.

PROGRESS TO DATE

Coming to terms with past abuses: children and transitional justice

The term 'transitional justice' refers to the "full range of processes and mechanisms associated with a society's attempts to come to terms with a legacy of large-scale past abuses, in order to ensure accountability, serve justice and achieve reconciliation. These may include both judicial and non-judicial mechanisms, with differing levels of international involvement (or none at all) and individual prosecutions, reparations, truth-seeking, institutional reform, vetting and dismissals, or a combination thereof."[156]

In implementing any of these mechanisms, the participation of children and adolescents must be a priority. Experience since the 1996 Machel study has confirmed that policies and practices supporting children's involvement in transitional justice measures help improve accountability for crimes against them. Such actions also contribute to the development of child-friendly policies and procedures that protect children's rights.[157]

This section highlights key developments and challenges for children in special tribunals, the ICC and national courts and informal systems as part of transitional justice processes and mechanisms.

The work of criminal tribunals

"People all over the world want to know that humanity can strike back – that wherever and whenever genocide, war crimes or other such violations are committed, there is a court before which the criminal can be held to account; a court that puts an end to a global culture of impunity; a court where 'acting under orders' is no defence; a court where all individuals in a government hierarchy or military chain of command, without exception, from rulers to private soldiers, must answer for their actions." – Former UN Secretary-General Kofi Annan, speaking at the Rome Conference of Plenipotentiaries for an International Criminal Court, 17 June 1998.

The development of special criminal tribunals. During the past decade, one of the most noteworthy successes in achieving accountability has been the establishment of a wide range of special criminal tribunals. Through these mechanisms the international community seeks to stop and prevent the recurrence of violations of human rights and humanitarian law, bring those responsible to justice and ensure a measure of justice and dignity for victims. Criminal tribunals can also play an important role in helping societies transition from conflict.

The institutional models that have emerged include ad hoc tribunals, such as the International Criminal Tribunals for the former Yugoslavia (ICTY) and for Rwanda (ICTR);[158] mixed tribunals, such as those for Bosnia and Herzegovina, Cambodia and Sierra Leone;[159] the use of international judges and prosecutors, such as in the courts of Kosovo; and panels with exclusive jurisdiction over serious criminal offences, such as those established by the UN Transitional Administration in East Timor.[160]

These special tribunals have not only set new precedents in holding perpetrators accountable for grave violations of child rights. They have also contributed to the development of an important body of jurisprudence that can strengthen and inform future practice. Thanks to the deliberations of tribunals for the former Yugoslavia and Rwanda, for example, there is now greater clarity on questions of rape as a war crime and crime against humanity, the elements of genocide, the definition of torture, the nature of individual criminal responsibility and the doctrine of command responsibility.[161]

The Special Court in Sierra Leone is considered the first war crimes tribunal to explicitly expose and administer justice for abuses perpetrated on or by children.[162] As of June 2007, the Special Court had convicted and sentenced three former leaders of Sierra Leone's Armed Forces Revolutionary Council – and three months later, a member of the Civil Defence Forces militia – for the recruitment and use of children.[163] Previously, the same court indicted the former president of Liberia, Charles Ghankay Taylor, for war crimes and crimes against humanity.[164] The prosecution of sexual violence and rape as war crimes and an instrument of genocide by

JUSTICE FOR CHILDREN: WHAT IT WILL TAKE

Achieving justice for children requires a continuum of standards at the international, national and local levels and the implementation of these standards by respective duty bearers. Ensuring that national systems conform with international standards for the protection and rights of children, and that the necessary institutions are established to implement them, is a vital first step.

Respect for the rule of law, including in conflict and post-conflict situations, is essential to lasting peace and security. This point was recognized by Member States at the 2005 World Summit. A functioning justice system – which includes legal, judicial and law-enforcement institutions, and non-formal mechanisms – is central to the rule of law. Furthermore, this system must seek to fulfil the rights of children at every stage of the legal process. This view was recently endorsed in the 'UN Approach on Justice for Children',[165] adopted in September 2008, which aims to ensure that all UN entities reflect child rights, as elaborated in international norms and standards, in their rule-of-law activities. The approach emphasizes that child justice must be addressed in national planning processes; legal, institutional and policy reform efforts; and capacity building, training and accountability programmes. In addition, collaboration should be sought with other sectors, particularly social protection, which has a crucial role to play in prevention of child rights violations and social reintegration.

In the context of armed conflict, strategic interventions to protect children's rights must be undertaken at the earliest possible opportunity. Among the actions recommended in the UN Approach is strengthening systems of justice and social services. This includes measures to build knowledge on the specific rights of particular groups of children (such as girls and indigenous children) and to recognize the different impact the justice system may have on them. Another area of concern is promoting restorative justice, and diversion and alternatives to deprivation of liberty, so that a child's reintegration into society can be achieved as quickly as possible.

the tribunals in former Yugoslavia and Rwanda set equally important precedents that recognized the gravity of sexual violence and the imperative of combating impunity.[166]

The establishment of the International Criminal Court. The adoption of the Rome Statute in 1998, and the subsequent establishment of the ICC, represents one

IMPROVING CHILDREN'S ACCESS TO JUSTICE

A variety of interventions can improve children's access to justice, both in situations of armed conflict and in the transition process that often follows. They include promotion of child rights and legal awareness among children, their families and communities; support for community-based legal and paralegal services for children; and encouraging children's participation, such as through projects that ensure children's involvement from the outset of transitional justice mechanisms and in restitution/reparation programmes. This participation in turn requires interventions that promote child-sensitive procedures in judicial, administrative or community-based processes, including non-state justice mechanisms.

Other interventions that can improve children's access to justice include reforms of the judicial and security sectors. Measures may also be required to deal with the proliferation of small arms in wartime. Training and legislative reforms are also usually needed to address discriminatory attitudes in relation to juvenile justice and gender issues and to curb abusive practices.

In addition to ensuring that children's concerns and interests are included in transitional justice mechanisms, it is vital to engage in interventions that prevent infractions of justice in the first place. These include: developing the capacity of civil society to design and run programmes that seek to provide justice for children in emergencies; supporting the capacity of non-state justice mechanisms,[167] which often play a crucial role in periods of crisis; and ensuring that children's concerns are included from the start in peace agreements or joint UN assessments and planning missions. Such interventions can be instrumental in mitigating further harm to children in conflict situations.

of the single most significant developments in ending impunity for perpetrators of crimes against children. This accomplishment is all the more impressive considering that the United Nations recognized the need for such a court as early as 1948.[168] Although the Rome Statute only entered into force in 2002,[169] it is already having an impact: It has established a vital channel to address impunity by codifying grave violations of international law, including against children. It has put would-be violators on notice. And it has served as a catalyst for the adoption of national laws against the most heinous of international crimes.[170]

The ICC has jurisdiction over genocide, crimes against humanity, war crimes and the crime of aggression. The definition of these crimes includes various references to children. For example, the definition of 'enslavement' as a crime against humanity makes particular mention of children. One of the violations cited as a war crime is conscripting or enlisting children under age 15 or using them to participate actively in hostilities (article 8). The Rome Statute was also the first legal instrument to codify sexual violence as both a crime against humanity and a war crime.

In order to facilitate and regulate the involvement of children in the proceedings of the ICC, both child-friendly and protective measures have been put in place to ensure the safe involvement of child witnesses in court proceedings. These include, for example, adoption of closed sessions and establishment of a victim and witness protection unit that takes into account the special needs of children, including those who have experienced trauma or sexual violence.

In the past couple of years the ICC has also broken new ground in prosecuting crimes against children by charging and indicting warlords from the Democratic Republic of the Congo and Uganda with recruiting and using children in hostilities.[171] The ICC is seeking arrest warrants for Ali Kushayb and Ahmad Mohammed Harun for their role in facilitating the Janjaweed's attacks on Darfur's civilian population. And in May 2007, the Court announced the opening of an investigation in the Central African Republic on allegations of rape

"In Somalia, we now have 'seafarers' who offer us the false promise of a better life, when we pay them to take us across to Yemen. Many of our friends, brothers and sisters do not survive these trips, as they are often ordered to swim the last part of the journey." –
Age and sex not specified, Somalia

and other acts of sexual violence perpetrated against hundreds of reported victims.[172]

The role of national courts and informal administration of justice systems. Although international criminal tribunals represent progress in ending impunity and restoring a measure of justice and rule of law, "no ad hoc, temporary or external measures can ever replace a functioning national justice system," according to a 2004 report of the UN Secretary-General.[173] At its core, the rule of law is based on a strong judiciary that is independent; properly financed, equipped and trained; and empowered to uphold human rights, even under difficult circumstances.

National legal mechanisms must also be able to address civil claims and disputes, such as property disputes, citizenship/nationality questions and other legal issues that arise in post-conflict situations. Regarding children, it is not enough for national legal systems to be aware of violations and legal issues particularly affecting children in the context of armed conflicts. They must also have juvenile justice systems in place that can treat children involved in criminal or civil procedures in accordance with recognized international standards.

In terms of criminal prosecutions related to children in situations of armed conflict, several concerns have come to light. One, in many instances children have not received compensa-

tion or redress for the suffering they have experienced, and two, States have not prosecuted those alleged to have violated children's rights. Three, there is concern that despite provisions in the CRC and UN guidelines on juvenile justice, some States have detained children for alleged war crimes. And they have done so in a manner that is not sufficiently distinguished from the adult justice system, does not focus on children's reintegration and has involved long pretrial detention in very poor conditions.[174]

Furthermore, in many countries, large sections of the population have

little knowledge about or contact with formal justice systems. They have long used less formal conflict-resolution and justice mechanisms. Ignoring these local traditions will exclude large sectors of society from accessing any form of justice, especially in post-conflict situations where formal legal institutions may be weak and seriously under-resourced. Supporting these informal mechanisms to better meet international standards, ensure special protections for children and take account of gender sensitivities can therefore be a key element in a comprehensive national justice strategy. In some cases, independent

Chad © UNICEF/NYHQ2007-0246/Pirozzi

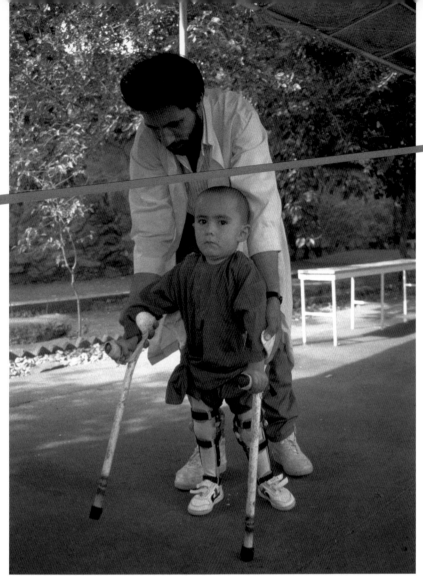

Afghanistan © UNICEF/NYHQ1996-0199/Hartley

national human rights commissions can also complement national courts during transitional periods and play a critical function by providing accountability, dispute resolution, redress and protection.[175]

The national courts of countries not involved in armed conflicts are also playing an increasingly prominent role.[176] Through adoption of extra-territorial provisions, for example, they may be able to prosecute those accused of crimes against children committed in another country. They may also take legal action against companies involved in illegal trade. Asylum cases involving the care and protection of children have been brought before national and administrative courts. In recent years, an unprecedented number of cases

have also been brought to the national courts of third-party States under the universality principle.[177]

Other transitional justice mechanisms

Despite the successes and benefits of international criminal courts, and the growing capacity of national courts, it is also true that most crimes committed in conflict situations go unpunished. As reported by the Secretary-General in a 2004 report: "In the end, in post-conflict countries, the vast majority of perpetrators… will never be tried, whether internationally or domestically."[178] For this reason, the report goes on to say, prosecutorial policy must be strategic, public expectations must be based

on sound information, programmes must be in place to protect and support victims and witnesses, and future international or hybrid tribunals must give consideration to an ultimate exit strategy.[179] "Moreover," the report continues, "other transitional justice mechanisms … may need to be put in place in order to overcome the inherent limitations of criminal justice processes – to do things that courts do not do or do not do well."[180]

Other transitional justice mechanisms are also necessary to promote national reconciliation, encourage moderate forces and ensure that those responsible for human rights violations or for aiding in repression are removed from jobs in the justice and security sectors.[181]

A holistic transitional justice strategy must ensure that child rights and concerns are adequately addressed from the outset. This must include due regard for relevant international standards and guidelines, such as the UN Guidelines on Justice in Matters Involving Child Victims and Witnesses of Crime. At the same time, such a strategy must take into account gender sensitivities and the best interests of the child, while embracing the principles of participation, non-discrimination, empowerment and accountability.

Truth and reconciliation mechanisms. It is now widely recognized that truth commissions, which are often undertaken together with reconciliation processes, can be a positive complement to criminal prosecutions.[182] Truth and reconciliation commissions are temporary, non-judicial mechanisms mandated to investigate and document human rights abuses and to produce a report on violations. In addition to promoting national reconciliation, they can recommend institutional reform and reparations for victims and help re-establish confidence in the rule of law.[183]

Reconciliation processes and truth commissions can be forums in which children and adolescents[184] can express themselves, relate their experiences and contribute as citizens to community efforts towards accountability, reconciliation and reintegration. The past decade has brought greater understanding of how children are affected as victims and witnesses of systematic human rights abuses, and with it, greater focus by truth commissions.[185] For instance, reporting on specific violations committed against children has demonstrated that children are not only indirect victims of the conflict but also direct targets of cruel violence.[186]

Traditional approaches to justice and reconciliation. Alongside these formal reconciliation processes, local approaches to justice and reconciliation are playing a larger role in transitional justice strategies. These are important because they are products of local

CHILDREN'S PARTICIPATION IN TRUTH AND RECONCILIATION COMMISSIONS

The lessons drawn from the involvement of children in truth and reconciliation commissions in Sierra Leone and Timor-Leste have provided insight into the opportunities of child-friendly procedures – and the challenges that remain. For example, it is clear that special measures are necessary to ensure proper protection and support for children and adolescents who participate in such commissions. And training is needed to ensure specialized staff can address the specific needs and capacities of children. Child protection agencies in particular can play a positive mediating role by assisting such commissions in developing child-friendly measures, facilitating children's involvement and ensuring follow-up. While children can be key contributors in justice and reconciliation efforts, their right to participation and their right to protection must be mutually supportive.[187]

The Sierra Leone Truth and Reconciliation Commission, in particular, offers a comprehensive model of child and adolescent participation.[188] Children gave confidential statements, participated in thematic hearings, prepared an official submission to the Commission and contributed to the preparation of a child-friendly version of the Commission's report. The creative strategies developed to encourage children's involvement throughout that process are now part of a legacy that continues to enrich international practice.

The involvement of children is also being encouraged in Liberia's reconciliation process. For example, the Liberian Truth and Reconciliation Commission Act specifies children's participation and protection; children's awareness workshops have been held and found successful as an outreach strategy; statements are being obtained from children by officials trained in child rights and child-friendly procedures; and children's hearings are being planned. Efforts are also under way to link the Commission with education through a curriculum component. These encouraging steps have been facilitated through close collaboration between the Truth and Reconciliation Commission and the Liberian Child Protection Network.

Meanwhile, important research initiatives are under way to promote further involvement of children in transitional justice mechanisms, especially truth and reconciliation commissions.[189]

> **"The Truth and Reconciliation Commission helped a great deal. People have had the opportunity to apologize for crimes committed and have received forgiveness, and this has been one good step towards keeping the peace."** –
> Young people, 15–19, sex not specified, Sierra Leone

culture and because state and international responses to massive human rights violations have built-in limitations. Local approaches have been implemented in a number of countries, including Angola, Mozambique, Rwanda, Sierra Leone, Timor-Leste and Uganda. They have taken a variety of forms, including informal courts and traditional ceremonies. Because they focus on transformation rather than punishment, they are considered particularly

Lebanon © UNICEF/NYHQ2006-1061/Brooks

suited for children. Reconciliation ceremonies in northern Uganda, for instance, were a strategic cultural mechanism for dealing with abducted children who were both victims and perpetrators of violence.[190]

In research conducted in Sierra Leone by the Women's Commission for Refugee Women and Children for this publication,[191] local actors cited the most positive reconciliation experiences as those that included traditional approaches. Children compelled to commit atrocities during the conflict reported that they had gained acceptance in their communities through traditional healing mechanisms. Although it is important to ensure that such traditional ceremonies conform to international standards, this experience shows that they complement and extend the reach of formal mechanisms at the community level.

Reparations to children. The question of reparations for harm suffered by victims as a result of armed conflict is a central issue for transitional justice, applying to both judicial and non-judicial mechanisms. A trust fund has been established at the International Criminal Court for victims and their families; it will give priority to the most vulnerable, including children.[192]

Yet comprehensive guidelines have been missing for implementing large-scale reparation programmes, and the interests and participation of

children in particular have long been neglected. In December 2005 the United Nations General Assembly adopted the Basic Principles and Guidelines on the Right to a Remedy and Reparation for Victims of Gross Violations of International Human Rights Law and Serious Violations of International Humanitarian Law, also known as the Van Boven/Bassiouni Principles.[193] Though non-binding, these principles now provide a comprehensive guide to standards and principles related to the right to remedy and reparation.

Reparations can take many forms and address various post-conflict challenges, such as the loss of property and land by refugees and displaced persons. They can be individual or collective (or both) and exercised legally through a lawsuit or as a result of political and diplomatic pressure. However, reparations can also include non-monetary elements, such as the restitution of a victims' liberty and other legal rights, reintegration programmes, physical or psychological assistance, the adoption of preventive measures and other guarantees of non-repetition, as well as symbolic acts such as commemorative ceremonies and official apologies. Under the Van Boven/Bassiouni Principles, the State responsible for the violations continues to be the primary source of reparations, but persons (corporate or individual) can also be held responsible.[194]

USING CULTURALLY SENSITIVE APPROACHES TO RECONCILIATION AND SOCIAL JUSTICE

A process of reconciliation is often necessary before children formerly associated with armed forces and groups are welcomed back into their communities. Such processes can be important in restoring a child's sense of well-being and even ensuring their protection. Yet little attention is often paid to reconciliation and social justice issues in programmes for children's reintegration into society following a conflict.

A community-based reintegration programme in Sierra Leone focused on these two themes when attempting to elicit cooperation between formerly recruited children and village members – who both feared and mistrusted each other. The programme began by facilitating dialogues in which local people described their suffering during the war. In doing so, they developed empathy towards each other and began to create the psychological space needed to allow them to work together. Further dialogues were subsequently undertaken on the subject of children's needs and community projects that could best address them. If the group decided, for instance, that education and the construction of a school were priorities, joint teams of those who had and had not been recruited worked together on construction, while earning an income.

This process of developing empathy, planning collectively and working together on a project that contributed to their livelihoods succeeded in reducing tensions, altering preconceptions and building social cohesion. Formerly recruited youth reported that the programme helped them improve their relations with the community, which appeased their fears and reduced their stigma – two major sources of psychosocial distress. The experience demonstrates the value of a reintegration approach that includes community reconciliation and provides children with psychosocial support.

In the Northern Province of Sierra Leone, tradition calls for those who have harmed a community to make some form of restitution – in other words, if reconciliation is to last, social justice must be achieved. One method of doing so, identified during dialogues on traditional healing, was considered especially valuable by one community: Upon returning to his village, a boy tells his family what happened to him during the war. The parents then go to the village chief and ask him to speak to the boy. If the chief agrees, the boy lies face down on the floor and, while holding the chief's ankles, tells him his story. If the chief believes him and thinks he should be allowed to return, he may give the boy a task that is helpful to the community. He also assigns him to a mentor.

Acceptance by the parents is the first step in this community reintegration process. In his interaction with the chief, the boy's posture of submission symbolizes his break with his military past and his recognition of local authority. Through community service, the boy seeks to repair the wrongs he has done to the village (the greater the wrongdoing, the greater the service required). This allows villagers an opportunity to view the boy in a new light. The mentor is also there to guide the boy in re-establishing social relations and readjusting to civilian life.

A number of insights can be drawn from these two examples. First, reintegration is not simply an individual process or one of reuniting children with their families and communities. It is an inherently communal process of creating social acceptance and building reconciliation through social justice. Communities themselves have to make the transformation towards peace. Thus it is vital that national reconciliation processes be backed by local reconciliation processes. Second, reintegration often requires social justice, which is based on traditional practices. Finally, such experiences show that community reconciliation work is an important aspect of assistance to formerly recruited children.

Source: Drawn from notes provided to the Machel review by the Christian Children's Fund on two of its projects in Sierra Leone, February 2008.

"[Disarmament, demobilization and reintegration] is good, but they train us and send us to work in communities that do not trust us. The people give us no jobs, so some of us sell our tools to live. They should address trust in communities." –
Young man, 19, Liberia

Predictably, however, many challenges remain. Who among the victims should be compensated? What types of harm should be considered and how much compensation should be awarded? How can different types of harm be quantified and compared? How can a community provide compensation to children who have taken part in hostilities, and perhaps been forced to commit crimes against their own communities, without triggering a sense of injustice on the part of their victims? For example, survivors of sexual and gender-based violence in armed conflicts, including children, have long been neglected in reparations programmes.

In 2007, the Committee on the Rights of the Child expressed concern as to whether the budgets for national reparation programmes were adequate. It recommended that States parties allocate appropriate resources towards comprehensive reparations measures, ensuring that they take gender into perspective.[195]

While the involvement and consideration of children in reparations programmes continue to pose difficult challenges,[196] there is also growing realization that children are entitled to reparations in their own right. Children, therefore, must be involved from the outset in identifying the issues at stake, and their representation must be

ensured in restitution processes. Moreover, it has become apparent that no single form of reparation can provide entire satisfaction to victims, especially children. A timely and sensitive combination of reparation measures will generally be required as a complement to other transitional justice mechanisms, such as criminal prosecutions and truth commissions.[197]

According to a 2004 report of the Secretary-General: "States have the obligation to act not only against perpetrators, but also on behalf of victims – including through the provision of reparations. Programmes to provide reparations to victims for harm suffered can be effective and expeditious complements to the contributions of tribunals and truth commissions by providing concrete remedies, promoting reconciliation and restoring victims' confidence in the State."[198]

Institutional and security sector reforms. Post-conflict situations are not only characterized by a lack of capacity to deliver basic services; the police, the judiciary and other key institutions may themselves be a source of public insecurity, mistrust and past violations of human rights. Profound reforms are often required, including a vetting process that screens out individuals associated with past abuses.

However, a vetting process is only one element of wider justice and security reforms. Such reforms also represent a critical opportunity

Democratic Republic of the Congo © UNICEF/NYHQ2005-0431/LeMoyne

to highlight child rights and the responsibility of state institutions, including the security and law enforcement sectors, as duty bearers in child protection.

Special protections for children involved in justice mechanisms

In addition to advances in prosecution, progress has also been made in the treatment of children in justice processes. A key principle in international law is that children involved in judicial proceedings, including transitional justice mechanisms, require special measures that protect their rights and take into account their vulnerability and best interests. This applies whether they have been perpetrators, victims or witnesses.

The special protections afforded child victims and witnesses are spelled out in the 2005 UN Guidelines on Justice in Matters Involving Child Victims and Witnesses of Crime. These guidelines, based on rights outlined in the CRC and other inter-national instruments, reiterate such principles as respect for the child's dignity; the best interests of the child; and the child's right to be heard, express his or her own views and contribute to decisions affecting his or her life.[199] A child-friendly version of the UN guidelines has also been prepared in all UN languages to help children understand and access their rights.

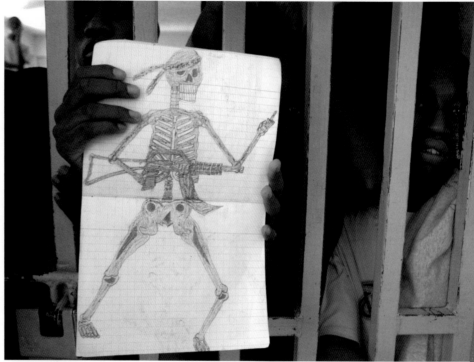

Haiti © UNICEF/NYHQ2005-1912/LeMoyne

Special protection provisions for child victims and witnesses can include hearings on camera, pre-recorded testimonies, the use of pseudonyms to protect the child's identity, videoconferencing and gender-sensitive approaches. International courts and tribunals have witnessed considerable progress in this area. As described above, both the Special Court for Sierra Leone and the ICC have adopted protective measures and child-friendly procedures to facilitate participation by child victims and witnesses.

Important protections also exist for children who must undergo criminal proceedings. Article 40 of the CRC, in particular, details minimum legal guarantees for these children and requires States to set a minimum age of criminal responsi-bility, provide alternative measures besides judicial proceedings or institutional care, and promote the

establishment of a distinct system of juvenile justice aimed at reintegrating children into a society in which they can play a constructive role. This provision should be read together with articles 37 and 39 of the CRC. Article 37 bars certain punishments[200] and provides that any restriction of liberty must be as a last resort and for the shortest possible time. Article 39 relates to the child's physical and psychological recovery and reintegration.

Significant strides have been made in developing implementation guidelines for the administration of juvenile justice, especially through a range of related UN rules and guidelines.[201] The Committee on the Rights of the Child has repeatedly advocated for the establishment of juvenile justice systems in conformity with these international standards and guidelines. It has also provided detailed comments expressing concern that country practices are not in line with international standards.[202] Most recently, in Comment No. 10 of 2007, it articulated the leading principles (articles 2, 3, 6 and 12) and core elements for a comprehensive policy on juvenile justice.

Children as perpetrators

A contentious question in recent years concerns accountability for crimes allegedly committed by children during armed conflict. A new standard is emerging based on the practice of the ad hoc tribunals in the former Yugoslavia and Rwanda, the policy of the Special Court for Sierra Leone and the Rome Statute for the ICC. It specifies that children under age 18 should not be held criminally responsible in international tribunals or courts for grave violations of international humanitarian law.[203] The Special Court for Sierra Leone, established in 2002, included provisions to prosecute persons 15 years or older, but the prosecutor elected not to prosecute children below 18. He stated that he preferred to "prosecute the people who forced thousands of children to commit unspeakable crimes."[204] The Rome Statute of the International Criminal Court does not allow for prosecution of persons below the age of 18 for war crimes, crimes against humanity or genocide.[205]

This emerging standard has recently been supported in the Paris Principles. The Principles maintain that children accused of crimes under international law allegedly committed while they were associated with armed forces or armed groups should be considered primarily as victims of offences against international law, not only as perpetrators. They must be treated in accordance with international juvenile justice standards and norms and within a framework of restorative justice and social reintegration.

Counterterrorism measures

A growing problem related to children in justice processes concerns counterterrorism policies, especially detention practices. While interna-

"When I saw the people responsible for organizing the killings of many people and destroying their homes... I was happy, because they were now in a tight place. I felt it was an opportunity to represent the voiceless, and my story told their story."– Former child soldier and witness to the Special Court of Sierra Leone, testifying through a video link in Freetown, June 2007

tional law requires the treatment of children to focus on reintegration, the counterterrorism measures being increasingly applied and the practice of national courts have sometimes resulted in prolonged detention of children and other violations of international juvenile justice standards.

For example, in April 2003, US authorities revealed that children as young as 13 were among the foreign nationals being held at Guantanamo Bay. One widely publicized case involves a boy who was arrested in Afghanistan in 2002 for crimes he allegedly committed when he was 15 years old. He was subsequently transferred to Guantanamo Bay, where he has been held for over five years as of February 2008.[206] Children are held in "administrative detention" in Aghanistan, Iraq and Israel. In Nepal, children were detained under the Terrorist and Disruptive Activities Ordinance, which has no set minimum age and grants security forces wide powers to arrest and detain any person suspected of being associated with armed groups, including children.[207]

Countless other examples from around the world are regularly reported. International law requires States to provide children with special safeguards and care including legal protections appropriate to their age. These obligations cannot be superseded by security measures. As the Committee on the Rights of

Uganda © UNICEF/NYHQ2004-1153/LeMoyne

the Child has recently cautioned, measures to prevent and combat terrorism should not result in retroactive or unintended punishment for children.[208]

REMAINING GAPS

Significant progress has been made in developing a global normative framework to protect children's rights in conflict situations. But a troubling dichotomy remains between the advances in norms at the international level and the prevalence of serious violations of children's rights on the ground. Reports are rampant of children's recruitment and use in conflict and other grave child rights

violations, including killing, maiming, abduction and sexual violence.

Even in cases where countries have ratified or acceded to international treaties, the enactment of national legislation is lagging, and the absence of will or capacity to implement standards leaves innumerable violations against children unpunished. In many cases, national legislation is undermined by practical and operational challenges. Formal justice systems in post-conflict countries are often dysfunctional or plagued by a lack of resources; sometimes they are virtually non-existent.

A comprehensive approach to transitional justice that adopts a

"Orphans and street children join militias at clan checkpoints to rape, loot and kill people. They are security guards of the warlords. The oldest of them is 17 years old. They are sent by the warlords. If you try to advise them they will kill you." – Girls and young women, 14–17, Somalia

variety of complementary mechanisms is needed to meet the different needs of society, communities and individual victims. While important efforts have been made towards facilitating the participation of children in these mechanisms, challenges remain, such as the involvement of girls – especially survivors of sexual violence.

Many years after war has ended, children will continue to search for healing and accountability, material reparations and emotional support, truth and reconciliation. It is incumbent upon citizens everywhere

to 'build back better' and to integrate children's concerns into broader efforts to re-establish the rule of law – now recognized as a principal keystone in promoting security and lasting peace.

RECOMMENDATIONS

The review of the Machel study presented to the General Assembly in 2007 made four principal recommendations that concern this chapter. The first appears on page 65; the other three are outlined below, along with additional complementary recommendations.

Lebanon © UNICEF/NYHQ2006-1148/Brooks

End impunity for violations against children.

1. **Adopt specific measures to end impunity.** States not involved in conflict should also adopt specific measures that end impunity for violations against children in armed conflict. Such measures may include adopting extraterritorial provisions for relevant crimes; ensuring that national provisions comply with the rules and provisions of the ICC; applying the universality principle where relevant; ensuring that domestic legislation criminalizes arms trade to countries with a record of illegally recruiting and using child soldiers; and adopting provisions that address money laundering and permit freezing the assets of persons or legal entities accused of serious violations against children in armed conflict.

GA RECOMMENDATION 3
Prioritize children's security.

2. **Reduce arms proliferation.** States should review their domestic legislation and practice in order to abolish arms trade to countries where children take part in armed conflict, including trade in small arms and light weapons. Violations of arms embargoes should be criminalized and prosecuted. States should implement existing legal instruments that address landmines and explosive remnants

of war and are encouraged to ratify the newly adopted Convention on Cluster Munitions and actively support its implementation. In addition, Member States should include in their national reports under the UN Programme of Action information on measures taken or needed to protect children from the scourge of small arms.

GA RECOMMENDATION 4
Promote justice for children.

3. **Ensure coordination and sustained efforts to move from crisis to long-term development.** The international community and UN agencies in particular should ensure coordination among themselves as well as with other actors (such as donors, NGOs, national governments) in working to (re)establish as quickly as possible the rule of law and a justice system that includes a distinct system for juvenile justice. The latter should be consistent with international standards and supported by institutional links with the social sector/child protection systems. Efforts by different actors at different stages of the process – from crisis to early recovery to development – should be sustained and should build on one another.

4. **Apply an integrated approach to justice for children.** The policies and programmes of UN agencies should be in line with the UN Common Approach on Justice for Children. Both States and UN agencies should aim to integrate children's concerns in legislative, judicial and security sector reforms, including those of law enforcement institutions, such as the police.

5. **Support the participation of children in justice processes.** States and the international community should support the participation of children in transitional justice processes by drawing on established principles, such as the best interests of the child, and good practices identified to date with regard to child protection measures and child-friendly procedures. They should also provide adequate resources to support transitional justice processes and related programmes for children and children's inclusion in reparations programmes.

6. **Improve children's access to justice.** The UN and NGOs should support community-based legal and paralegal services for children, families and communities along with programmes that establish diversion, alternatives to justice and restorative justice. ■

KEY RESOURCES

International Committee of the Red Cross, *Customary International Humanitarian Law,* edited by J.-M. Henckaerts and L. Oswald-Beck, ICRC/Cambridge University Press, 2005.

UN Security Council, 'The Rule of Law and Transitional Justice in Conflict and Post-conflict Societies: Report of the Secretary-General', S/2004/616, 23 August 2004.

United Nations Children's Fund, 'Expert Discussion on Transitional Justice and Children', 10–12 November 2005, outcome document and background documents (annexed), UNICEF Innocenti Research Centre, Florence, 2005.

United Nations Children's Fund, *Implementation Handbook for the Convention on the Rights of the Child,* third edition, UNICEF, Geneva, September 2007.

No Peace Without Justice and UNICEF Innocenti Research Centre, *International Criminal Justice and Children,* NPWJ and UNICEF Innocenti Research Centre, New York and Florence, September 2002.

UNICEF and the International Center for Transitional Justice, 'Children and Truth Commissions', Innocenti Research Centre, Florence (forthcoming).

EVOLUTION OF EFFORTS TO STRENGTHEN CHILD PROTECTION

Almost every action taken on behalf of children affected by armed conflict is rooted in a system – the combination of international treaties, national policies and programmes, funding strategies, and monitoring and evaluation structures that underpin official response to violations of the rights of these children. This chapter addresses developments and challenges from the perspective of these systems. Their components support every sector or issue in caring for and protecting conflict-affected children. (The more specific sectors and issues are discussed in chapter 8.) Despite the continuing challenges in protecting and caring for children affected by armed conflict, the global system of response has evolved significantly since the 1996 Graça Machel study.

This system is built on a foundation of standards and norms. The Convention on the Rights of the Child and its optional protocols covering armed conflict and sexual exploitation; the Geneva Conventions, which limit the barbarity of war; and the Rome Statute establishing the International Criminal Court – all of these, along with the many others mentioned in chapter 5, codify the rights of children and their need for special protection in situations of armed conflict.

'A World Fit for Children', the final document adopted at the 2002 UN General Assembly Special Session on Children, includes in its Plan of Action a key goal on children affected by armed conflict.[209] It states that governments will "protect children against the impact of armed conflict and ensure compliance with international humanitarian law and human rights law."[210] The document goes on to outline 13 actions that can be taken to achieve this goal.

Further key elements of the United Nations' efforts to protect children from armed conflict are the landmark Security Council Resolutions 1539 (2004) and 1612 (2005). These have led to the development of a system-wide Monitoring and Reporting Mechanism on the six grave violations against children in armed conflict (discussed later in this chapter). UN efforts have also resulted in a working group, comprised of all members of the Security Council, that regularly assesses progress by parties to conflicts in developing action plans to release children associated with armed forces and groups. This working group is also mandated to suggest further action should sufficient progress not be made. This mechanism and other efforts by partners have improved coordination, data collection and monitoring. In turn, these advances have led to more focused responses and prevention strategies.

ROLES AND PARTNERSHIPS

The impact of armed conflict on children, the 1996 Machel study stressed, "must be everyone's concern and is everyone's responsibility." Built on the foundation of norms, standards and goals are the operational and programmatic guidelines, policies and procedures steering the specialized organizations and technical groups that work on behalf of children affected by armed conflict. The system benefits from the diverse nature of the entities involved – from Member States of the United Nations to community groups, including non-governmental organizations (NGOs), traditional structures, women's organizations, youth groups and religious leaders. They are all essential in a chain that extends from the Security Council to the most isolated village. The mandates and partnerships are complementary, and they include children themselves, as discussed earlier in this publication. This chapter highlights key developments in this system of response.

Key drivers in the UN system

The roles of the Office of the Special Representative of the Secretary-General for Children and Armed Conflict (OSRSG-CAAC) and UNICEF, as well as other UN agencies, are widely acknowledged as fundamental to the United Nations' global work on children and armed conflict. The key agencies are described below.

Office of the Special Representative of the Secretary-General for Children and Armed Conflict. This office, established by the General Assembly, is one of the key results of the 1996

Sri Lanka © UNICEF/NYHQ2006-1591/Noorani

Machel study. The mandate of the office includes assessing "progress achieved, steps taken and difficulties encountered in strengthening the protection of children in situations of armed conflict"; raising awareness about the plight of affected children; and working closely with and fostering cooperation between governments and intergovernmental bodies, the Committee on the Rights of the Child and notable UN bodies and mechanisms, as well as non-governmental organizations.[211] The OSRSG offers a vital independent, moral voice for children affected by armed conflict around the globe. The office also plays the lead role in bringing the UN system together on behalf of the Secretary-General, in initiating and sustaining with UNICEF the global Monitoring and Reporting Mechanism, and in maintaining dialogue with Member States and relevant parties to conflict. In conjunction with UN country teams, the OSRSG advocates for the development of action plans to cease the recruitment and use of children in conflict, and to address all other grave violations against children.

The work of the OSRSG has been central to maintaining the Security Council's engagement on children's issues. With the support of UNICEF and key UN system and NGO partners, it has played a central role in generating political consensus for the Monitoring and Reporting Mechanism in the UN Security Council and beyond.

The SRSG has invested considerable time and effort on high-profile field missions to places affected by armed conflict, and these visits have served to enhance global advocacy for protection efforts. She has also engaged with governmental and non-state entities on issues of accountability and compliance in situations where UN system partners and other actors may have been constrained by practical field realities. Following a number of field visits by the Special Representative of the Secretary-General, parties to conflict have made commitments to formulate action plans to end children's participation in armed conflict.

The OSRSG presides over a Task Force on Children Affected by Armed Conflict. It works to mainstream the issue throughout UN agencies, offices and mandates, and it identifies trends and policies that need to be discussed. A chief responsibility of the Task Force is vetting the Secretary-General's annual report on children affected by armed conflict.

UNICEF. As the lead UN agency for children, UNICEF is responsible for developing policy around children's issues; supporting advocacy; developing guidelines and working tools; increasing capacity; and developing and maintaining effective responses for children, including those affected by armed conflict. UNICEF has consistently argued for an agenda that does more than simply respond to

the needs of children fighting in armed forces. It also aims to promote a rights-based approach to ensure a protective environment for all children affected by armed conflict. UNICEF's response is grounded by its 2004 Core Commitments for Children in Emergencies.

In response to the 1996 Machel study's recommendation to increase capacity to serve children affected by armed conflict, UNICEF has developed a team to focus on policy and systems development. Along with the Monitoring and Reporting Mechanism, this team addresses prevention of recruitment and release of children associated with armed forces and groups, sexual violence, child protection and psychosocial issues. In most countries affected by armed conflict, UNICEF and partners have gradually begun to dedicate specific human, financial and material resources to this issue. In addition, they work to help governments raise their capacity to respond, which is of utmost importance in developing sustainable, integrated mechanisms to prevent and respond to the six grave violations and to additional ones.

In collaboration with the OSRSG, UNICEF has taken the lead in working with the Monitoring and Reporting Mechanism Steering Committee to develop systems and tools to improve the quality and sustainability of the mechanism. UNICEF is also the lead agency for the Child Protection Working Group in the Inter-Agency Standing Committee Global Protection Cluster, dealing with the situation of children in emergencies, including those caused by armed conflict.

Other UN entities also have key roles and responsibilities regarding children. The 1996 Machel study called for all "United Nations bodies [to] treat children affected by armed conflicts as a distinct and priority concern."[212] Successive Secretaries-General have emphasized the need for collective responsibility to ensure that the issue is not regarded as specific to one agency and to ensure the UN family works with governments and civil society throughout the humanitarian community. In September 2004, then Secretary-General Kofi Annan submitted to the General Assembly a Comprehensive Assessment of the United Nations System Response to Children Affected by Armed Conflict.[213] Much of what was noted in that assessment remains relevant today.

Department of Peacekeeping Operations (DPKO). DPKO has significantly expanded the incorporation of children's issues in peacekeeping operations. This includes more coverage of child rights and protection in training for peacekeepers, as recommended by Mrs. Machel in 1996. It has also led to another important development: the inclusion of child protection advisers in peacekeeping missions. Beginning with the deployment of a single adviser in Sierra Leone in 2000, DPKO currently deploys more than 60 advisers in seven peacekeeping missions and one political mission.[214] A recent evaluation by DPKO, 'Lessons Learned Study: Child Protection – The impact of child protection advisers in peacekeeping operations', recognized the important work done by child protection advisers in raising attention to the rights of war-affected children. In many locations, child protection advisers have been instrumental in implementing the Monitoring and Reporting Mechanism and documenting child rights violations. They have also engaged in dialogue with parties to conflict and conducted advocacy on politically sensitive issues.[215]

Through such work, DPKO supports operational partners who may be unable to engage in overt political advocacy on child rights violations without jeopardizing their long-term work. As a follow-up to the lessons learned study, DPKO has recruited a child protection focal point at Headquarters to develop a policy within the department. This person will work with child protection advisers in the field and collaborate with such key partners as UNICEF and the OSRSG.

Office of the United Nations High Commissioner for Human Rights (OHCHR). OHCHR's function is evolving from advisory to operational. Its field presence in Nepal and Uganda and its role in providing human rights monitors to peacekeeping missions have made important contributions to improving the monitoring and reporting of violations and in raising the level of expertise in formulating response strategies and actions. OHCHR has played a major part in monitoring and reporting on grave violations against children in its Nepal and Uganda operations. It has also placed a dedicated child rights

focal point in its Nepal country operation. Similar child focal points should be established in all OHCHR country operations where practical.

Another recommendation calls for OHCHR to employ a full-time focal point on children and armed conflict at Headquarters to better integrate its field-based monitoring and advocacy activities. OHCHR also facilitates the work of UN human rights mechanisms, such as the Human Rights Council and the treaty bodies monitoring compliance with international human rights treaties – including the Committee on the Rights of the Child. As recommended in the Secretary-General's 2004 assessment report to the General Assembly, OHCHR is urged to recruit more expertise on child rights at Headquarters.

United Nations High Commissioner for Refugees (UNHCR). UNHCR has played a major role in drawing attention to the needs of children displaced by conflict within or across borders. As part of the humanitarian reform process, UNHCR is taking on new responsibilities to protect and deliver services to internally displaced persons, and has taken the lead in protection, emergency shelter and camp coordination and management. In the early 1990s, UNHCR added a Headquarters-level officer to coordinate issues pertaining to child refugees. It now requires annual participatory assessments as part

Kenya © UNICEF/NYHQ2008-0470/Cranston

of its age, gender and diversity mainstreaming strategy – an important example to other agencies. UNHCR reviews implementation of the Machel commitments for children every two years. It has been encouraged to expand its field child protection staff to better monitor, report, advocate around and respond to grave violations against children for populations of concern under its mandate.

UN Development Programme Bureau for Crisis Prevention and Recovery. The Bureau is mandated to provide a bridge between humanitarian response and longer-term development following a country's recovery from conflict. Its growing work on youth and conflict is an area calling for even further collaboration, both across the UN system and with

other partners, to improve policy and programme coherence for this priority age group, 15 to 24 years old.

Office for the Coordination of Humanitarian Affairs (OCHA). OCHA works through a network of field offices that support UN humanitarian coordinators and country teams. OCHA's work on protection of civilians and follow-up to Security Council resolutions and reports of the Secretary-General on that theme are an important component of international policies supporting initiatives for children and armed conflict. OCHA also leads the process of soliciting donor support for UN humanitarian programmes, mainly through the Consolidated Appeals Process and the Central Emergency Response Fund.

Other UN entities essential to children and related armed conflict issues include: the Department of Political Affairs, which could contribute to more consistent inclusion of children's concerns in mediation leading to peace agreements; the UN Office for Disarmament Affairs, especially in connection with the impact of small arms and light weapons; the United Nations Development Fund for Women, especially in its role spear-heading the campaign to end violence against women; and the United Nations Populations Fund (UNFPA), with its focus on reproductive health, gender-based violence and HIV.

Monitoring and reporting mechanisms

One of the most significant develop-ments during the past 10 years has been the creation of the UN Monitoring and Reporting Mechanism (MRM), as called for in Security Council Resolutions 1539 and 1612. The new system was crafted in part to address the lack of an effective child rights enforcement mechanism in situations of armed conflict. It created a channel to link information collected at the country level with reporting to the Security Council and to other organi-zations that can press actors to comply with international child rights and protection standards. The aim is to provide the Security Council with accurate, reliable and timely information on the recruitment and use of children by parties to armed conflict in violation of international law. In addition, it will provide information on other grave violations against children in situations of armed conflict as the basis for appropriate action.

As specified by the 2005 Secretary-General's report on the situation of children and armed conflict,[216] the mechanism concentrates on six categories of grave rights violations:

- Killing and maiming of children;

- Recruitment and use of children associated with armed forces and groups;

- Abduction;

- Rape and other acts of grave sexual violence against children;

- Attacks on schools and hospitals;

- Denial of humanitarian access.

The MRM Steering Committee, co-chaired by the OSRSG and UNICEF, is an inter-agency initiative. It is meant to guide country task forces on monitoring and reporting, including on their review of draft reports, iden-tification of policy issues, provision of guidance and development of working tools. Most recently, the committee has focused on technical issues related to building a common vision and understanding for the mechanism's global guidelines. The Steering Committee's work needs to be planned more systematically to ensure inter-agency commitment to the MRM initiative globally and in the field.

The Monitoring and Reporting Mechanism has achieved notable initial success, although it is more labour-intensive than anticipated and demands serious investment in human, financial and material resources. MRM country task forces have been established in 11 countries. Each is led by the most senior UN staff member in the country, whether the Special Representative of the Secretary-General or the Resident Coordinator. Most task forces for children and armed conflict are co-chaired by the UNICEF Representative; some by other agency heads. The SRSG-CAAC for children and armed conflict plays a crucial role in advocating for the monitoring and reporting exercise to remain a true inter-agency process involving all UN and child rights and protection institutions.

A workshop organized by UNICEF and the OSRSG-CAAC in Pretoria (South Africa) in April 2007 provided a unique opportunity for exchange of experiences and lessons learned among members of the country task forces, Headquarters staff and other repre-sentatives. This work contributed substantially to the MRM global guidelines, which call for developing a 'state of knowledge' study to identify all potential sources of information. It should assess the risk of imple-menting the mechanism for those who provide and gather information as well as for witnesses and victims.

Philippines © UNICEF/NYHQ2006-1460/Pirozzi

RECOMMENDATIONS

GLOBAL RESPONSE SYSTEM

1. **Make information available at all levels.** The United Nations should facilitate access to the latest research by UN agencies, international and local NGOs, Member States and other stakeholders. This will aid the development of national policies and support scaling up projects, leading to a sustainable impact on children.

2. **Generate more knowledge.** Stakeholders, including academic and research institutions, should increase their investment in generating and managing knowledge related to children and armed conflict.

3. **Develop a common set of indicators and an information management system.** To enable more accurate analysis of trends over time, global and field-based indicators are needed. It is crucially important to develop a baseline of data and a system to manage information (both quantitative and qualitative) on all relevant issues.

4. **Build a stronger evaluation system.** It is vital to improve documentation and analysis of the impact of prevention and response activities on the well-being of children.

MONITORING AND REPORTING MECHANISM

1. **Prepare practical guidelines for field workers.** In close consultation with country task forces, the MRM Steering Committee should prepare a concise field manual for those responsible for data collection, reporting and analysis, as well as for prevention and response activities at the country level. MRM task forces should ensure that the selected data collection tools complement the approaches outlined in the guidelines.

2. **Build the capacity of national and local partners.** Donors, UN agencies and international NGOs should support efforts to build capacity among the child protection partners (national and local) who will participate in the monitoring and reporting mechanism. Skills can be developed through traditional training courses, but mentoring is also effective. Training packages should be developed in collaboration with the MRM Steering Committee.

3. **Take steps to ensure the security of victims, witnesses and communities.** Safety and security issues related to the mechanism should be assessed globally. Such a project, convened by the OSRSG, UNICEF, OHCHR and other

global partners, should start with agreement on the precautions that data collectors should take in the field. It should also train field staff in security, establish a security incident monitoring system and develop contingency plans to respond to incidents. Global guidance, field manuals and training should, at a minimum, clarify field monitors' obligations and methods for safeguarding the identities of victims and witnesses.

4. **Support the mechanism with resources.** A successful Monitoring and Reporting Mechanism cannot be implemented within existing resources, as indicated in Resolution 1612. MRM country task forces will need to continue to strengthen capacity by recruiting dedicated, skilled staff and ensuring that all involved in the process are trained and kept informed about policy developments. All key stakeholders, including Member States, donors, UN entities and NGOs, are urged to dedicate greater levels of human and financial resources to consolidate the monitoring, reporting and response mechanisms. Donors should continue to fund prevention and response activities because they are an integral part of the mechanism.

5. **Integrate child protection advisers into missions by DPKO and the Department of Political Affairs.** In countries implementing

the Monitoring and Reporting Mechanism, the heads of peace-keeping and political missions co-chair the UN country task forces along with UNICEF. The child protection advisers should be integrated into all relevant peacekeeping and political missions to make sure that all staff incorporate a child rights approach into performance of their functions.[217]

INTER-AGENCY COLLABORATION AND HUMANITARIAN REFORM

The 1996 Machel study emphasized that protection of children "must be central to the humanitarian, peacemaking and peacekeeping policies of the United Nations, and should be given priority within existing human rights and humanitarian procedures." It also called for inter-institutional mechanisms to give sufficient priority to children.[218] Improvements have been made in mainstreaming and prioritizing children's concerns in United Nations decision-making, including discussions of UN executive committees.

Along with the Secretary-General's Policy Committee, the Executive Committee on Humanitarian Affairs (ECHA) and on Peace and Security (ECPS) are the most central to decisions that involve response to children affected by armed conflict.[219]

Established in General Assembly Resolution 46/182 of 19 December

1991, the Inter-Agency Standing Committee (IASC)[220] is the primary mechanism for inter-agency coordination of humanitarian assistance. IASC is unique in that it includes principal UN entities and non-UN partners. Under the leadership of the Under-Secretary-General for Humanitarian Affairs and Emergency Relief Coordinator, the committee works to:

- Develop and agree on system-wide humanitarian policies;

- Allocate responsibilities among agencies in humanitarian programmes;

- Advocate for humanitarian principles;

- Identify areas with gaps in mandates or lack of operational capacity;

- Develop and agree on a common ethical framework for all humanitarian activities.[221]

IASC's growing role in children's issues is reflected in the number of guidelines it has issued during the past decade.

At the field level, the 1996 Machel study called for children and armed conflict to "be reflected in the terms of reference for resident and humanitarian coordinators and those with political responsibilities, such as special representatives of the Secretary-General."[222] Leadership and engagement on children's concerns from these representatives of the UN system

> "Our home was damaged during war and we migrated to Pakistan. We lived for 10 years in Pakistan. We came back to Afghanistan. We have a place to build a house, but have no money to pay for it. We have rented a house and live there now, but it is very hard for us to pay for it." – Young man, 17, Afghanistan

have improved during the past decade. For example, special representatives and humanitarian coordinators more consistently advocate for child-specific concerns and provide leadership for monitoring, reporting and responding to grave violations against children. Interviews conducted for the strategic review[223] found that the number of agencies concerned with children and armed conflict issues has increased. Now concerns related to children are raised by UN entities in the field in addition to UNICEF, in particular by OCHA, peacekeeping operations, the United Nations Development Programme (UNDP) and UNHCR.

The United Nations is undergoing an institution-wide process of reform in which the humanitarian sector has advanced considerably. The reform process is intended to clarify accountability across sectors, prepare common standards and guidelines, improve information collection, and develop new emergency and post-conflict funding mechanisms.

In 2005, IASC adopted the 'cluster approach' to inter-agency cooperation. It aims to increase response capacity and effectiveness in emergencies by building global capacities and providing predictable leadership, stronger inter-agency partnerships, greater accountability, and improved field-level coordination and priority setting.[224] This approach has improved the delivery of services to conflict-affected children.

Reinforcing civil society and social support structures

In conflict-affected countries, civil society – including the media, local NGOs, faith-based organizations, and private sector and community groups and networks – often operates in parallel to governmental and international relief efforts. Civil society shares the burden of delivering services and protecting children from harm. These groups are frequently the first ones on the ground and often provide aid when others cannot.

Advocacy networks. In addition to operational agencies, numerous advocacy networks have emerged or consolidated during the past decade. These networks – which include the Coalition to Stop the Use of Child Soldiers, the Inter-Agency Network on Emergency Education and the Watchlist on Children and Armed Conflict – have provided significant help in reaching out to children and generating action to prevent and abolish the abuse of children in situations of armed conflict. The Coalition to Stop the Use of Child Soldiers, for example, produces a comprehensive report every four years on the recruitment and use of children by armed forces and armed groups. Although not specific to children, Landmine Monitor reports, an initiative of the International Campaign to Ban Landmines, contain information relevant to the impact of war on children.

Local non-governmental organizations. Even closer to the front lines for conflict-affected children are local NGOs. Women's groups, faith-based organizations, cultural groups and other community associations regularly provide aid or help monitor the situation of children. By utilizing their access to and understanding of local situations, they play a vital role in delivering services, monitoring and advocacy. Civil society organizations often proliferate in response to a crisis and may continue to operate after the conflict. But without coordination they may work at cross purposes.

As elaborated in chapters 3 and 9, youth groups and children themselves are an important resource, supporting each other and working to build peace. Like NGOs, these groups do not always have sufficient resources to carry out their work. But investment in training, mentoring and collaborative partnerships can empower them to contribute more effectively to protection and care of children in their communities.

Religious leaders and organizations. Faith-based entities can be a wellspring of resilience and communal strength during a crisis. They need more attention from international agencies to improve understanding of how and when to work with and support them. Religious leaders and institutions can also play a key role in peacebuilding and reconciliation. Examples include Bishop Desmond Tutu's role in

South Africa and beyond, and a coalition of church groups in the Philippines that worked as an intermediary between the Government and the National Democratic Front. They can also play a key role in children's protection. Religious leaders and faith-based organizations often have access to wide global networks, useful in mobilizing people around the care and protection of children.

The media. The media has a role in raising awareness of children's rights, reporting violations against children, and providing children and youth the opportunity to express their own ideas and opinions. Search for Common Ground has initiated Youth Voice radio projects in Angola, Burundi, the Democratic Republic of the Congo, Liberia and Sierra Leone. These projects encourage dialogue by allowing youth to express their opinions on a range of issues affecting them, such as demobilization of children associated with armed forces and armed groups, child rights and inter-ethnic conflict. Similar projects have been undertaken in Nepal.

Harnessing the power of national media as partners in information sharing, advocacy and awareness raising is key to promoting peace and driving positive change. Also needed are efforts to sensitize the media about ethical reporting on children's issues and best practices in covering child-related issues. Given the delicacy of issues relating to children

affected by armed conflict, all media coverage should reflect a code of conduct focused on safeguarding the best interests of the child and abiding by the 'do no harm' principle.

The private sector. With growing recognition of the role of business and 'war economies' in situations of conflict, private sector involvement is crucial. UN investigations in the Democratic Republic of the Congo and Sierra Leone, for example, exposed the complicity of some international corporations, and in response, corporate actors began to regulate trade flows and support human rights standards. The Peace Diamond Alliance in Sierra Leone brought two major buyers together with the Government, NGOs and donors. They now jointly regulate diamond production, monitor violence and ban the use of child labour.[225]

Analyses for the Machel strategic review identified some important new areas for action. One is that private sector companies need to be viewed as duty bearers – those with obligations to help fulfil child rights. This requires promotion of a wider understanding of corporate social responsibility and of child rights in situations of armed conflict. Some of the most promising measures involve cooperation among Member States and multinational enterprises. The Voluntary Principles on Security and Human Rights, for example, promote

human rights risk assessments and training of security providers. The Extractive Industries Transparency Initiative establishes a degree of revenue transparency in the taxes, royalties and fees companies pay to host governments. The Organisation for Economic Co-operation and Development (OECD) Guidelines for Multinational Enterprises and the UN Global Compact represent important partnerships in which children's rights should be part of the criterion.[226]

Child protection networks. In many countries, child protection networks perform a variety of roles, including advocacy, coordination among sectors, information sharing and harmonizing programme approaches.[227] Such networks have commonly been formed to address a particular issue, such as release and reintegration of children connected with armed groups, or separated children. Their memberships tend to be broad, including UN agencies, government departments and civil society groups.

Usually these networks do not take on child rights monitoring and reporting, but in some instances they have been mobilized to contribute to the UN Monitoring and Reporting Mechanism. Community groups in Somalia, for example, have organized to help document grave violations against children and to collect information on internal displacement and the impact it has on communities.

Iraq © UNICEF/NYHQ2007-2322/Kamber

Developing national systems

Central to the idea of protecting children's rights in times of conflict is the primary responsibility of the State to respect, protect and fulfil the human rights of all persons within its territory. The Convention on the Rights of the Child, like all other major human rights instruments, reiterates State responsibilities, including in times of war and internal conflict.

Clearly, however, national governments in conflict-affected countries are constrained in delivering essential services and reaching populations in need. Major emergencies attract large-scale international action, which can quickly evolve into capacity substitution rather than capacity building. When these international actors withdraw, a country can be left bereft of protection capacities for such initiatives as conducting family tracing and reunification or assistance to link victims of gender-based violence with public services. Solutions to such issues include development of the skills needed to gradually integrate services into national programmes and plans.

Within national systems, capacity building to protect children against violence, exploitation and abuse faces particular constraints. Because such issues can be culturally sensitive, politically charged or focused on marginalized groups, the political will to prioritize them may waver.

Even when governments want to be involved, the State may lack capacity in justice and social welfare systems, and national human rights commissions.

An approach emphasizing integrated systems and a coordinated response involving national government, civil society and international agencies could help scale up services. This requires long-term commitment; it cannot be achieved through short-term emergency funding. National governments should work closely with the MRM task force to build capacity to prevent violations, respond to them and ensure that strong accountability mechanisms are in place.

Recommendations

1. **Continue mainstreaming within the United Nations and other organizations.** Senior child protection focal points should be designated within all relevant UN agencies, departments and offices, and in field operations. Periodic assessments should be undertaken to gauge progress in mainstreaming against specific criteria: (a) the extent to which the issue of children affected by armed conflict is brought to the highest levels of decision-making of Member States and the UN system, including the governing boards of agencies, funds and programmes; (b) senior management commitment to and promotion of concerns around this issue; (c) integration of these concerns into doctrine and policy frameworks, strategic plans, operational mandates, and programmes and activities; (d) adequacy of in-house knowledge, expertise and training to inform policies, strategies and operations; and (e) adequacy of resources to support these actions.

Myanmar © UNICEF/NYHQ2008-0344/Dean

6. **Decentralize partnership mechanisms.** The United Nations, international NGOs and local civil society should establish partnership mechanisms at the national and/or subnational levels. A number of countries with functioning child protection working groups or national networks have already taken steps in this direction, but the model could be adapted and expanded. In particularly large and complex countries, the model can be mirrored at the subnational level, as has been done for cluster mechanisms in the Democratic Republic of the Congo.[228]

SETTING GLOBAL STANDARDS

The 1996 Machel study stressed that in armed conflicts, "everyone concerned with children must practice a consistent set of principles, standards and guidelines."[229] Thanks to increased international cooperation, numerous inter-agency standards have been developed over the past decade. Many of them have been developed through broad consultative processes, which aids their acceptance and authority. This growing body of policy standards and practice guidelines extends the international legal framework to the level of implementation.

In February 2007, the French Ministry of Foreign Affairs and UNICEF organized the ministerial

2. **UNHCR and OHCHR agencies: Recruit more expertise on child rights at Headquarters.** OHCHR should employ a full-time focal point on children and armed conflict at Headquarters to better integrate its field-based monitoring and advocacy activities.

3. **Build and strengthen national structures and systems**. Through cluster assessments, work plans and training, UN agencies and international NGOs should help transfer functions to government and civil society. This calls for gradually integrating actions into national policies, plans and programmes. It also requires helping governments and civil society deal with challenges such as lack of resources.

4. **Coordinate responses.** Integrated systems facilitate coordination among national government, civil society and international agencies. This, in turn, allows activities to be scaled up and provides greater benefits to a broader group of children. Donors and international partners must acknowledge that this process will be long term, and they must commit resources to its success.

5. **Provide technology.** Donors, international organizations and private companies should collaborate to identify affordable information and communication technology appropriate in crisis situations. They should ensure that this technology is transferred to national and local actors, and that staff are trained to use and maintain it.

meeting 'Free Children from War'. It culminated in a global consultative process to update the Cape Town Principles and other technical guidance on children associated with armed forces and groups. The first outcome document, endorsed by 66 governments, was the Paris Commitments (discussed in chapter 4). It reaffirms States' commitments to international standards on protection of children associated with armed forces and groups, and to good practices to support their release and reintegration. The second document, the Paris Principles, incorporates current knowledge and lessons learned on disarmament, demobilization and reintegration. It aims to help practitioners ensure that these processes lead to better quality of care for and protection of children.[230] Together, the Paris Commitments and Paris Principles comprise a new set of standards and guidelines. They provide coherence between governmental promises, international obligations, and programme principles and best practice.

The standards and guidelines developed during the past decade include:

- Sphere Humanitarian Charter and Minimum Standards in Disaster Response (1997);

- Guiding Principles on Internal Displacement (1998);

- International Guidelines for Landmine and Unexploded Ordnance Awareness Education (1999);

- The Secretary-General's bulletin on special measures for protection from sexual exploitation and sexual abuse (2003);[231]

- Inter-Agency Guiding Principles on Unaccompanied and Separated Children (2004);

- Inter-Agency Network for Education in Emergencies Minimum Standards for Education in Emergencies, Chronic Crises and Early Reconstruction (2004);

- IASC Guidelines for HIV/AIDS Interventions in Emergency Settings (2004);

- United Nations Guidelines on Justice in Matters involving Child Victims and Witnesses of Crime (2005);

- IASC Guidelines for Gender-based Violence Interventions in Humanitarian Settings (2005);

- Integrated Disarmament, Demobilization and Reintegration Standards (2006);

- IASC Guidelines on Mental Health and Psychosocial Support in Emergency Settings (2007).

Challenges in converting policy into practice

The new standards and guidelines have helped unify approaches. This, in turn, improves consistency in advocacy and programmes, and aids coordination and development of common strategies among partners. Results are being seen. For example, in an evaluation of implementation of minimum standards developed by the Inter-Agency Network for Education in Emergencies, respondents noted improvements in community participation and coordination, analysis, adoption of a more holistic approach to education, and attention to advocacy and capacity building.[232]

Humanitarian actors have tried to extend their accountability and predictability beyond voluntary adherence to standards. IASC's 2005 adoption of the cluster approach to inter-agency cooperation was key (it is discussed further below). Through a set of indicators to measure improvement, more attention has also been given to monitoring and evaluation of programmes for children and youth in armed conflict settings, and the implementation of standards and guidelines. For example, UNICEF has been developing a performance monitoring system for its Core Commitments for Children in Emergencies.[233]

It is clear that the improved body of standards and guidelines (only some of which are outlined here) have gone a long way towards implementing the 1996 Machel study's key findings. As a whole, however, the application of standards in the field needs to be strengthened

"If you go to the Fourah Bay road there are many beggars and they are assisted by children. When I see them I never feel good because the children are all my peers. Why shouldn't they go to school, why shouldn't they get the opportunity? And most of them are war affected. Their mothers are dead or they only have one parent who probably has amputated limbs. So please, they should build homes for them, and then educate them." – Young woman, 16, Sierra Leone

and institutionalized at all levels. Experience has shown that locally adapted and translated guidelines are indispensable, along with greater investment in training and capacity building, as discussed below.

Recommendations

1. **IASC should ensure issues pertaining to programmatic response for conflict-affected children are incorporated in new cluster guidance, common standards, guidelines and assessment tools.**

2. **Further the implementation of standards and guidelines.** Member States, civil society organizations, UN agencies and international NGOs should concentrate on incorporating standards into their organizational policy and operations documents, such as standard operating procedures, manuals and strategic plans. Progress towards harmonizing inter-agency, government and donor standards should be systematically monitored through a framework of indicators and benchmarks. It would be useful for the Committee on the Rights of the Child to consider implementation of these standards and guidelines in reviewing Member States' efforts to translate international law into domestic law.

ENSURING CAPACITY FOR RESPONSE

Across all areas of work on children affected by armed conflict, the strategic review found common gaps and constraints. These include inadequate human resources; insufficient funding, especially in terms of timeliness and flexibility; poor adherence to standards and guidelines; and insufficient monitoring, evaluation and documentation. This section highlights developments concerning human and financial resources.

Investing in human resources

UN agencies and civil society groups need more personnel to monitor, report on and respond to issues pertaining to children and armed conflict, as well as to increase coverage and strengthen child protection systems. Protection of children affected by armed conflict is extremely labour-intensive and requires specialized skills and experience. Human resources support is required across all levels – including the Security Council working group on children and armed conflict, UN agencies dealing with these issues at Headquarters and in the field, NGOs and community-based organizations.

Furthermore, the humanitarian community needs to do more to develop the capacities of national authorities so they can assume their responsibilities to protect children. Where possible, UN agencies and

donors should facilitate an assessment of national human resources needs and work with governments to develop strategies for human resource development and management. In areas affected by conflict, innovative strategies will be needed to retain qualified civil servants, who may also need on-the-job support.

Training is an important tool for improving the implementation of standards and the quality of response for children. Despite the extensive training being offered around the world, many sectors still lack adequately trained personnel. The IASC global clusters have been working to map capacity gaps for humanitarian action in emergencies for each sector and to develop strategies to address these gaps.

A noteworthy inter-agency training initiative, Action for the Rights of the Child, was launched by UNHCR and the International Save the Children Alliance in 1997; UNICEF and OHCHR joined in 1999. It consists of 14 training modules, including one covering international law and its application for children and specific issues such as separated children, disability, education, landmine awareness, sexual and reproductive health, and abuse and exploitation. Based on the results of an independent evaluation in 2006, the steering committee decided to revise the entire initiative. This work is still in process and offers an excellent opportunity to integrate recent developments in standards and practice into the training module.

Also in 2007, the inter-agency modular training package 'Introduction to Child Protection in Emergencies' was published. UNICEF and the other partners[234] now conduct regional trainings throughout the world on child protection in emergencies.

Rosters are one way of addressing personnel shortfalls and providing quick deployment in emergencies. The IASC global clusters for education, health, nutrition, protection, and water and sanitation have established or are establishing rosters of personnel to serve as cluster coordinators and provide technical support. ProCap, administered by the Norwegian Refugee Council, is a roster of protection specialists who can serve in crisis situations. It has an agreement with UNICEF to help fill the need for senior child protection officers. DPKO also maintains a roster of child protection experts, from which it draws child protection advisers. It is important to provide training and to explore ways to maximize use of the rosters.

Increasing financial resources

Donor countries have recognized that financing quality prevention and response measures for children affected by armed conflict is crucial, and they have generally supported such programmes. However, as noted in the strategic review report to the 2007 General Assembly,

"the gaps in resources for children affected by conflict are so extreme that it is clear that a quantum leap in funding is needed."[235]

Since the Machel study, commitment to strengthening coordination between donors has grown. This makes disbursement of humanitarian funds more predictable, including for 'forgotten emergencies'. It also enables longer-term support and aid to projects that fall in the gap between emergency response and post-conflict transition, and it ensures greater transparency.

Changes in the UN humanitarian financing system during the past decade, including those within the recent frame of humanitarian reform, all need to better incorporate child-specific priorities and tracking:

Consolidated Appeals Process (CAP). Administered by OCHA, the CAP is key to humanitarian funding. It has become the main tool for coordinated planning, implementation and monitoring of humanitarian actions, and it has improved cooperation between governments, donors, aid agencies, the International Red Cross and Red Crescent Movement, and NGOs. On average, since 1992, the Consolidated Appeals Process has sought $3.1 billion per year and received $2.1 billion per year (68 per cent).

Common Humanitarian Action Plan (CHAP). When OCHA develops

a consolidated appeal on behalf of a country or region experiencing a humanitarian emergency, CHAP is the foundation. It is unfortunate that not all have included child-specific analysis in their rationale or objectives. CHAPs for several African regions affected by conflict have not mentioned children or child-related issues in their sections on "strategic priorities for humanitarian response."[236] Explicit inclusion of child-focused programming in all CHAPs would be a valuable way to bring children's issues to the fore in the UN appeals process. The IASC Needs Assessment Format, which guides preparation of the CHAP, should help; it has a child protection subsection, and the education section addresses such issues as attacks on schools and teachers.

Central Emergency Response Fund (CERF). CERF is a financial instrument designed to ensure predictable funding for rapid response and underfunded emergencies. As of September 2008, CERF has committed $926 million for almost 1,000 projects in 62 countries.[237] It could be a mechanism for funding forgotten emergencies and crises too small to attract the attention of bilateral donors and larger NGOs. Yet only a small amount of humanitarian aid flows through the CERF, so its impact is limited. Concerns have also been expressed about the 'life-saving' criterion for CERF projects and whether it is consistent with the human rights approach to humanitarian assistance. The definition of life-saving may diminish CERF's flexibility and therefore its ability to provide adequate resources for education and protection activities.

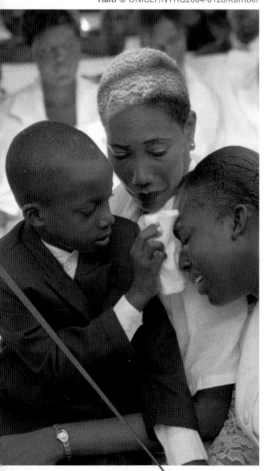

Emergency Response Funds. This mechanism enables NGOs (which cannot access CERF) and UN agencies to respond quickly to emergencies by making start-up funds available in cases of rapidly changing circumstances and humanitarian needs.[238] Typically the amount is $250,000 or less. Countries that have used these funds include Angola, the Democratic Republic of the Congo, Ethiopia, Indonesia, Liberia and Somalia. An early OCHA evaluation of the mechanism found that it has provided the greatest value in the middle phase of an emergency, filling gaps in humanitarian response, increasing humanitarian access and enabling NGOs to scale up their activities.[239]

Common Humanitarian Fund/Pooled Funds. These funds were tested in the Sudan[240] and the Democratic Republic of the Congo to quickly and flexibly provide resources before Consolidated Appeals Process funds became available and to give humanitarian coordinators greater flexibility. An independent evaluation found that the success of the decentralized allocation processes depended on cluster capacity, which varied widely. It recommended a more streamlined management process that would give the humanitarian coordinator more discretion.[241]

Multi-donor Trust Funds. The increasing use of these funds represents a direct application of the aid effec-

tiveness agenda and UN reform initiatives. They provide flexible, coordinated and predictable funding to support national priorities. In their governance structure and operations, these funds are consistent with objectives of the Paris Declaration on Aid Effectiveness,[242] national ownership, alignment with national priorities and coordination.[243]

The total amount of humanitarian aid is hard to quantify, but it has been estimated that around 10 per cent is now delivered by new mechanisms. The evidence is not conclusive as to whether these new mechanisms will effectively pool funding impartially and rapidly as well as direct funds to priority needs. There is a concern that they could introduce another layer of bureaucracy and transaction costs without resulting in improvement.[244]

For a complete picture of humanitarian resources it is necessary to include funds from governments that are not members of OECD, funds channelled through military forces for humanitarian activities, remittances from the various diasporas responding to crises, funds raised from the public by NGOs, corporate and foundation contributions, and the consistently underappreciated contribution of affected States, local communities and households. Most of these data are either not collected or not collated. It has been estimated that donors outside the Development

Assistance Committee now contribute 12 per cent of official humanitarian financing.[245] They focus on humanitarian engagement in neighbouring countries and maintain a strong preference for bilateral aid, including the Red Cross/Red Crescent Movement, over multilateral mechanisms.[246]

Funding continuity

Donors continue to provide resources for prevention, response and post-conflict reconstruction in three distinct envelopes. This lack of funding continuity continues to hamper interventions on behalf of children affected by armed conflict. Short-term emergency relief remains the preference, with time frames as short as three months. Short-term, piecemeal funding has not been conducive to a systematic approach to sustainable programming. This approach also contradicts the concept of flexible financing expressed in the concept of Good Humanitarian Donorship, a well-publicized commitment by 24 donor bodies to ensure that sufficient emergency aid is available at the right time.[247]

Assessing the impacts of humanitarian funding reforms, the Humanitarian Policy Group has noted that "global humanitarian funding to date does not appear to be growing more predictable or needs-based. On the contrary, donor governments' funding trends run counter to the stated requirements of the interna-

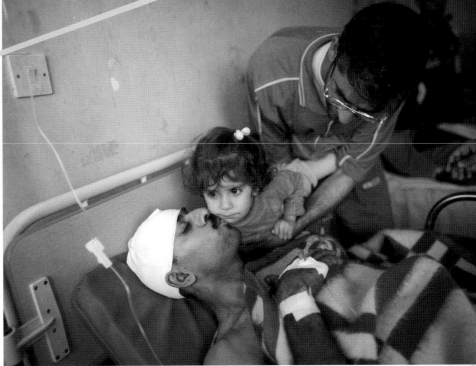

Iraq © UNICEF/NYHQ2007-1625/Kamber

tional humanitarian system."[248] A background paper presented to IASC and Good Humanitarian Donorship in July 2007 noted that the reforms of the United Nations, donors and NGOs of the past decade may have improved individual components of the system, but its overall structure is still inherently inefficient.[249] Donors frequently make decisions without consulting each other, and collective efforts to pool funding and make joint decisions about needs assessment are viewed as inefficient and inimical to rapid service delivery.

The challenge lies in how to determine whether aid is reaching children. Obtaining data to determine whether more aid is reaching children is not easy. Many of the new mechanisms do not explicitly refer to children or disaggregate their data by age. Child-focused funding is

often masked within broad categories of aid going to 'affected populations' or 'vulnerable groups'. Reporting by Common Humanitarian Fund, Pooled Funds and CERF should include indicators of humanitarian aid specifically benefiting children affected by conflict.

A review of the Consolidated Appeals Process for 11 countries revealed a wide disparity in how children's issues are articulated.[250] Each CHAP was analysed using the following criteria: (a) analysis of children's issues in the section on 'context and humanitarian consequences'; (b) child-focused objectives included in strategic priorities or objectives at the country level; and (c) child-focused objectives included in response plan objectives.

All but one CHAP included general descriptions and statistics on children's issues in the section on context and humanitarian consequences. In the section on strategic priorities for humanitarian response, several countries or regions (the Democratic Republic of the Congo, the Great Lakes Region, Somalia and West Africa) did not mention children or child-related issues. Children and child-focused programming was, however, included in numerous plan objectives. Although the trend seems to be to mainstream children's issues across sectors/clusters, their explicit inclusion, particularly in strategic priorities, is a valuable way to bring children's issues to the fore and to ensure they receive priority.

An additional funding problem is the tendency to allocate funds to projects addressing the needs of a narrow subgroup of young people, such as disarmament, demobilization and reintegration funds dedicated exclusively to work with children formerly associated with armed forces and armed groups rather than for community work in areas where these children return and where non-combatant young people may be even more vulnerable. This problem is noted across all sectors and undermines best practice on multi-sectoral and community-based approaches.

Recommendations

1. **Enhance human resources and build the base of expertise at all levels.** Key stakeholders such as Member States, regional organiza-tions and UN entities should invest significant resources in building the base of expertise on child protection, including for monitoring, reporting and responding in both programming and advocacy. They should give priority to investing in additional human resources to meet the growing needs of child protection entities at UN Headquarters, and at regional and country levels.

2. **Expand access to training at all levels.** Humanitarian staff and peacekeeping personnel should have access to training – and so should local service providers, such as teachers, health workers and staff of national institutions. Member States, donors, the United Nations and international NGOs should offer or support training in conflict-affected countries, which will allow greater access by staff of local NGOs and government agencies. These inter-national and national entities should also support local NGO leaders to participate in interna-tional training programmes and conferences. The impact of training should be routinely evaluated by such methods as knowledge assessments before and after training and assessments of how the knowledge is applied.

3. **Incorporate analysis of issues in planning documents.** OCHA, with support from UNICEF, should ensure that CHAP guide-lines require clear articulation of child-related strategic objectives.

4. **Ensure continuity of funding through crisis and recovery.** Donors and implementing agencies should identify ways to manage funding to ensure continuity and sustainability of critical programmes. Donors should allow implementing agencies greater flexibility and a broader time frame to use funds.

IMPROVING PROGRAMME RESPONSE, MONITORING AND KNOWLEDGE SHARING

Studies, assessments and day-to-day observation by the international humanitarian and human rights community have raised awareness of the devastating effect armed conflict has on children. Although broad agreement exists on the necessity of accurate and comprehensive information, the true extent of the impact remains elusive.

Two of the key themes in the 1996–2000 Machel strategic review were the need for improved moni-toring and reporting on child rights violations in conflict, and improving information, data collection and analysis on children in conflict.[251] Many systems and initiatives have been launched over the past decade to improve the monitoring, reporting and response. Yet an effective global framework to guide the work and support the regular collection and consolidation of information has not been fully developed. Due to insufficient global coordination of data collection and collation, this body of work has not been readily available to all in one central location.

The monitoring, reporting and response components of the mechanism are essential to ensure that children receive the maximum impact of programmes. But they also present practitioners with numerous logistical, conceptual and methodological challenges in situations of conflict. Logistical challenges include the difficulty of collecting data in insecure environments with shifting populations. Problems of impact assessment are made even more complex when baseline data are lacking and access to populations in insecure environments poses methodological constraints and personal risks to researchers.

Common programme monitoring framework

A common programme monitoring framework would improve the level of programming across the global system. Efforts to develop one should build on existing work and emphasize a division of labour, with data being collected through different agencies and processes.

A clear starting point would be the framework offered in 'A World Fit for Children'. To implement its goals and monitor its progress,

governments should prepare national plans of action. Progress would be reviewed through regular reports of the Secretary-General to the General Assembly.[252] A global five-year progress report was prepared at the end of 2007, but it contained very little data on children affected by conflict.[253] An examination of data from the Millennium Development Goals and World Fit for Children databases for conflict-affected countries, as begun in chapter 2 of this review, should be expanded and made more systematic.

The mechanisms in place to monitor compliance with the Convention on the Rights of the Child and its optional protocols represent another important system.[254] The UNICEF Multiple Indicator Cluster Surveys provide rich data on the situation of children. But due to resource and other constraints, data have not always been disaggregated to reveal displacement or other effects of armed conflict.

Because impacts reach across all sectors, a mapping exercise would identify existing initiatives and systems that could provide data on children. A gap analysis, which should be done as a part of the mapping, would reveal incomplete information.

Among existing initiatives and systems to draw from is the registration database software. Using it, UNHCR can generate statistics and other information on separated and unaccompanied children as well as children and adolescents at risk.

This category includes ex-combatants, children in conflict with the law, child heads of households and their siblings, children with special educational needs and children at risk of not attending school. OCHA's plans to collect data across the clusters could also contribute to a consolidated system, as long as it incorporates disaggregation by age and gender. In 2003 in Sri Lanka, UNICEF launched (and continues to operate) a database to monitor recruitment of children into armed groups. Much information has been collected – the challenge now is to make it accessible.

Strengthening information and knowledge sharing

Knowledge must also be used to inform policy and programming. The humanitarian community produces an extensive amount of documentation and data related to conflict-affected children. But much of it remains invisible to humanitarian workers and researchers because it stays at the local level, available only in hard copy or inaccessible due to issues of Internet access reliability and affordability.

The Machel study helped to invigorate academic and practitioner interest in research. It resulted in numerous initiatives to document the impact of armed conflict on children. However, much of this research remains generated by institutions from the North, and its

Central African Republic © UNICEF/NYHQ2008-0468/Holtz

outputs are often hard to access by people in the South. An innovative attempt is being made to link research and learning by Columbia University along with four international NGOs (Christian Children's Fund, International Rescue Committee, Save the Children Alliance, and Women's Commission for Refugee Women and Children), UNICEF and several local organizations. In 2008 they plan to launch the Care and Protection of Children in Emergencies Agency Learning Network. The aim is to build consensus on definitions and standards, design assessment tools, develop knowledge of community protection programmes, promote effective policies and programming, foster organizational collaboration and mobilize resources.

More independent financing and a commitment to rigour, including a peer review mechanism for research,

are required. Research can contribute to many goals, including debunking myths and bolstering a particular advocacy or institutional agenda. Children and armed conflict is an emotional issue, and war inevitably politicizes the research context. Given these realities, the highest standards of rigour and peer review are essential if research is to contribute to evidence-based policies.

BOLSTERING THE SYSTEM: THE WAY FORWARD

Hopeful new initiatives and the atmosphere of reform hold much promise for improving the lives of children affected by conflict. There are many opportunities to ensure that their needs are represented in structures, policies and programmes.

Passage of UN Security Council Resolution 1612 marked a critical threshold: The age of enforcement of

norms, agreements and instruments has arrived. In a relatively short period of time, the international system needs to expand its efforts to give children the protection that is their legal rights. Generating norms without ensuring adequate implementation does not effectively challenge impunity.

'A World Fit For Children' offers a strong foundation for a global agenda that maintains its focus on ending grave violations against children while taking a step further to encompass the many other ways in which war hinders children's development, such as through loss of education, health, nutrition, water and hygiene services. The humanitarian reform process will continue to offer opportunities to re-evaluate past work and improve response. Innovative funding mechanisms, if supported by better needs assessment data, could fill gaps. National and local actors, the centrepiece of any response to help children in need, must be given greater support. Groups and individuals at all levels of the system should continue to build links that will allow them to harmonize their efforts and work towards common goals while respecting each others' differences.

The elements of the system to help children affected by armed conflict are now clearly established. The new institutions, standards and mechanisms hold much promise for alleviating the suffering of children.

Addressing children affected by armed conflict goes beyond recruitment and use of children and the six grave violations. Building a protective environment for children is key to addressing the concerns of all children affected by armed conflict. The elements of this protective environment include:

- Building government commitment and capacity;

- Facilitating passage and enforcement of legislation;

- Changes in attitudes, customs and traditions to ensure that it becomes universally unacceptable to harm children;

- Open discussion that breaks down taboos against discussing such subjects as sexual abuse and exploitation;

- Greater use of children's own capacity to address the key issues, craft coping strategies and develop solutions;

- Mobilization of the capacities of families and communities;

- Strategic targeting of services, especially to keep children in school, and provide women and girls with food, shelter and water so they are not compelled to engage in 'survival sex';

- Efficient systems for birth registration and tracing for family reunification.

Those who wish to strengthen and otherwise engage in work in conflict-affected environments must ensure that aid does not serve to exacerbate the conflict or entrench corruption. OECD's 'Principles for Good International Engagement in Fragile States and Situations'[255] offer guidance for ensuring that proper planning precedes interventions and continues during programmes, for installing safeguards in relief activities and for initiating preventative action to ward off future instability. All operations must ensure that the best interests of the child are central to any effort and that a rights-based approach is utilized. ■

KEY RESOURCES

United Nations, 'A World Fit for Children', UN document A/RES/S-27/2, New York, 11 October 2002, <www.unicef.org/worldfitforchildren/files/A-RES-S27-2E.pdf>.

United Nations, 'Report of the Secretary-General: Comprehensive assessment of the United Nations system response to children affected by armed conflict', UN document A/59/331, New York, September 2004.

United Nations Children's Fund, 'Protecting Children during Armed Conflict', Child Protection Information Sheet, UNICEF, New York, 2006, <www.unicef.org/protection/files/Armed_Conflict.pdf>.

B. Verhey, *What are Child Protection Networks? Global mapping and analysis in view of actions on monitoring and reporting of child rights violations in conflict-affected areas*, UNICEF Innocenti Research Centre, Florence, February 2006, <www.unicef-irc.org/research/pdf/cpn_report_final_2006.pdf>.

Watchlist on Children and Armed Conflict, *The Power of Partnership: Guiding principles for partnerships to end violations against children during armed conflict*, Women's Commission for Refugee Women and Children, New York, July 2006, <www.watchlist.org/advocacy/policystatements/the_power_of_partnership.pdf>.

Women's Commission for Refugee Women and Children, *Youth Speak Out: New voices on the protection and participation of young people affected by armed conflict*, WCRWC, New York, 2005, <www.womenscommission.org/pdf/cap_ysofinal_rev.pdf>.

R. Williamson, 'Children and Armed Conflict: Towards a policy consensus and future agenda – Ten years after the Machel study', Wilton Park Paper, West Sussex, UK, April 2007, <www.wiltonpark.org.uk/documents/conferences/WP840/pdfs/WP840.pdf>.

Refugee Studies Centre, 'Education and Conflict: Research, policy and practice', *Forced Migration Review* (supplement), July 2006, <www.fmreview.org/FMRpdfs/EducationSupplement/full.pdf>.

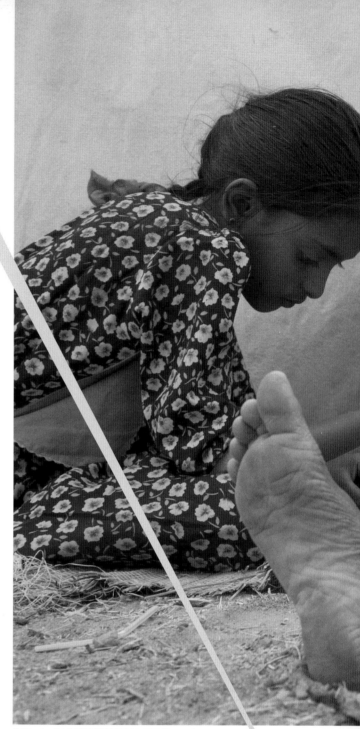

Sri Lanka © UNICEF/NYHQ2006-1583/Noorani

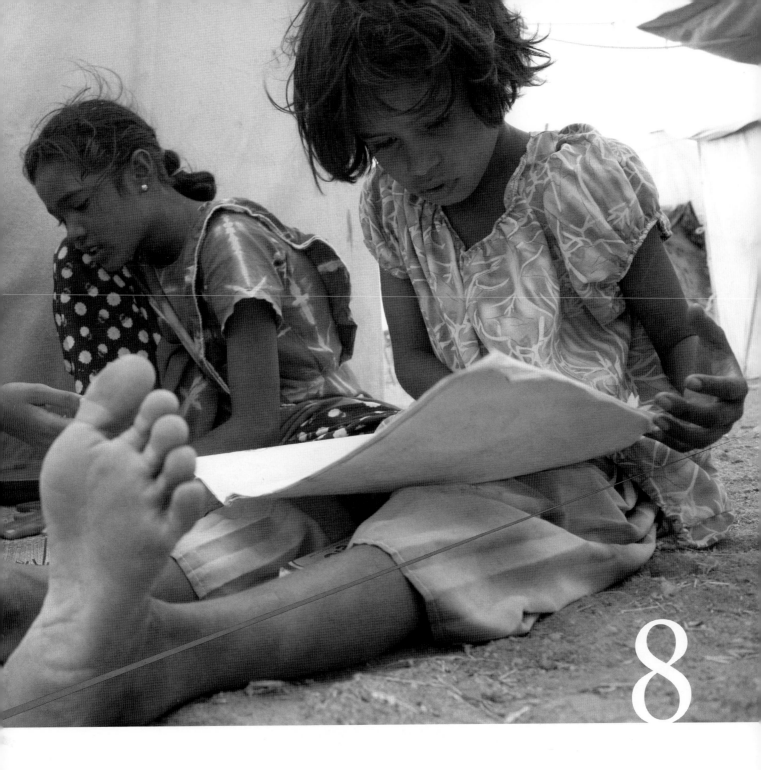

8

THE CARE AND PROTECTION
OF CHILDREN

"Armed conflict [may be] finished, but we still have other types of wars – poverty, illiteracy, unemployment, youth delinquency and many more." – Young man, 16, Angola

8.1 PRINCIPLES AND APPROACHES

"War violates every right of the child," the 1996 Machel study declared, "the right to life, the right to be with family and community, the right to health, the right to development of the personality and the right to be nurtured and protected."

In the decade since the report, efforts to address the plight of war-affected children have focused on particular thematic areas of concern, sometimes in connection with specific countries. Since then, there has been growing recognition of the report's insight that there can be no long-term protection and care for children in armed conflict without addressing the whole mosaic of factors affecting all children, in all conflict situations.

For example, interventions in such areas as health, nutrition, education, and water and sanitation are vital. But their proven benefits will not ultimately help children with differing experiences and needs unless they are accompanied by cross-cutting services such as mental health and psychosocial counselling.

In the years since 1996, experience has continued to show how armed conflict can disrupt the social fabric of a community. It increases children's vulnerability, jeopardizes their right to survival and development, and increases their risk of marginalization, abuse and exploitation. Part of the solution is longer-term community-based care and protection – and the education that is every child's right. The more insecure and fragile the context, the more these rights are at risk

of being violated and left unfulfilled.

Efforts to address these issues gained momentum when the Machel study offered the first comprehensive look at the impact of war on children. This chapter provides an overview of the principles and approaches that have become increasingly common to all sectors and response areas since that time. They take into account the primacy of children's rights and the realities of their diverse needs and capacities.

THE LEGAL FRAMEWORK FOR PROTECTION

As discussed in chapter 6, the framework of international norms and standards for children and armed conflict, especially the Convention on the Rights on the Child (CRC), provides the foundation for response. The Convention commits States parties to respect the rules of international humanitarian law that are relevant to children, ensure protection and care of children who are affected by armed conflict, and take all appropriate measures to promote children's physical and psychological recovery and social reintegration.

States parties to the Convention must ensure that the rights it pledges are extended to every child under their jurisdiction, including refugees and those internally displaced, without regard to their status or that of their parents. But while the State retains primary responsibility for ensuring

the rights of the child, circumstances may leave it ill-equipped to properly carry out its role. Armed conflict often leaves central governments struggling to provide such public services as education, health care, welfare, water and sanitation, and security, and unable to ensure the quality of these services or their equitable delivery. In such situations, a greater burden may fall to municipal and local authorities.

Others also have responsibilities for the care, protection and development of children. Parents, community-based organizations, religious groups and the private sector all play key roles in realizing children's rights. Beyond these groups, the magnitude of children's unmet needs in conflict-affected countries has long led international actors to respond. Efforts to create a coherent system across these organizations – all of which have their individual mandates – were detailed in chapter 7.

RESPONDING TO THE UNIQUENESS OF EVERY CHILD

The 1996 Machel study stressed the importance of ensuring that every response recognizes children's diversity. Children and young people are not a homogeneous group. Young children and adolescent girls, for example, have very different needs. But while each child affected by armed conflict has had a multiplicity of experiences, all of them, without exception, share the same rights.

Children and adolescents also have very different capacities, and the lines between them are often blurred. In a child's early years, the focus is on survival, with special attention needed in health, nutrition and protection. Research shows, however, that cognitive development is equally important.[256] Young children have special vulnerabilities, and their protection requires close collaboration with and support of caregivers.

As children get older and begin to enter school, greater emphasis is placed on socialization, intellectual growth and skills development. Regular attendance at school can be an important source of protection. During adolescence, young people begin to assume adult roles, including experimenting with sex and seeking a vocation. Peer group pressure, political consciousness and socially constructed roles such as 'breadwinner' or 'fighter' also become more apparent.

Gender plays an important part in defining the experience of childhood, and boys and girls have significantly different security and protection needs in conflict situations. Boys, for example, may be more vulnerable to recruitment by armed groups, and they are often expected to begin earning an income at an early age. Girls typically face greater risk of sexual violence and abuse, and they are commonly expected to

take on household tasks and be the first to forgo schooling.

The ways in which children respond to the stress of armed conflict also depend on their particular circumstances. These in turn are affected by such factors as age, sex, personality type, personal and family history, and cultural background. Moreover, armed conflict often pushes children into roles beyond their capacity. It can also prolong certain transitions for young people. Because children are agents of their own protection, and appropriate coping mechanisms require specific cognitive competencies, a key priority is supporting children's cognitive development through various life stages.

The different ways in which armed conflict may have already shaped children's lives can expose them to additional risks. Children can be especially vulnerable if they are living with a disability, with HIV or on the street, or if they lack access to school or health care. Similarly, separation from family, the experience of gender-based violence, internal displacement or refugee status, and current or former association with the armed forces or other armed groups can heighten the risk of further violations. A child's reaction depends on the accumulation of risks, and also on her or his coping skills, available sources of support and other resources.

EARLY RELIEF EFFORTS INSPIRED A FOCUS ON CHILDREN'S RIGHTS

Throughout history, efforts to respond to the suffering of those affected by war have played a large role in drawing attention to children's rights. Shocked by the aftermath of battles in 17th century Europe, Swiss businessman Henri Dunant became concerned with the plight of non-combatants and prisoners of war. His work led to the founding of the Red Cross as well as the 1864 Geneva Convention, which remains the basis of international humanitarian law today.

Half a century later, Eglantyne Jebb organized emergency relief for children affected by the Allied blockade following World War I and formed the foundation of what has become the International Save the Children Alliance. She went on to become a leading advocate for children, and was the author and a main force behind the Declaration of Children's Rights in 1923. This document was an inspiration for the 1989 Convention on the Rights of the Child. Among other rights, the original Declaration stated that "the child must be the first to receive relief in times of distress."

"There is no summer camp for this year. We cannot get together with our friends any more. That is so sad." – Girl, 13, Iraq

GIVING CHILDREN THE RIGHT START IN LIFE, EVEN IN THE MIDST OF WAR

Research suggests that critical brain development related to intelligence occurs during the first three years of life. This process is influenced by a child's nutritional and health status, exposure to stimulation, and interactions with people and objects in his or her environment. A child's experiences in the first few years can therefore have a lifelong impact.

Field experience and research conducted during the past few decades indicate that interventions to promote physical, intellectual and emotional development in early childhood, particularly in times of stress, make a difference for young children and their caregivers, both immediately and over the long term. Early childhood development programmes can both support caregivers and ensure the quality care needed for children to survive and thrive.

In situations of armed conflict, it is crucial to return children to a normal routine as quickly as possible. In such circumstances, the survival and development of young children tends to depend even more heavily on their mothers or other caregivers and the stability of the emotional bond they forge. Emotional proximity to the caregiver, in fact, is equally important as health and other factors.

Early childhood development interventions should always work within the target population's cultural constructs of childhood. Such interventions should aim to address the differing needs of young children, based on their stage of development. It should take into account the effects of war on the women, families and communities on whom children depend. A variety of approaches can be used. They include parenting classes, community-based centres, preschool programmes, psychosocial support, and early stimulation and play activities. Programmes involving these and other approaches to early childhood development have been used in conflict zones from Chad to Lebanon and from the Balkans to Iraq.

PROGRAMMING GROUNDED IN CHILDREN'S RIGHTS

At the time of the 1996 Machel study, the CRC was still relatively new and untested. Yet it clearly offered a fresh, multidisciplinary perspective that demonstrated the interdependence of all children's rights. During the past decade, there has been increased learning in programme approaches that best help to protect children's rights.

What has become known as 'child rights programming' is now used by UN agencies and others to help realize the ideals embodied in international humanitarian and human rights law. Although child rights programming has been less extensively applied in conflict situations than elsewhere, a consensus has developed around the importance of using an inclusive and community-based approach involving multiple sectors. Such methods, applicable across a range of responses, are essential in minimizing children's vulnerability, strengthening their resilience, and mitigating the impact of armed conflict on their lives and future prospects. This is true whether applied to specific sectors, such as education and health, or for specific protection issues, such as psychosocial support or responding to the recruitment of children by armed forces and groups.

Child rights programming differs from needs-based programming. The needs-based approach is likely to respond only to immediately apparent needs. The rights-based approach seeks to create an 'enabling' environment that is conducive to children's overall well-being. In addition to encouraging practical actions and delivery of services, child rights programming is balanced with efforts to protect children against abuse and exploitation, encourage their participation, build the capacity of institutions and systems, support community networks and hold authorities to account.

The fact that children bring with them a multiplicity of experiences and identities must be reflected in how their needs are addressed. Programming that addresses only one experience – such as that of being a child mother or having been recruited into a fighting force – is likely to ignore the range of needs as well as the rights and individual capacities of each child. It would also tend to ignore the root causes of the child's circumstances and might not prevent re-recruitment or other forms of exploitation.

Taking a community-based approach. The 1996 Machel study asserted that "children's well-being is best ensured through family and community-based solutions ... [and] those solutions work best when they are based on local cultures and drawn from an understanding of child development." Since that time, community-based approaches have been reinforced through experience. Building on existing community

structures – including at the family, local and national levels – this approach aims to ensure that services and protection reach all children in a community. Evidence to date has shown that community-based programming is more appropriate to the context and more sustainable in benefits for war-affected children and families than traditional, needs-based programming.

Implementing community-based programming and protection means addressing multiple factors. Does the community have the capacity to identify and implement its own response? Would involvement imply significant costs to already stretched

families? Is the community being asked to provide a basic service, such as health or education, which is typically the responsibility of the State? Is the participation of all members of the community being ensured, or are community 'leaders', who may not represent the range of needs and capacities present in the community, the only interlocutors? These questions can often be addressed during programme design. The inherent flexibility of a community-based approach makes it an important tool in a response that fosters local ownership.

The humanitarian community has long debated whether it is best to target responses to those perceived to

---

EMERGENCY SPACES FOR CHILDREN

'Emergency spaces for children' arose to provide integrated support for children in emergencies where services were weakened or absent. The spaces are designed to offer a mixture of protection, non-formal education, early learning, psychosocial support and access to basic services, geared to a child's developmental age. This multi-sectoral programming approach supports children's well-being during and immediately after an emergency.

Variations on the model, sometimes called 'child-friendly spaces' or just 'safe spaces', have been widely used since 1999 in places including Aceh Province in Indonesia, Afghanistan, Albania, Darfur (Sudan), Liberia, Sri Lanka, The former Yugoslav Republic of Macedonia and Timor-Leste. They are intended to complement other mechanisms needed to protect children in dangerous circumstances. Emergency spaces can safeguard children by providing a protected area and adult-supervised activities. Involved adults tend to develop an awareness of risks to children and learn to create protective environments for them.

Christian Children's Fund Uganda, for example, has organized emergency spaces for children aged three to six in a camp for internally displaced persons in the northern part of the country. Communities decided on relevant activities and selected adults to organize learning sessions and recreation. They also disseminated messages about basic hygiene, nutrition and protection. A comparison of two camps that had and did not have emergency spaces for children showed that the children who had access to them were less likely to be harmed while left at home alone, were better prepared for school, less likely to fight, and more likely to be regarded as 'well' according to local norms.[257]

Challenges to creating such spaces include the fact that children of primary school age typically receive better support than younger children and adolescents. Moreover, in some cultural contexts, the participation of either girls or boys lags significantly behind the other. The concept also needs to be expanded to better serve adolescents. Levels of quality control, community engagement and links with other protection processes also vary considerably.

Nonetheless, experience has shown that the intervention's strengths can include flexibility, rapid start-up, the ability to scale up, low cost, adaptability to different contexts and utility in mobilizing communities. A next step forward is to strengthen the evidence base regarding the implementation of emergency spaces for children and develop inter-agency guidelines on their use.

be the most vulnerable or to provide assistance to the community as a whole. When it comes to children and young people, there is growing consensus that an inclusive approach best addresses the mix of needs faced by all those affected by armed conflict.

In reality, attempts at targeting have sometimes fallen short, partly because it is difficult to measure vulnerability. Where certain children require assistance, it has been found that free access to a service may be more acceptable to the community than visible aid for a specific group. In addition to broadening access, an inclusive approach to programming avoids stigmatizing anyone, including specific groups such as survivors of sexual violence or children formerly associated with armed forces or other armed groups.

The Machel study also advocated for an approach involving multiple sectors, arguing that a range of factors – disease, malnutrition, over-crowding, and lack of food and clean water, as well as poor sanitation and inadequate shelter – all contribute to child mortality in emergencies. The study cautioned that "only a multi-sectoral approach to health and nutrition can protect young children." In the intervening years, the understanding of this approach has expanded to embrace many other types of interventions, including those involving education, early childhood development, water and sanitation, HIV prevention, livelihoods, justice and child protection.

Experience shows, for example, that the best early childhood development programmes deal holistically with physical, intellectual and emotional needs – all of which are interrelated. Early childhood development programmes carried out during emergencies clearly demonstrate increased impact when health, education, nutrition, water, sanitation and hygiene are addressed simultaneously. In northern Uganda, adding stimulation and play activities in the children's early years to nutrition, health and rehabilitation programmes appeared to speed up recovery among children affected by conflict.

REMAINING GAPS

Although there has been progress in developing and applying child rights approaches and programming during armed conflict, much remains to be done. Authorities in affected countries cannot always be relied upon to protect the rights of all children. Moreover, in times of crisis, humanitarian workers sometimes revert to programming based on needs rather than on children's rights.

While the value of community-based, inclusive and multi-sectoral approaches is acknowledged, implementation does not always follow. Agreed-upon standards are not always respected, in particular by new, less experienced actors in the

humanitarian field. During the years since the Machel study, responses have been constrained by additional issues that have received limited attention. These include the inability to scale up initiatives, cost-related barriers and concern for the security of humanitarian workers.

Scaling up response. How to expand programmes across large and often insecure geographical areas has emerged as a key challenge in recent years. It is particularly significant in view of the international community's growing focus on those who are internally displaced and who may not necessarily

TAKING EMERGENCY HEALTH INTERVENTIONS TO SCALE[258]

Early experience and guidelines on health programming during emergencies have been largely limited to activities conducted in refugee camps. Today, relief workers are beginning to adapt this experience to serve populations displaced within their own countries as a result of armed conflict. Providing public health services over large geographic areas, often with poor infrastructure, presents a challenge very different from operating in a refugee camp.

No one agency can deal with such demands. To cover large areas requires even greater coordination and operational partnerships. One successful example is a nationwide measles vaccination campaign in Afghanistan that was carried out in 2002 and 2003. The campaign, which aimed to reach all children aged six months to twelve years, vaccinated more than 95 per cent of the target population. It may have contributed to saving 30,000 lives per year. This multi-agency initiative, involving UN agencies, NGOs, Afghan ministries of health and education along with religious leaders, among others, provides lessons for the future.

Democratic Republic of the Congo © UNICEF/NYHQ2005-2171/Pirozzi

grapple with these issues if there is to be progress in respecting, protecting and fulfilling children's rights in armed conflict situations.

Extending good practice. Humanitarian actors have a responsibility to build awareness among both state and civil society representatives about human rights and international humanitarian law, child rights programming and international development goals, as well as community-based, inclusive and multi-sectoral programming. The State is the primary 'duty bearer' in protecting the rights of children. But it often needs support in fulfilling this role, whether through enhancing technical capacity, bolstering coordination mechanisms or providing additional sources of funding. Moreover, to maintain credibility and advance progress, international entities must demonstrate good practices in programmes, policy and advocacy, and build a body of evidence to show the impact of their work.

States themselves need to deliver on their promises. And there is an ongoing need for civil society and communities to engage in advocacy, protection of children and, at times, delivery of services. At all levels, more efforts are needed to involve children and young people in a meaningful way. This means, in part, listening to their views and acting upon their priorities and recommendations.

be living in camps. While the challenges are not unique to one sector, lessons from the health sector, as shown in the box on page 109, can provide insights.

Eliminating cost barriers. The need to eliminate or reduce costs for access to basic services such as education and health in difficult environments is another common challenge. The tension is especially apparent in situations of ongoing armed conflict or a fragile peace. With key donors now explicitly stating that their policies do not support cost recovery, questions of how to finance these services are vital when the State itself has a limited budget. Moreover, most programmes struggle with short-term funding that does not address the

long-term nature of securing child rights in areas affected by conflict.

Preventing the targeting of aid workers. Another constraint is the fact that civilians and humanitarian workers are increasingly the target of deliberate attacks during armed conflicts. Attacks on personnel in Afghanistan deprived certain populations of health services; others had limited access to education for long periods of time. In Afghanistan, Somalia and the Balkans, military forces have played a prominent role in the response to humanitarian emergencies. This trend is expected to increase, thus compromising the perception of impartiality of humanitarian agencies and their workers. All actors will need to

"There are no trees to play under and no playground to go to." –
Girl, 10, in a transit centre for internally displaced persons in Sri Lanka

RECOMMENDATIONS

As part of the 10-year review of the Machel study presented to the General Assembly in 2007, a number of recommendations were made to better care for and protect children in armed conflict. These centred on ensuring access to basic services, supporting inclusive reintegration strategies and ending gender-based violence. Core principles and approaches were highlighted, including an integrated package of basic services, removal of all barriers to access, including costs, and alignment with government systems. An inclusive approach emphasizing long-term sustainability and community-based approaches was regarded as key. Further recommendations to forward an agenda of better care and protection for children affected by armed conflict follow:

1. **Build response around children's diversity.** Relevant ministries, UN agencies and NGOs should ensure that all responses respect children's diverse needs and capacities, taking particular care to reach young children and adolescents. The use of participatory assessments addressing age, gender and diversity should be widely adopted.

2. **Mainstream child rights programming in emergencies.** Members of the Inter-Agency Standing Committee (IASC) should further mainstream child rights programming in response to emergencies. They should continue to foster inclusive partnerships and collaboration at all levels to promote learning across locations and organizations and identify proven and promising practices.

3. **Ensure use of community-based, inclusive and multi-sectoral approaches.** Humanitarian actors should continue to apply community-based, inclusive and multi-sectoral approaches in their work, with a special focus on building a base of evidence regarding impact.

4. **Improve the quality and accountability of response.** Agencies focused on assisting children and youth in armed conflict, in addition to ensuring application of existing standards and guidelines, should improve monitoring and evaluation in ways that promote greater learning, accountability and coordination.

5. **Address emerging and common challenges of scaling up, reducing access costs and responding in insecure environments.** UN Member States, UN agencies and NGOs should work collaboratively to develop common approaches to dealing with these fundamental challenges. Specific efforts to advocate for improved humanitarian access should be made. ■

KEY RESOURCES

Office of the United Nations High Commissioner for Refugees, 'Practical Guide to the Systematic Use of Standards and Indicators in UNHCR Operations', second edition, UNHCR, Geneva, February 2006.

Save the Children, *Stolen Futures: The reintegration of children affected by armed conflict,* Save the Children UK, London, November 2007.

T. Slaymaker and K. Christiansen, with I. Hemming, 'Community-based Approaches and Service Delivery: Issues and options in difficult environments and partnerships', Overseas Development Institute, London, 2006.

United Nations, 'UNICEF Child Protection Strategy', UN document E/ICEF/2008/5/Rev. 1, United Nations, New York, June 2008.

United Nations, *The Millennium Development Goals Report 2008,* United Nations, New York, 2008.

8.2 PROTECTING THE RIGHT TO EDUCATION

War-affected children and their communities regard education as paramount. In countless assessments involving displaced populations, refugee leaders and community members have specifically identified schooling as an immediate need and a priority humanitarian intervention for their communities, even before food, water, medicine or shelter.[259]

Since publication of the Machel study in 1996, a number of global initiatives have emerged to protect the right to education. The MDGs and the Education for All commitments aim to ensure universal basic education of good quality. Although the momentum around these comprehensive frameworks has increased the number of children with access to educational opportunities, children living in conflict situations still make up a disproportionate number of those out of school.

Based on available figures, the latest UNICEF research shows that nearly 60 million children are not attending primary school in 33 countries affected by conflict. This represents 46 per cent of the children of primary school age living in these countries and two thirds of the total number of children out of school globally. While 10 conflict-affected countries are on track to achieve universal primary education by 2015 (MDG 2), 19 have made no progress at all.[260]

In addition, it is certain that many out-of-school young people aged 12 and older are unable to return to school once the conflict has ended. Others who have completed their primary education and wish to enter or resume secondary school are unable to do so. Children in conflict situations are often prevented from attending school because of school closures, lack of safety and security in or en route to school, family poverty, bureaucratic obstacles or lack of access to the next level of education.

Even when children are able to go to school, the quality of the education they receive is often poor. It is still common to see students sitting in cramped conditions, with few books or materials, listening to a teacher who has very little professional training. Teachers themselves may be suffering from the trauma of war, unable to provide children with the psychosocial support they need. Particularly in emergency and post-crisis settings, the curriculum needs to be enriched with survival

Syrian Arab Republic © UNICEF/NYHQ2007-0720/Noorani

"I was in fifth grade when the war came to my village 10 years ago. Since then, I have not gone back to school. I cannot go back now and sit in the same class; I am too old for that. But I still want to learn." – Young woman, 22, Liberia

messages and life skills that promote health and safety, peace, human rights and citizenship.

On the other hand, crisis can also be the path to opportunity. Rehabilitation efforts following an emergency can provide an opening to 'build back better' – that is, to rebuild schools to a higher, child-friendly standard and to create environments that are clean, safe and inspiring for children.

While the number of children without access to primary education is staggering, the situation worsens significantly after primary school: According to the UN High Commissioner for Refugees (UNHCR), 70 per cent of 1.1 million camp-based adolescents were not enrolled in formal secondary education in 2007, compared to 20 per cent of the 1.9 million children of primary school age who were out of school. Investment in secondary education is especially critical in post-conflict transitions. Like younger children, youth have psychosocial needs during and after conflict that can be addressed in part by quality education. Education also provides them with the skills they need to work towards peace and the development of their communities and countries.

The issues of gender and disability, which have practical implications for all sectors, pose particular challenges for education in conflict and post-crisis environments. Girls' education lags behind that of boys in many

developing countries due to such factors as early marriage, exploitation by teachers, and traditional gender roles and responsibilities. During a crisis, the constraints on girls' education – most notably the lack of physical security – usually intensify. For disabled children, social institutions such as schools provide important environments for developing and promoting their capabilities. But even in the best of times, children with disabilities are often 'forgotten' and further marginalized.

WHAT THE MACHEL STUDY SAID

The 1996 Machel study emphasized that access to quality education is critical to the welfare of children and young people in crisis situations and should be a key component of the humanitarian response. The study highlighted children's need for continuity in schooling. It stressed that the right to quality education does not lapse under circumstances of crisis or displacement, within the country or in refugee contexts. "Support for the re-establishment and continuity of education must be a priority strategy for donors and NGOs in conflict and post-conflict situations," the study pointed out.

Not only did the study reassert that education is a basic human right; it also stressed that the structure education provides can help meet children's psychosocial needs in the most extreme circumstances. The

Sudan © UNICEF/NYHQ2006-0895/Furrer

study found that education can play a critical role in restoring normalcy for younger children, as well as for adolescents who are entering an important developmental stage in their lives. The study further urged that education providers should better prepare teachers both to cope with the effects of stress on children and to impart vital survival information, such as details about the emergency, landmine safety and HIV prevention.

The Machel study also observed that schools are often targeted during war, and it unequivocally stated that

GLOBAL STANDARDS RAISE EDUCATION QUALITY IN EMERGENCIES

Perhaps one of the most significant changes the field has seen since publication of the Machel study is the development of the INEE Minimum Standards for Education in Emergencies, Chronic Crisis and Early Reconstruction, launched in late 2004. Modelled on the Sphere Minimum Standards, the INEE Minimum Standards were developed through a highly consultative and broadly based process. The standards articulate a minimum level of educational quality and access for those affected by crisis. They provide a global framework for coordinated action, good practice and concrete guidance to governments and humanitarian workers on issues related to: community participation; analysis; access and learning environments; teaching and learning; teachers and other education personnel; and education policy and coordination.

Used in more than 80 countries and translated into 14 languages to date, these standards have increased the quality, coordination and accountability of education interventions. Although more work is needed to institutionalize the INEE Minimum Standards, they represent a major development in the approach to education in times of crisis. The holistic framework they provide is particularly relevant in complex and chronic emergencies, where the effects of insecurity and violence on children and the education system are multifaceted.

governments and the international community must protect educational facilities from attack. "All possible efforts should be made to maintain education systems during conflicts," the study said. "The international community must insist that Government or non-state entities involved in conflicts do not target educational facilities and indeed promote active protection of such services."

CHANGES IN APPROACH AND UNDERSTANDING

In 1996 the field of education in emergencies was newly emerging. The very inclusion of education within the Machel study provided an important impetus to this effort. The study had a significant influence on development of the field and has served as a strong foundation for the programming and advocacy work that has taken place during the decade since its publication. In a 2001 follow-up review to the General Assembly, Graça Machel extended this influence, stating, "It is important that education programmes be viewed as a central part of the continuum from emergency relief to reintegration and development."

Moving from peace dividend to essential aspect of humanitarian aid. Education was once considered part of longer-term development and a peace dividend, rather than an essential part of humanitarian aid. During recent years, however, education in emergencies has emerged as a structured, institutionalized and priority field. Much of this progress has resulted from the collaborative work of the Inter-Agency Network for Education in Emergencies (INEE). As a follow-up to the Education for All Dakar Conference in 2000, UNHCR, UNICEF and the United Nations Educational, Scientific and Cultural Organization (UNESCO) were mandated to reinforce preparedness and response in education during emergencies. This led to creation of INEE later that year. It has grown into an open global network

> **"Often during armed conflicts, schools and other education institutions are closed for one reason or another. This has a negative impact on children and young people's state of mind."** – Girls and young women, 13-20, Iraq

of more than 2,300 practitioners, students, teachers and staff from UN agencies, non-governmental organizations, donors, governments and research institutions.

As a result of the original Machel study and the 2001 review, and subsequent advocacy work by INEE members and partners, education in emergencies is now considered a relief intervention that can be both life-saving and life-sustaining. Illustrating this shift was the December 2006 decision of the IASC Working Group to apply the cluster approach to the education sector. Subsequently the IASC education cluster was established.

Co-led by UNICEF and the Save the Children Alliance, creation of the education cluster indicates recognition by the international community of education's critical role in humanitarian response. It also demonstrates willingness to support a strengthening of the humanitarian response capacity, leadership, accountability and partnership in the education sector.

Education is also now recognized as a sector that can provide continuity across the relief-to-development continuum. Education programming often cuts across the traditional boundaries of relief, recovery, development and preparedness activities. It can address the key issue of how to protect and insulate

GETTING GIRLS AND BOYS INTO SCHOOL IN SOUTHERN SUDAN

In Southern Sudan, a major programme was launched in April 2006 to rebuild the education system and bring 1.6 million children into the classroom. The Go to School Initiative, supported by UNICEF, initially focused on enrolment. But it soon shifted to education quality as a means to encourage both girls and boys to stay in school.

people and societies from the shock of crisis. Education practitioners and policymakers strive to ensure that recovery after crisis offers more than a simple return to the status quo.

PROGRESS IN POLICY AND PRACTICE

These new understandings and institutional developments have influenced policy and practice, but it is clear that a degree of influence goes both ways. Progress in such key areas as gender strategies, community capacities, teacher compensation policies, back-to-school campaigns and links across sectors is illustrative.

Becoming more gender sensitive. Humanitarian actors recognize that emergencies are experienced differently by girls and boys, women and men. Formation of a Gender Working Group within the IASC education cluster, along with the ongoing work of the INEE Gender Task Team, has had two important results: It has ensured that education programming in emergencies addresses gender issues from the outset, and that this responsiveness is reflected in efforts to raise resources and develop training and research. The United Nation Girls' Education Initiative also collaborates on gender and education in emergency efforts.

COMMUNITIES IN IRAQ HELP RESTART EDUCATION

Working in Iraq with people who had been internally displaced, an international non-governmental organization (NGO), anonymous for security reasons, has had positive results using the INEE Minimum Standards relating to community participation. The NGO facilitated the formation of a local Community Education Committee, and the two groups worked together to rehabilitate schools and improve children's access to them. Following the guidance in the INEE standards, particular effort was made to ensure that the committee included both men and women as well as members of internally displaced and host communities.

The Community Education Committee was instrumental in rehabilitating schools, providing security advice and negotiating fair rates with local contractors. Once the schools were completed, the committee identified security as a major obstacle to girls' attendance. They subsequently agreed on proactive measures to ensure girls' safety by arranging for them to walk to school in groups or be accompanied by an escort.

Source: Inter-Agency Network for Education in Emergencies Gender Task Team, 'Case Study: School rehabilitation in Iraq', INEE, New York, 2007.

Growing gender awareness has revealed that the number of female teachers in a school is a key indicator of safety in the classroom. As a result, greater efforts are being made to raise both the status and the proportion of female teachers in crisis contexts. An example of good practice comes out of West African education programmes for refugees. Since it was not possible to recruit a sufficient number of adequately qualified women teachers, the International Rescue Committee developed a transitional model of female classroom assistants in the region. The assistants work in the classroom alongside their male counterparts while also completing their own teacher education.

Broadening community participation. Some of the strongest feedback from users of the INEE Minimum Standards has been on the usefulness of guidance encouraging community participation in all phases of programming for education.[261] Humanitarian actors and educational personnel are often unfamiliar with the broader roles that communities can play.

Consequently, emergency programming tends to be 'top down'. Typically, for example, affected communities are asked to provide only manual labour such as ground clearance and classroom construction.

As the INEE guidelines point out, it is vital to build strong community education committees and/or parent-teacher associations through local training and advocacy. This is especially true when education systems lack resources and external communications are poor. Active community and family support can enhance resilience, so schooling can continue despite security or economic problems that interrupt the normal functioning of the education system.

Ensuring adequate compensation for teachers. A looming threat to education worldwide, but especially in conflict-affected and fragile States, is a projected shortfall of 18 million primary school teachers in the coming decade.[262] Ensuring that all teachers are compensated appropriately is ultimately the role of the government. However, in circumstances of emergency, fragility or conflict, the government may be unable or unwilling to carry out this role because of weakened capacity, damaged infrastructure, limited budgets, breakdown of mechanisms to disburse funds and the movement of refugee populations beyond state jurisdiction. As a result, the international community and local populations are often asked to provide temporary support for displaced and conflict-affected populations, including coordinating the education process and compensating teachers.

Securing adequate, consistent funding for teachers' salaries is a critical problem. But there are many other challenges to be addressed in establishing and sustaining effective systems for teacher compensation. To address some of them, the International Rescue Committee, Save the Children Alliance, Women's Commission for Refugee Women and Children, UNESCO, UNHCR and UNICEF are working together to develop guidance notes on compensating teachers in situations of displacement, early reconstruction and fragile States.

Jump-starting education through back-to-school campaigns. School attendance campaigns – involving major advocacy and communication efforts to mobilize donors, governments, partner organizations and affected populations – have helped jump-start education in countries facing conflict. First launched in Rwanda following the 1994 genocide, back-to-school initiatives have become a key strategy to restore education in emergency situations and beyond. Typically led by a ministry of education through the support of UNICEF and others, they have been carried out in places as diverse as

Afghanistan, Angola, Burundi, Grenada, Liberia, the Occupied Palestinian Territory, Pakistan, Southern Sudan and Timor-Leste.

In recent years, multi-phase initiatives – back to school, go to school and stay in school campaigns – have been implemented in countries including Uganda, where they aim to foster long-term commitment to building sustainable education systems. Back-to-school campaigns respond to the immediate need to restore education after a crisis while incorporating a longer-term perspective.

Addressing education holistically. The establishment of an IASC education cluster has reinforced the links across sectors, which is vital in addressing children's needs holistically. An inter-sectoral approach to education is especially critical in conflict and post-conflict contexts because it can provide a safe space for learning – offering physical protection against exploitation and harm as well as a sense of normalcy and psychosocial support.

Because of these characteristics, schools have also become a focus for

REVIVING EDUCATION IN AFGHANISTAN

After the fall of the Taliban in Afghanistan, the Government, working with local communities, non-governmental organizations and the international community, began rebuilding the country's education system. As schools across the country opened their doors in March 2002 for the first time in years, UNICEF mounted one of the largest back-to-school campaigns in its history. The campaign succeeded in bringing more than 3 million children, one third of them girls, into the classroom. The number of students has continued to increase, despite some recent violence. By 2007, an estimated 6 million Afghan children were enrolled in school.

"No new schools are opened, the old ones are closed. Parents don't have money to send their children. Children have nothing to do, they learn nothing." – Young men and women, 15–19, Haiti

delivering other important services, such as providing food, an area in which the World Food Programme has been active. Children's nutrition can be improved through school feeding programmes and a 'food for education' strategy in emergencies. Such interventions have proved particularly challenging, however, and must be carefully managed to

Afghanistan © UNICEF/NYHQ2007-1081/Noorani

ensure that they are appropriate in a particular context as well as sustainable.

Schools, whether permanent or temporary, are also places where children can receive safe and reliable health services, advice on hygiene and life-saving information. Safe water and sanitation facilities for both girls and boys are an essential aspect of healthy, protective environments.

Providing a safe place for education in emergencies not only reduces children's vulnerability to trafficking and other forms of exploitation; it also engages them in positive alternatives to military recruitment and involvement in gangs and drugs. In addition, it provides a place for identifying children with special needs, such as those dealing with trauma or family separation, and facilitates their social integration.

Education in camp environments helps recreate elements of a social structure that children may have lost. At the outset of the emergency and in collaboration with the camp management, it is important to identify areas for schools, play and other forms of recreation, and child-friendly spaces. Guidance on such standards as adequate sanitation is important to ensure safe and protective environments.

School shelters can be anything from tents or other temporary structures to reconstructed education infrastructure. But they must be carefully planned to ensure that they

comply with minimum standards for size, safety of construction, lighting, and other essential elements.

REMAINING GAPS

While progress has been made since 1996, much remains to be done to promote education during emergencies. Many of the actions recommended in the Machel study still require concerted effort on the part of Member States and the international community to ensure that the educational rights of children affected by conflict are met.

Preventing the targeting of schools. Despite the normative frameworks that protect educational facilities in times of conflict, a lack of systematic effort to monitor and address violations severely undermines the right to education of children affected by conflict. According to a recent UNESCO study, the frequency of attacks on schools, students, teachers and other education personnel is rising. While accurate global figures for the numbers of teachers and students killed each year are not available, nationally reported assassinations, bombings and burnings of school buildings have risen dramatically during recent years.[263]

The monitoring and reporting mechanism for Security Council Resolution 1612 focuses specifically on six grave violations that, in line with the Machel recommendations, include attacks on schools. Its current scope and capacity are limited and efforts should be made in improving, monitoring, reporting and responding to this grave situation.

Financing education in emergencies. The Machel study called on donors to give priority to supporting the re-establishment and continuation of education in conflict and post-conflict situations. More than a decade later, however, donors still tend to prioritize more traditional emergency sectors. And even when education is part of the humanitarian response, funding allocations fall far below what is required.

A recent analysis by the International Save the Children Alliance showed that conflict-affected fragile States received only 18 per cent of total education aid from 2003 to 2005, though they account for around half of the world's out-of-school children.[264] Middle-income countries received 49 per cent of aid, while 33 per cent went to low-income countries.[265]

Furthermore, although awareness is increasing about the need to support education in humanitarian crises, it remains one of the least funded sectors. In 2006, the education sector received only 1.1 per cent of humanitarian assistance, although it represented at least 4.2 per cent of humanitarian needs.[266] Only five donor governments explicitly refer to education as part of their humanitarian policy: Canada, Denmark, Japan, Norway and Sweden.[267]

Rwanda © UNICEF/NYHQ2007-1387/Pirozzi

Some governments are now committing substantial funding for educating children in countries affected by conflict. But despite a number of pledges by the Group of Eight industrialized nations, a huge shortfall remains in funding for education in emergencies in terms of meeting the MDGs and Education for All commitments. Funding mechanisms such as the Central Emergency Response Fund and the Consolidated Appeals Process, which are accessed through the IASC cluster system, provide alternative channels for education funding in conflict-affected and fragile states. However, more flexible financing mechanisms are needed, along with sustained political will behind the funding. The goal is to meet short-term needs while supporting long-term development of systems and capacity.

Expanding educational opportunities for older children and out-of-school youth. The Machel study recommended giving special emphasis to appropriate educational activities for adolescents and youth affected by conflict. It also called for promoting secondary school access and providing learning opportunities for out-of-school youth.

Nevertheless, secondary and tertiary education for refugees and

Islamic Republic of Iran © UNICEF/NYHQ2007-2459/Noorani

internally displaced populations have been grossly underfunded in recent years. Making matters worse is a major gap in the availability of teachers at all levels. Post-primary education is nearly always fee-based, and families affected by conflict are often unable to meet these costs. So even when, against all odds, children affected by conflict are able to complete primary education, many find that access to secondary school is extremely limited.

Creating opportunities for adolescents and youth who have not completed primary school also remains a challenge. Some inter-

national NGOs now offer accelerated learning programmes and youth activities designed to provide relevant literacy, numeracy, life skills and vocational training. But given the large youth populations in many countries enduring conflict, these programmes are severely limited in scope.

Building a reliable database.
Finally, there is a gap in the data pertaining to education in situations of crisis and early recovery. Many agencies are collecting data, including the UNESCO Education for All coordination team, UNICEF and

key international NGOs. But challenges remain in coordinating and systematizing data collection in many contexts.

Developments in the IASC education cluster will help address gaps in the uniformity and timeliness of data collection. These advances include preparation of a common needs assessment format and toolkit as well as a comprehensive monitoring and evaluation system. The resulting quantitative data and strategic studies will aid advocacy as well as broad programme learning and better response.

Also needed is more evidence-based research on the value and impact of education in countries affected by conflict. Particularly challenging is collecting data on the role education plays in mitigating community and state fragility and strengthening social cohesion. Practitioners and academics should develop research strategies that include longitudinal studies and address the preventive role that education can play in reducing conflict and the impact of crisis.

RECOMMENDATIONS

The education sector has developed substantially during the decade since the Machel study, yet there are significant challenges ahead. The 10-year review presented to the UN General Assembly during 2007 recommended access to a continuous, integrated

> **"This is a year of ignorance."** –
> Young woman, 16, Occupied Palestinian Territory

package of basic services – including education – aligned with government systems. It called for more investment in building capacities and for donors to ensure early and multi-year funding, both key priorities for education. The importance of secondary and tertiary education was specifically highlighted. The study called for elaborating preventive approaches to conflict, including education. The following are priority actions for education in emergencies, chronic crises and early recovery in the coming years:

1. **Ensure preparedness, rapid education response and sustained provision.** Member States should work to guarantee the right to education by providing continuous schooling before, during and after times of crisis. Donor governments should create bridging structures to link the risk reduction, preparedness, humanitarian and development arms of their education assistance programmes.

2. **Improve coordination and capacity building.** Donors, governments, and humanitarian and development actors should increase coordination through participation in global frameworks, such as the IASC education cluster, INEE and, at national levels especially, sectoral mechanisms. They should enhance professionalism in education, ensuring adequate support to the development of 'surge capacity', gap

analysis, and creation of professional tools and training.

3. **Strengthen standards and accountability.** Donors, bilateral and multilateral organizations, and the humanitarian community should proactively support implementation of the global Minimum Standards and those developed at the national level, including within the IASC education cluster. They should develop an effective monitoring, reporting and evaluation system based on these standards, as well as covering attacks against schools, as part of the Resolution 1612 monitoring and reporting mechanism.

4. **Provide adequate and consistent funding.** Member States and donor governments should

increase the level and consistency of education funding for conflict-affected and fragile States. A substantial portion of new education funding for basic education should go to conflict-affected fragile States.

5. **Improve data collection and analysis.** Humanitarian actors should improve the timely collection and analysis of education data to demonstrate the magnitude of an emergency, guide response and measure its impact. Further, more systematic data collection is needed on the grave problem of attacks on schools. Longitudinal studies are needed to assess education's role in conflict prevention and peacebuilding. ▪

KEY RESOURCES

K. Tomasevski, *Education Denied,* Zed Books, London, 2003.

UNESCO International Institute of Educational Planning, 'Guidebook for Planning Education in Emergencies and Reconstruction', UNESCO IIEP, Paris, 2006.

Inter-Agency Network for Education in Emergencies, *Minimum Standards for Education in Emergencies,* 'Chronic Crisis and Early Reconstruction', INEE, London, 2004, <www.ineesite.org>; and Interactive INEE Minimum Standards Toolkit <www.ineesite.org/toolkit>.

United Nations Children's Fund, 'Education in Emergencies: A resource tool kit', UNICEF Regional Office for South Asia and UNICEF New York, 2006.

8.3 SAFEGUARDING HEALTH AND MANAGING DISEASE

The quality and accessibility of health care for war-affected children has improved since the 1996 Machel study. In fact, the entire technical field dealing with child health in conflict has become more professional in terms of guidelines, training opportunities and improvements in the evidence base of what does and does not work.

Yet it is a measure of how much work remains that 9 of the 20 countries with the highest under-five child mortality rates have also been affected by recent conflict.[268] Achievement of the health-related MDGs is unlikely unless the humanitarian response is scaled up dramatically and sustained, especially in protracted emergencies where high mortality rates persist over several years.

Since conflicts often occur in areas where children already suffer from malnutrition and ill health, including communicable diseases such as diarrhoea, acute respiratory infections, malaria and measles, these ailments continue to be a major cause of mortality.[269] In fact, available data suggest that these common childhood illnesses are responsible for the majority of childhood deaths in conflict situations, in some instances out-numbering deaths directly linked to conflict by a factor of 10 to 1.[270]

Lowering these rates requires rapid delivery of proven child survival interventions. The scale of these efforts is particularly relevant because armed conflict often involves major population displacements over large geographic areas. Appropriate distribution of services is also vital if children and other vulnerable groups that lack access to health services are to be reached.

In keeping with a human rights-based approach, strategies to engage affected children should be considered thoroughly in designing health programmes. Doing so will ultimately increase the use of services.

WHAT THE MACHEL STUDY SAID

The Machel study emphasized disparities between the horrific situations faced by children during armed conflict and the promise of article 24 of the Convention on the Rights of the Child, which stipulates that children have a right to the highest standard of health and medical care available. For children affected by war, the reality is grim. As the Machel study pointed out: "Thousands of children are killed every year as a direct result of fighting, from knife wounds, bullets, bombs and landmines, but many more die from malnutrition and disease caused or increased by armed conflicts…. Many die as a direct result of diminished food intake that causes acute and severe malnutrition, while others, compromised by malnutrition, become unable to resist common childhood diseases and infections."

In assessing the delivery of health services, the Machel study stressed the need to protect health workers and limit the disruption of services, including preventing the destruction of health facilities and the breakdown of supply lines. It also highlighted security on roads and access routes needed to ensure accessibility to such services.

The Machel study's specific recommendations for relief workers involved in nutrition and health were aimed at establishing links between emergency interventions and long-term development programmes.

CHANGES IN APPROACH AND UNDERSTANDING

Taking life-saving interventions to scale. The health community agrees that a limited set of proven interventions, taken to scale, can drastically reduce child mortality, even in areas facing conflict.[271] These interventions are increasingly carried out in emergency contexts, aimed at reducing child illness and death.

The intervention package includes measles immunization; vitamin A supplements; anti-malaria measures such as distribution of long-lasting insecticide-treated mosquito nets; prevention, early detection and treatment of malnutrition; adequate clean water and sanitation; appropriate community-based management of common illnesses (including oral rehydration salts and zinc for diarrhoea, artemisinin-based combination therapy for malaria and appropriate antibiotics for respiratory infections); standardized

"Our only hope is to pray that we do not get sick. If you do, only God can save you from dying." – Young man, 18, Sierra Leone

guidelines; and promotion of hygiene and correct infant and child feeding practices, including exclusive breastfeeding. These interventions have become mainstays of any emergency response.

Promoting multi-sectoral approaches. Advances have also been made in forging approaches that combine actions from diverse sectors. Public health, nutrition, food aid, water, sanitation, education and other relief programmes are now accepted as multiple elements in an emergency response because none of them is effective in reducing morbidity and mortality without the others. It is common, for instance, to distribute vitamin A supplements and deworming medications during immunization campaigns, as took place during the 2004 measles immunization campaign in Darfur.

Delivering health services effectively. Progress has also been made in appropriate delivery of child-health interventions in countries facing conflict with inadequate or inaccessible health services. The right mix of facility-based and community-based services is critical to ensuring wide coverage of life-saving interventions. Community-based delivery may include campaigns to offer a package of services – such as immunization and vitamin A supplementation – at regular intervals. For example, Ethiopia's Enhanced Outreach Strategy delivers a package of services twice a

year, accompanied by community mobilization efforts.

It is widely recognized that community-based activities are the future of public health implementation in resource-poor settings. Moreover, establishing community-based health activities prior to a conflict may help reduce the harm to children's health should a conflict arise. This approach also contributes to emergency preparedness.

However, emergency interventions will only reach children when the services provided are appropriate to the circumstances and accepted and understood by beneficiaries.[272] For this reason, active participation of key community members is critical. In Afghanistan, engaging religious leaders and using mosques as vaccination posts for a nationwide measles campaign contributed to the high coverage achieved in 2002.[273]

In many countries affected by conflict, national governments have limited capacity to provide health services. This remains the case despite growing recognition that strengthening health systems is critical, especially following protracted conflicts. In response, such groups as the GAVI Alliance (formerly the Global Alliance for Vaccines and Immunization) have relaxed their application and co-financing criteria for funding support targeted to strengthening health systems. The changes encourage fragile States with weak capacity to apply for these funds.

Building robust health systems is a long-term investment. Other strategies have also been tried, including performance-based contracting. Under this approach non-state entities such as NGOs contract to deliver a package of services, and their performance is monitored using a predefined set of indicators. Such strategies can lead to wide coverage of life-saving interventions. They also enable governments to focus on their normative responsibilities, such as planning, policy setting, financing and regulation, rather than on service delivery. Although further evaluation of this approach is required, preliminary results from experiences in Afghanistan and Cambodia are promising.[274]

PROGRESS IN POLICY AND PRACTICE

Controlling major diseases. Since the 1996 Machel study, progress has been made in disease control among populations affected by conflict, with new interventions available for use in complex emergencies. Malaria, for example, can be prevented and managed through using more effective medications (artemisinin-based combination therapy), rapid diagnostic kits, insecticide-treated mosquito nets and indoor spraying. Diarrhoea can be treated using oral rehydration salts in combination with zinc supplements.

Measles was once a devastating killer of children in emergencies.

But it is no longer a major cause of death in camps for refugees and the internally displaced since measles vaccination has become a priority in such settings. In non-camp emergency situations, measles still kills many children. Nevertheless, several measles vaccination campaigns have been successfully carried out nationwide or over large geographical areas in conflict situations, including in Afghanistan in 2003[275] and Southern Sudan in 2006–2007.[276]

Tuberculosis (TB) and AIDS were ignored for many years during complex emergencies. However, the importance of addressing these scourges, even in the midst of conflict is now recognized because HIV is endemic to a number of conflict-affected areas.

Progress has also been made in negotiating periods of peace and security with warring factions so that services can be provided to populations isolated by conflict. The successful negotiation of 'zones of peace' and 'days of tranquillity' have made it possible to conduct campaigns against polio and dracunculiasis (Guinea worm disease), for example, in countries including Afghanistan, the Sudan and Uganda.

Making reproductive health an integral part of the emergency response. The Machel study advocated a wide reproductive health agenda covering both men and women and placing special emphasis on girls.

This challenged the assumption that reproductive health was the responsibility of development programmes rather than a priority at the onset of complex emergencies. Reproductive health is now an integral part of an emergency response. The minimum initial service package, which includes condoms, universal precautions to prevent the spread of HIV, clinical management of rape and designation of a reproductive health coordinator, has been a major advance in camp settings. This is well outlined in the inter-agency Reproductive Health in Refugee Situations Manual, currently being revised.[277]

Setting technical standards. In recent years, a number of inter-agency guidelines have been developed to provide benchmarks and guide stakeholders in responding to malaria, AIDS and other health issues. These guidelines include: Malaria Control in Complex Emergencies: An inter-agency handbook (2005); Reproductive Health in Refugee Situations: An inter-agency manual (1999); the IASC Mental Health & Psychosocial Support Guidelines (2007); and the IASC Guidelines for HIV/AIDS Interventions in Emergency Settings (2004).

Along with the Sphere Project's minimum standards for health services in emergencies, these guidelines have contributed to more effective and standardized approaches. Since most were developed through an inter-

agency process, they have the support of a majority of stakeholders and are therefore widely used.

Many in the field of health in emergencies are trying to document experiences and lessons in a more systematic manner. Journals are encouraging submission of articles addressing health issues in emergencies, such as *The Lancet* series on complex emergencies in 2004. Some UN agencies and NGOs have also developed books and guidelines on appropriate health responses in emergencies, such as Médecins Sans Frontières' 1997 publication, Refugee Health: An approach to emergency situations, and UNICEF's Emergency Field Handbook. A guide for UNICEF staff, published in 2005. A number of new textbooks on the subject highlight child health needs in these settings. Given that the first textbook on refugee health was only published in 1983, this is a major accomplishment.

Other tools for improved response. In late 2005, when IASC introduced the cluster approach as a part of the humanitarian reform process, child health was a core focus area in the health cluster. This places child health needs firmly on the agenda of actors responding to health in emergencies. It also enhances coordination and complementarities among partners.

The health cluster is developing tools and guidelines to increase the efficiency and effectiveness of the

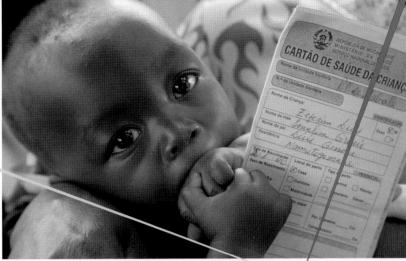

Mozambique © UNICEF/NYHQ2006-2234/Pirozzi

emergency humanitarian response. In addition to a multi-sectoral assessment tool to ensure a more consistent approach, other aids to identify gaps in health response and map health actors are under development.

Efforts are also under way to improve health statistics through uniform and timely processes to collect, validate and disseminate critical data. The IASC Health and Nutrition Tracking Service is expected to address gaps in this very important area. Although it is still too early to assess the impact of these tools, they will eventually be evaluated.

REMAINING GAPS

Despite more than a decade of progress in providing health care to children affected by conflict, a number of gaps remain. In particular, 'going to scale' with a package of proven, cost-effective interventions and sustaining them in areas of protracted conflict remains a challenge. The constraints include lack of adequate financing, insecurity and difficult access, and limited numbers of qualified staff. Areas such as chronic diseases, neonatal health and mental health also need more attention.

Moreover, current emergency thresholds need to be reviewed to determine whether they are relevant in today's emergency settings. If not, they should be revised to meet new realities. This goes hand in hand with the need to improve data collection

as well as dissemination and implementation of guidelines.

Taking proven interventions to scale. As new technologies become available, the humanitarian health community must continue to innovate to make them available to more people. A number of new vaccines – for Hib, pneumococcal disease, rotavirus and cholera – are now available and may have major applications in the future for reducing morbidity and mortality associated with pneumonia and diarrhoea, the top two causes of childhood death.

Community management of common childhood illnesses and therapeutic feeding have often been used in stable settings. But these techniques are now being introduced in areas caught up in complex emergencies, such as northern Uganda. Other proven interventions with potential for broader use include clean delivery of babies, and antenatal steroids and zinc supplementation to treat severe diarrhoea. But the human resources to carry out such interventions – especially finding the right mix of health-care workers – remains a key challenge.

Addressing chronic diseases. The humanitarian community has made a limited response so far to the threat of chronic infectious diseases such as HIV and AIDS and TB as well as to non-infectious chronic diseases such

as asthma and rheumatic heart disease. Although guidelines are now available to implement HIV and TB control programmes in emergencies, they are still not systematically used.

Promoting neonatal health. Failure to safeguard the health of newborns during crises is increasingly recognized as a cause of mortality and morbidity. This requires greater programmatic and research attention during the coming years.

Preventing and treating a range of psychosocial disorders. Mental and social aspects of health can be dramatically altered by conflict. Among the problems are risks to social health, including social relationships; distress or absence of well-being; mild to moderate mental disorders (including depression, anxiety and post-traumatic stress disorder); severe mental disorders (psychosis, conversion, severe depression); and hazardous alcohol and substance use. Addressing these requires a multi-sectoral response, including preventive and curative health care.

Removing barriers to access. Recognition has been growing of the critical need to remove barriers that hinder children from accessing services. One such barrier is cost, and every effort must be made to ensure that services are accessible and affordable. Abolishing user fees

Kenya © UNICEF/NYHQ2008-0231/Cranston

during a conflict, when populations are more vulnerable due to loss of livelihoods, has proved successful in increasing access to health services. Making this policy shift requires careful consideration of the consequences – without sufficient resources, services could be interrupted. Another challenge is ensuring that formal user fees are not replaced by informal or 'under the table' fees.

Responding in a timely manner.
A broader range of triggers needs to be considered to mount a timely emergency response. The crude mortality rate threshold of one death per 10,000 people per day has contributed decisively to defining the acute phase of a complex emergency.[278] This threshold was not appropriate, however, in defining an emergency in a middle-income country such as Kosovo.

Filling gaps in data collection. Gaps remain in the availability of data on

basic health indicators in complex emergencies. Many agencies are collecting data in the field, including Médecins Sans Frontières in the Niger and the International Rescue Committee in the Democratic Republic of the Congo. Others are compiling available data for easy access and use, such as a database on complex emergencies established by the Center for Research on the Epidemiology of Disasters. But challenges remain in systematically collecting, interpreting and using data for programmatic decision-making in all emergency contexts.

Making technical guidelines more accessible. Since the 1996 Machel study, many effective guidelines have been designed, but some health-care workers find them difficult to use.[279] Evidence-based guidelines should be locally adapted for health-care workers who don't have a high level of technical expertise; in most cases, local health-care workers provide the

direct care to children during armed conflict. New guidelines are also needed for managing asphyxia, prematurity and infections in neonates, for physical trauma in young children, and for finding and treating TB in children.

Encouraging children's participation. Finally, children's health problems, especially in emergencies, cannot be resolved by technical services alone. Health interventions need to reflect an understanding of how children themselves cope with armed conflict. Children, particularly those who are older and attending school, need to be fully involved in their health and that of their community.

RECOMMENDATIONS

Health services in emergencies and during recovery are a well-established humanitarian response. Recommendations from the 10-year strategic review presented to the UN General Assembly in 2007 reinforce this focus. They call for a proven, integrated package of basic services – including health – implemented on a wide scale. The review stipulated the need to ensure safe and unhindered access and delivery of humanitarian assistance to all children. It also called for investing in building capacity and knowledge acquisition and management as well as ensuring that appropriate operations research is conducted and documented, disseminated and applied. Additionally, the review

> **"Every week a woman dies in childbirth on the road to the hospital."** –
> Young woman, 19, Liberia

recommended strengthening monitoring and reporting; these activities should include information on all factors affecting children, and the data should be disaggregated by age and sex. The following actions should be a priority in complex emergencies to mitigate the effects on child health:

1. **Provide rapid and appropriate child-survival interventions.** Working with Member States and other key stakeholders, humanitarian actors should ensure rapid implementation of a package of evidence-based child survival interventions targeting the major causes of morbidity and mortality. These should be appropriate to the context and provided at an appropriate scale in a coordinated manner with high coverage.

2. **Continue development of guidelines and capacity building.** The humanitarian health community, including the IASC health cluster, should continue to develop and update user-friendly guidelines to ensure effective and standardized approaches. Since health and related responses in complex emergencies require highly skilled personnel, human resources capacity (both national and international) needs further development.

3. **Explore and apply new health technologies.** Health personnel

and researchers should continue to explore new technologies and innovative delivery strategies for conflict-affected settings. As new technologies become available, donors should support their application in complex emergencies and ensure they are independently evaluated. Lessons learned in the process should also be documented. Humanitarian actors should invest in operational research, focusing on key strategic areas where there is inadequate evidence and knowledge.

4. **Ensure timely collection and analysis of data.** Humanitarian actors should ensure that data, disaggregated by age and sex, are collected and analysed in a timely manner. This is important in demonstrating the magnitude of an emergency, guiding an appropriate response, measuring the impact of the response and advocating for resources. Systematic, continuous data collection is needed to monitor the health of affected populations, especially children.

5. **Commit adequate and consistent funding.** Donors should provide increased and sustained financing of humanitarian health responses focused on children in complex emergencies. ■

KEY RESOURCES

Inter-Agency Standing Committee, 'Health Cluster Working Group', <www.humanitarianinfo.org/iasc/content/cluster/health/default.asp?bodyID=20&publish=0>.

W. Moss et al., 'Child Health in Complex Emergencies', *Bulletin of the World Health Organization*, vol. 84, no. 1, January 2006, pp. 58-64, <whqlibdoc.who.int/bulletin/2006/Vol84-No1/bulletin_2006_84(1)_58-64.pdf>.

W. Moss et al., *Child Health in Complex Emergencies,* National Academies Press, Washington, D.C., 2006, <http://books.nap.edu/catalog.php?record_id=11527>.

P. Salama et al., 'Lessons Learned from Complex Emergencies over the Past Decade', *The Lancet,* vol. 364, 2004, pp. 1801-1813.

Sphere Project, 'Humanitarian Charter and Minimum Standards in Disaster Response', Sphere Project, Geneva, 2004.

World Health Organization, 'Consultation on Child Health in Emergencies', 2004, <www.who.int/child_adolescent_health/documents/chce_meeting/en/index.html>.

8.4 SAVING LIVES THROUGH SOUND NUTRITION

Armed conflict can have a devastating impact on human nutrition by threatening livelihoods and compromising food security, health and the ability of caregivers to provide for the young. During complex emergencies the prevalence of acute malnutrition is typically high, specifically wasting, nutritional oedema and micronutrient deficiency diseases. The situation can worsen if people are forced to rely on food rations lacking in vitamins and minerals, as demonstrated by the 2001 outbreaks of scurvy in Afghanistan and pellagra in Angola.[280]

Myanmar © UNICEF/NYHQ2008-0375/Dean

Of the 143 million children under age five who are underweight in the developing world, 98.5 million are living in emergency situations.[281] The level of acute malnutrition in many conflict settings is alarming: Of the 24 countries with national wasting levels above the 'critical threshold' of 10 per cent, 10 are affected by armed conflict (among the 33 countries listed in table 2 on page 27). These include the Sudan (with a wasting rate of 16 per cent), Chad and Sri Lanka (14 per cent) and the Democratic Republic of the Congo and Nepal (13 per cent).[282]

The latest data suggest that maternal and child undernutrition contributes significantly to child morbidity and mortality in complex emergencies. It dramatically increases fatalities among children and women suffering from common illnesses, such as malaria, diarrhoea and pneumonia. And it was one of the primary causes of death in children under five in camps in northern Uganda[283] as well as in the Democratic Republic of the Congo.[284]

WHAT THE MACHEL STUDY SAID

Both the 1996 Machel study and the 2001 review emphasized the effect of conflict on child nutrition as an area that cried out for greater attention and action. Similarly, both reports specifically advocated for continued access to affected children through 'days of tranquillity'. Negotiated

ceasefires during such days provide opportunities for services that include vaccinations and other health interventions, child-based needs assessments, food and nutritional support, and dissemination of information on child rights.

CHANGES IN APPROACH AND UNDERSTANDING

Working under the framework of public nutrition. Understanding of malnutrition has deepened since 1996. The focus has moved from the individual to the larger population and from a narrow set of interventions to a broad-based, problem-solving approach known as 'public nutrition'.[285] Many of the achievements in managing child malnutrition in conflict have been made under this framework.

Public nutrition addresses malnutrition in complex emergencies by combining an analysis of nutritional risk and vulnerability with action-oriented strategies involving policies, programmes and capacity development. This approach, which combines both nutritional and public health interventions, has proved to be especially relevant in complex emergencies, when insecurity and violence have multidimensional effects on child nutrition.

Managing malnutrition holistically. Changes in managing malnutrition reflect growing awareness of the importance of gender and child

"Our parents have lost their livelihood, and for us this means that we don't get food every day, that we are hungry sometimes." – Boy, 14, Sri Lanka

protection issues; psychosocial support and other care practices; and support for food security and livelihoods. Using this holistic approach to prevent and treat severe malnutrition in conflict has brought a number of improvements: It has enhanced prospects for children, helped protect and develop the self-esteem and care practices of mothers, and provided a stronger link between immediate hunger relief and long-term strategies for sustainable development. The effectiveness of integrated programming can be seen in Action Contre la Faim's nutritional programmes in Afghanistan, Darfur (the Sudan) and Southern Sudan, which combine therapeutic feeding with a basic package of care practices and mental health activities.

Devising new strategies to reach dispersed populations. Reaching internally displaced persons, who are likely to be dispersed across insecure areas, presents an additional challenge in humanitarian assistance. Compared to working in a traditional refugee camp environment, providing services to displaced and dispersed populations is often logistically difficult because of restricted access. The result can be low rates of coverage and effectiveness. In such situations, traditional nutrition programmes and protocols may not be appropriate. New strategies may be needed, such as decentralized services, reliance on community volunteers and locally based staff, and enhanced operational coordination.

Such strategies are now being tried out by GOAL in north-west Sudan and Darfur, among other organizations.[286] But it is clear that further work and experience sharing is needed.

PROGRESS IN POLICY AND PRACTICE

More reliance on community-based management of malnutrition. For many years the management of severe acute malnutrition relied on inpatient facilities known as therapeutic feeding centres. In the 1990s, experience from several humanitarian emergencies demonstrated that this model was largely ineffective.[287] NGO feeding centres established in response to the famine in Southern Sudan in 1998, for example, were able to reach only a small proportion of children suffering from this acute form of malnutrition.[288]

Community-based management of severe acute malnutrition is an innovative approach to treating the majority of these children at home with ready-to-use therapeutic foods. It has consistently achieved recovery rates of about 75 per cent, which are well within international humanitarian standards, and has increased coverage in emergency settings by as much as 70 per cent.[289] By 2006, more than 25,000 children with severe acute malnutrition and more than 130,000 children with moderate acute malnutrition were successfully treated using the community-based approach in

complex contexts, including those of Chad and Darfur.[290]

In these places community-based management of severe acute malnutrition is being promoted by district-level ministries of health, which provide a platform for scaling up programmes. And UNICEF, in cooperation with other organizations, is facilitating the development of national guidelines for managing severe acute malnutrition that include community-based approaches in various countries.

Addressing micronutrient deficiencies. Micronutrient deficiencies can easily develop or worsen during an emergency. This can happen due to loss of livelihoods or food crops, interruption of food supplies, diarrhoeal diseases (which cause nutrient losses) and infectious diseases (which suppress the appetite while increasing the need for micronutrients to help fight illness). For these reasons, it is essential to ensure that the micronutrient needs of people affected by complex emergencies are adequately met. The World Health Organization (WHO), UNICEF and the World Food Programme (WFP) have issued a joint statement on preventing and controlling micronutrient deficiencies in populations affected by emergencies through the use of multiple vitamin and mineral supplements for pregnant and lactating women and for children aged 6–59 months.[291]

Taking gender into account. Insecurity can create risks that have different effects on women, girls, men and boys, so it is crucial to understand how gender issues affect nutritional status and programming. This helps in promoting interventions that enable women to continue to care for their infants and young children, and it ensures that children benefit from emergency interventions.[292] Along with other agencies and NGOs, WFP has increased its commitment to giving women direct access to and control over food aid. They are also encouraging women to participate in all stages of an intervention – from analysing a problem and designing a solution to managing and monitoring the resulting action.[293] This has improved targeting of aid and appropriate use of it within the household.

The 2001 review of the Machel study highlighted sexual violence as a defining characteristic of contemporary conflict. This is attributed to the breakdown of social values and community structures, weakened response and prevention mechanisms, and significant population movements that typically accompany conflicts. In planning nutritional assistance, therefore, guidelines have been established to ensure that such programmes do not inadvertently increase risks for women and girls. These are outlined in a 2005 document prepared by the IASC Task Force on Gender, 'Guidelines for Gender-based Violence Interventions in Humanitarian Emergencies:

Focusing on Prevention and Response to Sexual Violence'.[294]

Stepping up international cooperation. Inter-agency collaboration and development of the Emergency Nutrition Network over the past 10 years have provided a catalyst for advancing the public nutrition approach. This collaboration has also facilitated standardizing procedures and sharing experiences in emergency response. Most recently, the IASC nutrition cluster, established in 2005, has provided a forum for improved coordination and analysis of gaps and constraints. It has also developed tools for prevention and care. These include evidence-based toolkits, a 21-module training package and instruments for initial rapid assessment. The latter, along with Save the Children UK's Household Economy Approach, are among the tools now being used to measure malnutrition and analyse vulnerability. Their development was carefully coordinated to minimize bias, ensure valid comparisons and review trends over time.

Unfortunately, standardized tools have yet to be developed for assessing micronutrient deficiency disorders in complex emergencies. The fact that certain staples have been linked with specific disorders (for example, maize-based rations have been linked to pellagra and rice-based rations with beriberi)[295] emphasizes the urgent need for more user-friendly methods and equipment.

Other frameworks and tools are improving the quality, accountability and effectiveness of nutritional programming in emergencies. These include new standards, such as those in the Sphere handbook on using multiple micronutrient supplements in emergencies, as well as technical guidelines on treating severe acute malnutrition,[296] and on infant and young child feeding practices in emergencies.[297]

REMAINING GAPS

Mounting an integrated, broad-based response. Ineffective responses to nutrition issues in complex emergencies are not surprising, given that they tend to be problematic even under normal circumstances. A long-standing challenge is defining where nutrition fits within government structures. Although it is a multi-sectoral issue, nutrition is often subsumed under ministries of health, without the necessary mechanisms to link it to other sectors.

Insufficient efforts to achieve integrated, broad-based programming for nutrition continue to compromise programme quality and impact. In Darfur, for example, malnutrition rates dropped significantly after food aid was provided, but nutrition problems linked to disease remained. This provides one example of disconnected programming that did not adequately meet the needs of children affected by conflict.[298]

In 2007, armed conflicts in Afghanistan, the Central African Republic, Chad, Darfur (the Sudan), the Democratic Republic of the Congo, Iraq, the Occupied Palestinian Territory and Somalia continued to wreak havoc on children's nutritional status and survival. These crises resulted in inadequate household food security, poor diet, an unsanitary environment, inadequate maternal and child care, and poor access to health services. For example, preliminary data on Darfur indicate that global acute malnutrition increased from 12.9 per cent in 2006 to 16.1 per cent in 2007. While the prevalence has not returned to levels reported in 2004 (21.8 per cent), it has crossed the emergency threshold of 15 per cent.

Democratic People's Republic of Korea © UNICEF/NYHQ2004-0537/Horner

Promoting breastfeeding. Exclusive breastfeeding during the first six months of life reduces illness and death from a range of infectious diseases, including diarrhoea. In complex emergencies, where hygiene and care practices might be compromised and overcrowding is common, the risk of diarrhoea and other infections is high. This makes breastfeeding even more essential. Adherence to good practice is often constrained, however, by an absence of institutional memory and failure of leadership and coordination. In complex emergencies it is difficult to guarantee the conditions required for safe use of breast-milk substitutes, including clean water,

facilities for hygienic preparation and a regular supply of substitutes, so the associated risks are higher.

During the 2006 crisis in Lebanon, for example, large quantities of breast-milk substitutes and infant formula were widely distributed. The dangers of untargeted formula feeding were exacerbated by poor hygiene following widespread bombing that destroyed water supply and sanitation facilities. The combination of factors resulted in an outbreak of diarrhoeal diseases.

Addressing acute malnutrition in adolescents. Substantial gaps also exist in understanding how to address acute malnutrition in adolescents. Inadequate reference population data and ethnic variation in adolescent development have hampered efforts to target older children for selective feeding programmes.

Counselling traumatized mothers. Another challenge is insufficient psychological counselling for mothers traumatized by armed conflict. A majority of these women report having 'not enough breast milk' when taking their infant children (under six months) to therapeutic feeding centres. In Afghanistan, approximately 40 per cent of admissions to such centres are infants less than six months old. The major cause of the severe acute malnutrition is insufficient breast milk, with psychosocial stress an underlying issue.

Developing early indicators for malnutrition. Rising rates of malnutrition are usually late indicators of a population's deteriorating nutritional status. Developing early indicators of nutritional crisis, therefore, remains an important challenge to timely and effective emergency response.

Liberia © UNICEF/NYHQ2007-0632/Pirozzi

Consistency in the quality and comprehensiveness of needs assessments has also been lacking. One example of this continuing challenge is the finding that only 6 of 67 surveys conducted in Ethiopia in 2000 recorded essential measles immunization status with anthropometric data.[299]

Promoting good practice. Inadequate support for documenting and disseminating information on good practice in infant and young child feeding in emergencies has resulted in missed opportunities. For instance, many humanitarian agencies continue to include infant formula in food and health kits, despite lack of safe water for preparing it. This kind of response conflicts with operational guidance on infant feeding in emergencies.

Moreover, it hinders breastfeeding practices and endangers the health of non-breastfed infants. The lack of information and effective tools to measure micronutrient deficiencies and to meet the needs of children and mothers living with HIV also pose significant obstacles to overall programme effectiveness.

RECOMMENDATIONS

Nutrition responses have progressed since the 1996 Machel study from a focus on a narrow set of interventions to the broad-based approach of public nutrition. Nevertheless, protracted conflicts, such as those in the Democratic Republic of the Congo, Somalia and the Sudan, hamper access to health and other social services. The result is deterioration of children's nutritional status.

Recommendations from the 10-year strategic review presented to the General Assembly in 2007 call for an integrated package of basic services – including nutrition – to be made available to all, continuously, during emergencies. Priority actions in addressing child nutrition in conflict and emergencies include the following:

1. **Support infant feeding in emergencies.** Humanitarian actors should protect and support early initiation of breastfeeding and exclusive breastfeeding in the first six months of life; targeted distribution of infant formula for non-breastfed infants, including education of mothers and families on appropriate use of infant formula and monitoring of its use; and timely introduction of nutrient-rich complementary foods. The upheaval surrounding complex emergencies may disturb normal breastfeeding patterns and result in less frequent feeding. It is critical that mothers receive support to re-establish breastfeeding as an emergency intervention. Women who are infected with HIV should also be supported in making informed decisions about appropriate infant feeding.

2. **Apply a three-pronged approach to treating children with acute malnutrition.** For children with severe acute malnutrition and medical complications, facility-based (inpatient) management is

recommended. For children with severe acute malnutrition without medical complications, community-based management is more appropriate. For children with moderate acute malnutrition, community-based management should be initiated and supplementary feeding provided. Community-based interventions need more support, since they reduce the opportunity costs of treatment and enable caregivers to continue their economic activities and family responsibilities, including caring for other children. When implementing community-based interventions, it is important to inform children, families and communities about them to increase access, coverage and effectiveness of such programmes in conflict situations.

3. **Scale up use of multi-vitamins and minerals.** In emergency situations, efforts should be stepped up to promote daily use of multi-vitamin and mineral supplements to meet recommended nutritional requirements and improve the quality of diets. In complex emergencies, all children under five should receive 'Sprinkles' (a blend of micronutrients in powder form), and pregnant and lactating women should receive daily multi-vitamin and mineral supplements. Monitoring should be carried out to assess coverage.

4. **Deliver deworming medication to reduce the burden of disease and enhance nutritional status.** In complex emergencies, deworming treatment and vitamin A should be delivered along with measles vaccinations. Treating worm diseases in both women and children through a few simple, single-dose drugs is an essential step to good health, particularly when combined with simple and inexpensive nutritional interventions, such as providing vitamin and mineral supplements to promote recovery.

5. **Strengthen partnerships.** Donors, international agencies and NGOs should strengthen partnerships and increase communication and coordination to support an accountable and effective humanitarian response. This can be done through existing coordination frameworks, such as the humanitarian reform and the IASC Cluster Working Group on Nutrition, the Standing Committee on Nutrition, Emergency Nutrition Network, the International Nutritional Anemia Consultative Group, the International Vitamin A Consultative Group and other nutrition networks. ■

KEY RESOURCES

IASC Nutrition Cluster, 'A Toolkit for Addressing Nutrition in Emergency Situations', 2008, <www.humanitarianreform.org/humanitarianreform/Default.aspx?tabid=74>.

IASC Nutrition Cluster, 'Harmonized Training Package for Nutrition in Emergencies', 2008, <www.humanitarianreform.org/humanitarianreform/Default.aspx?tabid=74>.

IFE Core Group, 'Infant and Young Child Feeding in Emergencies: Operational guidance for emergency relief staff and programme managers', version 2.1., Emergency Nutrition Network, Oxford, 2007, <www.ennonline.net/ife/>.

'WHO/UNICEF/WFP Joint Statement: Preventing and controlling micronutrient deficiencies in populations affected by an emergency', World Health Organization, Geneva, 2006, <www.who.int/nutrition/publications/WHO_WFP_UNICEFstatement.pdf>.

WHO, WFP, Standing Committee on Nutrition and UNICEF, 'Community-based Management of Severe Acute Malnutrition: A joint statement by WHO, WFP, SCN and UNICEF', New York, 2007.

Sphere Project, 'Humanitarian Charter and Minimum Standards in Disaster Response', Sphere Project, Geneva, 2004, <www.sphereproject.org>.

8.5 THE ESSENTIAL ROLE OF WATER, SANITATION AND HYGIENE

Water, sanitation and hygiene (WASH) are key elements in ensuring the health, development and welfare of children. Inadequate access to safe water and sanitation services, coupled with poor hygiene practices, is the cause of at least one quarter of all child deaths and one fifth of the total childhood disease burden globally.[300] Water, sanitation and hygiene are also linked to school attendance and performance (particularly among girls), safety and security of women and girls, and the economic and social development of communities and nations.

In situations of instability and conflict, community water and sanitation services are among the first to be disrupted, and facilities are often damaged or destroyed. When conflicts cause population movements, children and their families are cut off from water supplies and from hygienic means of excreta disposal. In addition, women and girls become highly vulnerable to attack, rape and kidnapping because of insecure routes to both water sources and private places for defecation.

The re-establishment of water and sanitation services is among the highest priority interventions during conflict situations in both communities and camps.[301] Unless adequate services are quickly provided to children and their families, there is a very high risk of diarrhoea, cholera and other diseases with high mortality and morbidity rates. And unless good hygiene practices are effectively promoted in camps and communities, the danger of outbreaks will persist.

During the past 10 years, the sectoral framework for water, sanitation and hygiene has evolved in response to studies and field lessons in both the emergency and the development arenas. Key changes to programme design include new emphases on behaviour change related to hygiene and on water quality, greater attention to gender disparities and marginalized groups, more focus on partnership frameworks and collaboration among sectors, and greater decentralization of authority, resources and planning.

WHAT THE MACHEL STUDY SAID

The 1996 Machel study examined water and sanitation from three perspectives: as a determinant of conflict, as a key prerequisite for reducing child mortality, and as a gender issue. These perspectives remain valid today as a framework for defining the nature of the problem and appropriate responses.

The study highlighted the importance of water as a factor in causing and exacerbating conflict. Since then, its importance has become even more pronounced due to increasing competition for dwindling freshwater supplies. The evidence is now clear: Global warming is reducing the availability of water, and water-scarce regions in developing countries will suffer disproportionately.[302]

At the same time, population growth, urbanization and intensive irrigation practices have significantly increased competition for water. This has further marginalized poor and vulnerable groups. Interruption of water, sanitation and hygiene services and destruction of facilities are all too common during conflict, in part due to the increasing value of water as it becomes more scarce.

The 1996 study noted that both water and sanitation are key interventions for reducing child mortality in camps and emergency-affected communities because they are linked to disease and malnutrition. Field manuals now clearly spell out the centrality of WASH interventions in humanitarian response. The lesson is also more frequently applied in practice: The global response to the 2004 Asian tsunami, for example, successfully prevented major disease outbreaks by prioritizing both water and sanitation interventions.

PROGRESS IN POLICY AND PRACTICE

Promoting hygiene. The importance of hygiene promotion in emergencies has become increasingly clear during recent years. This is in response to new evidence showing that hygiene (and hand washing with soap, in particular) can reduce diarrhoeal disease rates by more than 40 per cent.[303] As a result, hygiene promotion is seen as an integral part of emergency response.

Improving water safety. Similarly, the growing body of evidence showing the links between water quality and diarrhoea is prompting a new emphasis on water safety, both in the sector as a whole and in emergency response.[304]

Taking gender into account. As the Machel study highlighted, water and sanitation is a gender issue in conflict and camp situations. The report specifically noted that water and sanitation facilities in camps must be carefully designed to avoid creating "opportunities for gender-based aggression against displaced women and children." Although field experience shows that this threat to women and girls continues today, it is now a more widely recognized problem, and the security of facilities is more commonly reflected in design criteria.

Enhancing local and global coordination. Both globally and locally, progress towards more effective and equitable emergency response programmes in water, sanitation and hygiene have focused on improved coordination and preparedness planning, defining and refining standards, and improving management and implementation capacities.

The 2005 launch of the IASC cluster approach and the establishment of the

MAINSTREAMING HYGIENE PROMOTION IN EMERGENCY RESPONSE

Promoting the practice of hand washing with soap and water at critical times (immediately after defecation, after handling babies' faeces and before handling food) is key to preventing the spread of diarrhoeal diseases. Evidence shows that this is especially true in conflict and other emergency situations, where people are often living in cramped conditions and water and sanitation services are interrupted.

Humanitarian agencies are responding accordingly, and hygiene promotion is increasingly mainstreamed into emergency response. In UNICEF-supported programmes alone, examples during the past few years illustrate the extent of this effort:

- In Darfur and neighbouring areas in 2007, a door-to-door hygiene promotion and soap distribution campaign reached more than 1 million people; more than 3 million people had access to radio programmes that emphasized the importance of hygiene.

- In Somalia in 2007, 3,500 hygiene promoters were trained to encourage hand washing with soap among vulnerable populations.

- In countries in crisis and transition in eastern and central Africa, the number of reported cholera cases fell significantly from 2006 to 2007, in part due to continuing prevention programmes, which include hygiene promotion in some countries.

To help expand and improve the quality of emergency hygiene promotion efforts, the WASH cluster has identified capacity building for hygiene promotion as one of five key outcomes in its global work plan. In a related effort, UNICEF completed a comprehensive, multilingual training package for UNICEF staff and partners in 2007.

WASH cluster represent significant steps forward in coordi-nation, quality and accountability of humanitarian relief efforts. The WASH cluster is becoming the principal coordination mechanism among humanitarian response actors in water, sanitation and hygiene among the United Nations system, the International Red Cross and Red Crescent Movement and the NGO community.

The cluster mechanism is also important in its formal recognition of the valuable role played by NGOs in emergency response, ranging from policy formulation at the global level to field-level action. NGOs also act as 'protection agents' on the ground, working to minimize threats to women and girls through WASH-related interventions.

WASH clusters have been formed in about 20 acute and complex emergencies (conflicts as well as natural disasters) around the world since the launch of the cluster approach, helping improve coordi-nation and clarify roles and responsi-bilities. Coordination mechanisms for WASH emergency response need improvement, however, over and above the efforts already made through the cluster initiative.

Setting minimum standards. For the first time, through the Sphere Project, a set of minimum standards has been defined for water, sanitation and hygiene in emergencies. These standards are increasingly being used by global and local entities for both programme design, and awareness raising and advocacy. The wide use of the Sphere WASH standards by both humanitarian response agencies and governments is helping improve the quality and consistency of interventions.

Governments and response agencies are also defining their own humanitarian standards and norms, in most cases informed by the Sphere Project. For example, the 2004 UNICEF Core Commitments for Children in Emergencies include a set of interventions and standards related to water, sanitation and hygiene that is now the basis for all UNICEF interventions in the field. Moreover, a growing number of countries are revising their own national standards.

REMAINING GAPS

Applying established standards. Challenges remain in applying standards during conflicts and other emergencies. Due to a variety of constraints, ranging from funding shortfalls to poor access resulting from insecurity, standards are not commonly applied in practice. UNHCR, for example, estimates that between 2003 and 2005 standards were not met for water supply in 40 per cent of refugee camps and for sanitation in 25 per cent of camps.[305] These findings are reinforced by the field experiences of other actors, both in camp-based and community-based WASH humanitarian response efforts.

Strengthening emergency preparedness and response. Agencies involved in both development and emergency work are increasingly reflecting the importance of emergency preparedness and response in their policies and strategies. A recent UNICEF strategy paper on water, sanitation and hygiene, for example, places a much greater emphasis on emergency response than in the past.[306] At the same time, standard non-emergency references and guidelines – such as the 2006 WHO Guidelines for Drinking Water Quality – now specifically address emergency response.[307]

Raising the necessary funds. Mobilizing resources for humani-tarian response in conflict situations continues to be a key challenge for the WASH sector. This is especially the case in conflict-related complex emergencies not prominently covered by the media, such as the continuing crisis in the Democratic Republic of the Congo.

RECOMMENDATIONS

Understanding has grown during recent years regarding the role of water in conflict; the importance of adequate response in this area is also increasingly acknowledged. Recommendations from the 10-year strategic review presented to the General Assembly in 2007 call for a continuous, integrated package of basic services including water, sanitation and hygiene. They highlight the need to invest more in building international and national capacities as well as knowledge acquisition and management. A further call is made to give priority to protecting children from gender-based violence, a concern that relates closely to this sector. Priority actions related to water, sanitation and hygiene include the following:

1. **Strengthen WASH preparedness and coordination for more effective and timely response.** WASH cluster members and other humanitarian actors should continue to improve water, sanitation and hygiene preparedness and coordination through the cluster initiative and other collaborative frameworks. This includes developing robust policy and guidance material (including those specific to conflicts), improved information management, refinement and promotion of inter-sectoral and inter-agency coordination, and building global emergency stocks and qualified human resources pools.

2. **Ensure compliance with emergency water, sanitation and hygiene standards.** Member States and humanitarian actors should take steps to ensure that established emergency water, sanitation and hygiene standards are consistently met in conflict situations through the allocation of sufficient resources, enhanced technical support and improved monitoring systems.

3. **Take steps for the safety and security of girls and women.** WASH cluster members and other humanitarian actors should take steps to ensure that policy instruments, guidelines and response efforts stress WASH-related measures to improve the safety and security of girls and women in conflict situations. ■

KEY RESOURCES

L. Fewtrell et al., 'Water, Sanitation, and Hygiene Interventions to Reduce Diarrhoea in Less Developed Countries: A systematic review and meta-analysis', *The Lancet: Infectious Diseases,* vol. 5, 2005, pp. 42-52.

P. Harvey, *Excreta Disposal in Emergencies,* Water, Engineering and Development Centre, Loughborough University, UK, in collaboration with the International Federation of Red Cross and Red Crescent Societies, Oxfam GB, UNHCR and UNICEF, 2007.

S. House and B. Reed, *Emergency Water Sources,* third edition, Water, Engineering and Development Centre, Loughborough University, UK, 2004.

Sphere Project, *Sphere Humanitarian Charter and Minimum Standards in Disaster Response,* Sphere Project, Geneva, 2004, <www.sphereproject.org/>.

United Nations Children's Fund, 'UNICEF Water, Sanitation and Hygiene Strategies for 2006–2015', UN document E/ICEF/2006/6, United Nations Economic and Social Council, New York, 2006.

Websites

UNICEF Water, Environment and Sanitation, 'Emergency WASH', <www.unicef.org/wes/index_emergency.html>, and 'Emergency Coordination and the WASH Cluster Initiative', <www.unicef.org/wes/index_43104.html>

United Nations Humanitarian Reform Support Unit and Office for the Coordination of Humanitarian Affairs, Water, Sanitation, Hygiene 'Cluster Approach', <www.humanitarianreform.org/humanitarianreform/Default.aspx?tabid=76>

Water, Engineering and Development Centre, Loughborough University, 'Technical Notes for Emergencies' prepared for WEDC by the World Health Organization, <http://wedc.lboro.ac.uk/WHO_Technical_Notes_for_Emergencies/>

World Health Organization, <www.who.org>

> "We were scared working inside our home; we were scared working outside our homes. We never knew what was going to happen." –
> Girls and young women, 14–18, Nepal

8.6 PROMOTING MENTAL HEALTH AND PSYCHOSOCIAL RECOVERY

As the 1996 Machel study pointed out, armed conflict can be devastating to a child's mental health and psychosocial well-being. Being a victim of violence, witnessing violence against others, living in fear and uncertainty, and experiencing extreme hardship, such as lack of food, shelter and medical services, can cause severe physical and mental suffering – ranging from feelings of intense sadness to anxiety, loneliness and despair.

In fact, the accumulation of stress over time and the long-term consequences of distressing events – such as the risks associated with growing up without a caring, protective adult or having no access to education – may have a more damaging and lasting impact on a child's well-being and development than the events themselves.[308]

It should be noted that the reactions of most children in emergencies are normal responses to horrific events. They are not pathological in the clinical sense.[309] Moreover, in spite of often extreme adversity, most children show considerable resilience and ability to cope, provided their basic survival needs are met and they have sufficient security and emotional and social support.[310]

Yet it is these very systems of support that tend to break down in the chaos of war. The damage inflicted upon social, economic and political structures in conflict situations often leads to mass population movements; disruption of social services and insti-

tutions; loss of livelihoods; tension and divisions within communities; erosion of traditional values and practices; and the collapse of political authority and the rule of law. Any of these changes can undermine support systems, including those that reside in families and communities, that provide the nurturing and protective environment children need to develop and thrive.

Effective mental health and psychosocial programmes for children have therefore focused on restoring an environment that protects children from further harm and offers caring relationships and opportunities for development. Such programmes are multidimensional and include promotion of family unity and family-based care. They aim to strengthen children's attachment to caring adults, restore normal routines and structures at the earliest possible stage, and facilitate the role of culture, spirituality and social responsibility. This helps give children a sense of identity and purpose. Such programmes also encourage children's participation and engagement in meaningful activities. They advance security and mitigate further harm, enhance access to basic services and reinforce children's support networks so they can provide care and protection.

Even within a caring environment, children respond differently in the face of extreme adversity.[311] A small percentage will have severe mental health problems: They will continue

to experience emotional and mental distress, and their functioning will be impaired even in a protective family and community context. Severe mental health problems appear to result from a combination of factors, including the severity of the experience, level of support children receive, accumulation of loss and stress, pre-existing mental or physical illness or disability, and mental illness in family members.[312] These children require specialized interventions to address their suffering and help restore normal functioning and development. In addition to care from the child's existing support system, interventions such as community mental health services or traditional healing are often helpful and should be made available.[313]

WHAT THE MACHEL STUDY SAID

The 1996 Machel study outlined several aspects of an ethical and effective psychosocial response for children in armed conflict. These include building on and supporting a community's resources, beliefs and practices; mobilizing the community care network around children; and re-establishing a sense of normalcy through meaningful, structured and regular activities. It also warned against systematic use of "psycho-therapeutic approaches based on western mental health traditions [that] tend to emphasize individual emotional expression." This caution reflected the practice, then widespread,

Lebanon © UNICEF/NYHQ2006-1118/Brooks

of initiating large-scale psychosocial programmes that focused narrowly on specific clinical issues such as post-traumatic stress disorder. This approach failed to help establish a systematic and all-inclusive system of care. The study laid out the broad principles of a comprehensive, community-based response to the mental health and psychosocial needs of children in armed conflict.

CHANGES IN APPROACH AND UNDERSTANDING

At the time of the Machel study, the field of psychosocial and mental health programming for children in emergencies was deeply divided. It was characterized by diverse and often contradictory approaches that left affected populations open to interventions that were inappropriate and at times harmful, though well-meaning.

Experience during the past decade has brought a growing consensus within the humanitarian community on the main programmatic strategies that promote mental health and psycho-social well-being in children – and prevent further harm. At the core of this consensus is recognition of the need to address the immediate and long-term social as well as psychological effects of armed conflict on children.[314] There is also agreement on the important role of protective factors in mitigating the effect of armed conflict and in promoting mental health.[315] As described above, this involves strengthening caring relation-

ships, protection and opportunities for children to develop. Another area of understanding and agreement is the complementarity of social and psychological supports and the links between protective factors. These call for an integrated, multi-sectoral and many-layered response.

At the same time, recognition is growing of the thin evidence base for assessing the effectiveness and long-term impact of different kinds of mental health and psychosocial interventions in conflict and post-conflict settings. Most of the research has been conducted on clinical interventions carried out by well-trained mental health professionals in relatively stable countries. These have limited relevance to conflict settings. Assessments of interventions carried out in countries affected by conflict need to be pursued more rigorously and in an ethical and participatory way. Local understanding of distress and well-being must also be better integrated into the evidence base. Furthermore, it is increasingly acknowledged that capacities and coping skills, not only deficits, need to be considered.

Better understanding of the importance of strong evidence among field workers, managers and donors, combined with promising new approaches and tools, and more effective partnerships between researchers and practitioners, are among the most important recent developments.

PROGRESS IN POLICY AND PRACTICE

Strong recognition of the role of mental health and psychosocial support since the 1996 Machel study has led to more consistent implementation of programmes in the field. Psychosocial support programmes, for example, have been carried out in Afghanistan, northern Uganda and throughout the Middle East. Numerous psychosocial guidelines, policies and training work-shops have been developed, many specific to children. Significant levels of funding have also been made available.

Increasing inter-agency collaboration. There are many examples of collaboration in this field among UN agencies, from production of training manuals to implementation of joint programmes. At the global level, this has included the development of inter-agency guidelines on psychosocial support, networking initiatives such as the inter-agency Psychosocial Working Group and joint projects such as training in psychosocial support for child protection actors. At the local and regional levels, inter-agency initiatives have included regional networks,[316] development of local guidelines and standards (such as those developed in Aceh by the Psychosocial Working Group) and joint projects.

Providing strong policy guidance. The inter-agency consensus on mental health and psychosocial principles

"While I was playing football with friends, I heard an explosion. I rushed to the place where the explosion happened and I saw Hassan, our 14-year-old neighbour, who was dead. We collected his scattered body. I could not sleep for nights; I used to dream of people drenched in blood." – Boy, 13, Somalia

and practice that has emerged over the years was recently formalized in the IASC Guidelines on Mental Health and Psychosocial Support in Emergency Settings, launched in Geneva in September 2007. The guidelines were developed by staff from 27 agencies through extensive consultation and dialogue.

By providing strong policy guidance in a field formerly plagued by dissension about 'good practice', the new IASC guidelines are a significant step forward in protecting and promoting the mental health and psychosocial well-being of populations in emergencies. The guidelines recognize that how humanitarian aid is provided has a substantial impact on people's mental health and psychosocial well-being, and that protecting this sense of well-being is the responsibility of all sectors at the earliest possible stages of humanitarian response. The guidelines reiterate that most people are resilient when given adequate community support and services. Moreover, the guidelines focus clearly on building upon local resources and social interventions that reinforce existing ways that people in the community handle distress in their lives. They also include attention to protection and care of those with severe mental disorders, including severe trauma-induced and pre-existing disorders, as well as access to psychological first aid for those in acute distress.

The guidelines acknowledge the complementarity of approaches that focus primarily on strengthening social supports and those that focus on clinical assistance in the health sector. They therefore encourage establishment of a single coordinating body. In doing so they transcend the traditional divide between 'mental health' and 'psychosocial' actors.

REMAINING GAPS

Forging consensus on divergent approaches at the country level. Despite significant progress over the past decade, gaps remain. For example, although the IASC guidelines capture the consensus at the global policy level, debate continues at the country level regarding the relative weight to give to social, community-driven approaches versus psychological/clinical approaches. This contributes to varying quality of responses and risks undermining the progress made so far. Ineffective or harmful practices continue to be used. For this reason, a good deal of work remains to build understanding and ownership of this new consensus in the field and to adapt the guidelines to specific realities on the ground.

Filling gaps in coverage. Major gaps persist in coverage because current mental health and psychosocial programmes reach only a small percentage of conflict-affected children and their families. In addition, an enormous challenge remains in

identifying and reaching some of the least visible and most-at-risk children, such as sexually abused children, child domestic workers and children exploited by foster families. More work is required to find appropriate responses to severe mental distress that can be scaled up and adapted to local cultures and capacities.

Developing consistently high-quality programmes. Progress has been made in developing and using inter-agency tools and guidelines specific to psychosocial support for children, but more work is needed to ensure consistently high-quality programmes. For example, too little attention has been given to the differing needs and responses required for children at different stages of development. In particular, more work should be carried out to understand the needs and capacities of very young children (5 years and younger) and adolescents (12 to 18 years). Also needed is greater understanding of the impact of gender on psychosocial problems and on coping and resilience.

In addition, there has been insufficient documentation of programmes and sharing of promising practices and approaches and lessons learned. Peer support, on-the-job supervision and mentoring of psychosocial and mental health staff should also be strengthened.

RECOMMENDATIONS

The 10-year review of the Machel study presented to the General Assembly in 2007 noted that a consensus has been achieved on good practice relating to children's mental health and psychosocial well-being. It mentioned that social support systems, along with opportunities for play, development and clinical services for specific problems all constitute important aspects of programming. It also reaffirmed the role that sports, music and drama can play in restoring a sense of normalcy and routine to children whose lives have been altered by the tumult of war. Priorities relating to children's mental and psychosocial well-being follow:

1. **Implement mental health and psychosocial support guidelines.** Humanitarian actors should support the implementation of the IASC guidelines, while carefully monitoring and assessing their relevance and impact in different settings.

2. **Build up professional networks and peer support.** UN agencies and NGOs should strengthen networking among mental health and psychosocial actors. A global network on psychosocial support in emergencies should be established, and local and regional forums supported in conflict and post-conflict settings.

3. **Build capacity to implement mental health and psychosocial programmes.** Humanitarian actors should strengthen the capacity of child rights and humanitarian workers in countries affected by conflict to implement effective psychosocial and mental health programmes for children and their families. This requires development and provision of tools, training and on-the-job supervision.

4. **Strengthen the evidence base to improve programming.** In partnership with relevant research institutions, UN agencies and NGOs should develop a new generation of research on impact that is methodologically rigorous, based on the views of affected children and families regarding mental health and psychosocial well-being, and addresses sources of resilience, functionality and positive coping.

5. **Provide more flexible, longer-term funding.** Donors should provide more flexible, longer-term funding for psychosocial/mental health programming. Implementation of the principles contained in the IASC guidelines should be a prerequisite for funding in this field. ∎

KEY RESOURCES

Action Without Borders, website at <www.psychosocial.org/>.

Inter-Agency Standing Committee, 'Guidelines on Mental Health and Psychosocial Support in Emergency Settings', IASC, Geneva, 2007, <www.humanitarianinfo.org/iasc>.

Psychosocial Working Group, 'Psychosocial Interventions in Complex Emergencies: A conceptual framework', Psychosocial Working Group, Edinburgh/Oxford, 2003, <www.forcedmigration.org/psychosocial/>.

Save the Children Alliance, 'Promoting Psychosocial Well-being among Children Affected by Armed Conflict and Displacement: Principles and approaches', working paper no. 1, 1996, <www.savethechildren.org/publications/technical-resources/emergencies-protection/psychsocwellbeing2.pdf.>.

Sphere Project, 'Humanitarian Charter and Minimum Standards in Disaster Response', Sphere Project, Geneva, 2004, <www.sphereproject.org/>.

"When you are a girl, you think you'd [rather] die of a bullet than AIDS. So we go fight next to our brothers." – Young woman, 17, Burundi

8.7 LESSENING THE TOLL OF HIV

In 2006, 1.8 million people living with HIV were affected by conflict, disaster or displacement. An estimated 930,000 of them were women, and 150,000 were children under age 15.[317]

Vulnerabilities and risks associated with HIV may be heightened in crisis situations. HIV prevention centres and other public services, including education, are usually disrupted, and therefore inaccessible to those who need them. Moreover, whether the crisis is due to conflict or natural disaster, institutions and systems for physical and social protection may be weakened or destroyed. Families and communities become separated, resulting in a further breakdown of community support systems and protection mechanisms. All of these factors may increase young people's risk-taking behaviours and their vulnerability to HIV. In addition, women and children, in particular, are often targeted for abuse. They are the most vulnerable to exploitation and violence because of their gender, age and social status.

Other factors, however, may actually slow the spread of HIV during emergencies. These include a decrease in sexual networking because of limited mobility and accessibility, reduced urban migration, social or physical isolation, and relative poverty.

The ultimate result of the interaction between the HIV epidemic and a conflict situation will therefore be specific to the circumstances. This calls for careful assessment and understanding of HIV risk and vulnerability in each conflict setting.

WHAT THE MACHEL STUDY SAID

As the 1996 Machel study highlighted, the spread of sexually transmitted infections, including HIV, has the potential to rise dramatically during conflicts. The study also noted that all humanitarian responses in conflict situations must emphasize the special reproductive health needs of women and girls, including prevention and treatment of HIV and AIDS.

PROGRESS IN POLICY AND PRACTICE

Generating global commitment and national plans. The Declaration of Commitment that emerged from the General Assembly Special Session on HIV/AIDS in 2001 devoted an entire section to the HIV epidemic in regions affected by conflict and disaster. Among other things, the Declaration bound signatories to develop and begin implementing national strategies that address HIV and AIDS into programmes or actions that respond to emergencies and to factor these into international assistance programmes.

The UN Security Council also acknowledged the relevance of the HIV epidemic in addressing humanitarian and security issues, as reflected in the adoption of Resolutions 1308 and 1325 in 2000.

In recent years, the HIV-related needs of populations affected by emergencies have increasingly been considered within national AIDS strategic plans and other development frameworks, though mainly focused on refugees. Funding of HIV proposals within Consolidated and Flash Appeals more than doubled from 2002 to 2005, increasing from less than 10 per cent to 19 per cent. Still, HIV programmes in emergency settings are underfunded in relation to overall appeals for humanitarian aid, whose funding has remained stable at about 67 per cent.[318]

Establishing inter-agency guidelines. Guidelines for HIV/AIDS interventions in emergency settings have been developed by an IASC task force. The guidelines cover several programmatic issues related to children, such as protection of unaccompanied children and those separated from their families, prevention of and response to sexual violence, and access to education for every child. They also emphasize the importance of information, education and communication programmes for young people as well as communications programmes targeted at behaviour change.

Refining the programmatic response. In 2003, UNICEF further refined the core elements of its response to protecting and assisting children and women in conflict and unstable situations. The organi-

Occupied Palestinian Territory © UNICEF/NYHQ2007-0779/El Baba

zation's Core Commitments for Children in Emergencies include key elements of a programmatic response to HIV.

For example, the use of drugs to help prevent HIV infection after possible exposure has been shown to be an essential part of a package of standard precautions for service providers within and outside the health services sector; it is also part of a comprehensive strategy to address HIV prevention associated with gender-based violence. Programmes that include post-exposure prophylaxis in services for rape survivors have been implemented in a number of complex emergencies, including in Burundi, the Democratic Republic of the Congo and Haiti.

Interventions to prevent mother-to-child transmission of HIV have also been successfully carried out in emergency settings, as in northern Uganda. There, good results were achieved, even when compared with non-affected areas of the country. Still, many challenges remain, including insufficient skilled assistance during childbirth, complex protocols, lack of adherence to protocols and fear of stigma.

Although the use of antiretroviral therapy in conflict and post-conflict settings has been limited in scale, the outcomes achieved compare favourably to those found in non-conflict situations. This suggests that with adaptation and resources, it is possible to deliver comprehensive

care for persons living with HIV or AIDS in both post-conflict and chronic-conflict settings. Antiretroviral therapy has already been administered during complex emergencies in the Democratic Republic of the Congo, Haiti and Uganda.

Promoting protection and ethical conduct. Within the United Nations, norms are being established with regard to protection issues and ethical conduct. The Secretary-General's 2003 'Bulletin on special measures for protection from sexual exploitation and sexual abuse' provides clear definitions of these issues. The bulletin, aiming to protect the most vulnerable from harm, states that sexual exploitation and abuse constitute serious misconduct and are grounds for disciplinary measures, including summary dismissal for UN staff. It covers specific standards of behaviour, for instance, prohibiting sex with minors and the exchange of money, employment, goods or services for sex.

REMAINING GAPS

Increasing AIDS-related programming and funding. There is little doubt that HIV and AIDS have received insufficient programming attention in conflict situations: By the end of 2005, only half the proposals submitted to the Global Fund to Fight AIDS, Tuberculosis and Malaria by countries with significant refugee populations included specific activities addressing HIV or AIDS among

refugees. And the World Bank's Multi-Country HIV/AIDS Program included projects in only 19 of the 28 African countries hosting refugees.

AIDS-related programming and funding also remain low in post-conflict and recovery contexts, as suggested by a UNDP review of 85 countries affected by emergencies or hosting more than 5,000 refugees. The study analysed available Poverty Reduction Strategy Papers and found that only 14 of 49 countries (29 per cent) mention increased vulnerability to HIV among 'populations of humanitarian concern'. These include refugees, internally displaced persons and others affected by armed conflicts or disasters, including children.[319] Moreover, only a quarter of UN Development Assistance Frameworks in 74 countries studied included activities aimed at reducing or preventing HIV in the same population.[320]

Improving coverage of antiretroviral therapy. Not surprisingly, coverage of antiretroviral therapy is often lower in areas affected by conflict than nationally. Inadequacy of supply is compounded when paediatric demand is taken into account.

Implementing guidelines. Use of the inter-agency 'Guidelines for HIV/AIDS interventions in emergency settings' in the field has been uneven.

Mainstreaming HIV across sectors. Similarly, although HIV is a cross-cutting issue of the cluster approach

"Girls have been raped and this has resulted in HIV/AIDS." –
Young women, 19-29, Rwanda

being adopted as part of humanitarian reform, experience in recent crises suggests that HIV has too frequently been ignored, along with other issues that must be addressed through multiple sectors.

RECOMMENDATIONS

Understanding of HIV as a relevant concern for children in conflict has deepened since publication of the five-year review of the Machel study in 2001. Policy and programming have also advanced. Still, millions of children and young people remain vulnerable to HIV in conflict situations worldwide. To address the most urgent needs in this area, an agenda for action should encompass policy and programming involving all stakeholders:

1. **Increase support to national HIV programming.** UN agencies and NGOs should improve support and guidance to national HIV programming, with the objective of developing interventions that address populations of humanitarian concern.

2. **Integrate HIV and AIDS programming in the humanitarian framework.** Humanitarian actors should integrate HIV and AIDS into programming responses and the humanitarian framework, such as the UN Consolidated Appeals Processes and the UN Central Emergency Response Fund.

3. **Ensure HIV-related capacity building across clusters.** All IASC cluster leads should ensure that relevant personnel receive training on HIV and AIDS to build capacity in addressing the epidemic as part of humanitarian reform.

4. **Promote inter-agency guidance on HIV programming in conflict situations.** Humanitarian actors should adopt and disseminate inter-agency guidance on HIV programming in conflict situations. They should also develop additional guidance related to emerging programmatic areas as an essential step to ensure a predictable and coherent response to HIV in humanitarian settings.

5. **Ensure linkages in HIV programming throughout the emergency.** UN agencies and NGOs should ensure links in HIV programming through the various phases of an emergency as well as post-conflict recovery, transition and reconstruction. Links must also be established in programmes aimed at disarmament, demobilization and reintegration, and the return or repatriation of displaced populations. ■

KEY RESOURCES

M. Lowicki-Zucca et al., 'Estimates of HIV Burden in Emergencies', *Sexually Transmitted Infections*, vol. 84, 2008, pp. i42-i48, <http://sti.bmj.com/cgi/content/abstract/84/Suppl_1/i42>.

UNICEF Canada, 'HIV/AIDS, Conflict and Displacement,' conference report on the XVI International AIDS Conference affiliated event, Toronto, 12 August 2006, hosted by UNHCR and UNICEF, 2006, <http://data.unaids.org/pub/Report/2006/hiv_aids_conflict_displacement.pdf >

United Nations, 'Secretary-General's Bulletin: Special measures for protection from sexual exploitation and sexual abuse', UN document ST/SGB/2003/13, New York, 9 October 2003, PDF link <www.un.org/staff/panelofcounsel/pocimages/sgb0313.pdf>.

Inter-Agency Standing Committee, 'Guidelines for HIV/AIDS interventions in emergency settings', IASC, Geneva, 2004, <data.unaids.org/Publications/External-Documents/IASC_Guidelines-Emergency-Settings_en.pdf>.

Joint United Nations Programme on HIV/AIDS, 'Strategies to Support the HIV-Related Needs of Refugees and Host Populations: A joint publication of the Joint United Nations Programme on HIV/AIDS (UNAIDS) and the United Nations High Commissioner for Refugees (UNHCR)', UNAIDS Best Practice Collection, UNAIDS, Geneva, 2005, <http://data.unaids.org/pub/Report/2005/refugees_aids_strategies_to_support.pdf>.

8.8 BUILDING CHILD PROTECTION SYSTEMS

The 1996 Machel study highlighted particular risks that jeopardize children's protection during armed conflict. This section, and the three that follow, describe an emerging priority among child protection specialists – building national child protection systems – while maintaining a focus on specific issues. These include the unlawful recruitment of children, separation of families and gender-based violence.[321]

Child protection systems consist of laws, policies, regulations and services across all social sectors – especially social welfare, education, health, security and justice – that support prevention and response to protection-related risks. These systems are an aspect of social protection but extend beyond it. At the level of prevention, their aim includes supporting and strengthening families to reduce social exclusion and lower the risk of separation, violence and exploitation.

A systems approach to child protection responds to the gaps identified within 'issue-based' interventions. While such interventions have achieved coherence on standards and encouraged rapid, predictable responses, they have also led to duplication and isolated programmes targeting specific categories of children. A systems approach to child protection, on the other hand, aims to reduce the stigmatization of targeted children and adolescents, strengthen responses to other

important categories of vulnerable children, and ensure more equitable attention to various forms of violence, abuse and exploitation. It can build on synergies with development partners, in particular those working to improve social protection or strengthen the rule of law. Responsive child protection systems should build on the strengths of issue-specific programming by ensuring that distinct forms of vulnerability are addressed, including those related to gender, disability, HIV status and indigenous populations. They should also be able to measure outcomes for different groups.

A systems approach presents challenges, to be sure, particularly regarding the roles of ministries

and sectors. Social welfare ministries, commonly the cornerstone for protection, generally have few resources and often lack the staff to carry out even statutory responsibilities. The justice and security sectors tend to give scant attention to children. And despite their important role, the health and education sectors often lack child protection policies, codes of conduct and established procedures.

The following sections focus on progress and gaps in specific child protection issues, which are also being addressed within a broader context by child protection actors seeking to develop a systems approach that is better able to safeguard children, even in the midst of war. ■

KEY RESOURCES

Save the Children, *Stolen Futures: The reintegration of children affected by armed conflict,* Save the Children UK, London, 2007.

T. Slaymaker and K. Christiansen with I. Hemming, *Community-based Approaches and Service Delivery: Issues and options in difficult environments and partnerships,* Overseas Development Institute, 2006.

United Nations High Commissioner for Refugees, *Practical Guide to the Systematic Use of Standards and Indicators in UNHCR Operations,* second edition, UNHCR, Geneva, 2006.

United Nations, 'UNICEF Child Protection Strategy', UN document E/ICEF/2008/5/Rev.1, United Nations, New York, 2008.

United Nations, *The Millennium Development Goals Report 2008,* United Nations, New York, 2008.

8.9 FINDING APPROPRIATE CARE FOR SEPARATED AND UNACCOMPANIED CHILDREN

In all armed conflicts, children are at risk of being separated from their families, especially when fighting causes people to flee their homes and even their countries en masse.

Children separated during war often find themselves in the care of strangers and in danger. Having lost the protection of parents or guardians at a time when they most need it, these children are more likely to experience abuse, exploitation and neglect than those who remain with primary caregivers. Children living in child-headed households are especially at risk, as are those associated with the armed forces or other armed groups.

In broad terms, children affected by armed conflict can face two types of separation: involuntary or intentional. Involuntary separations typically occur when children and their parents are fleeing from danger, when parents or primary caregivers die, or when children are abducted. Intentional separations, on the other hand, include sending children away to work or to boarding school, abandoning children as a result of family destitution or emotional exhaustion, and placing children in orphanages or children's homes to access education and material assistance. In times of distress, some families entrust children to relatives or non-relatives, although the designated caregivers may also lack resources to survive wartime conditions.

Family separation can occur at any stage of an armed conflict, even months or years after the initial emergency phase – and after years of surviving in urban centres or camps for refugees and the internally displaced. It may also happen when protracted conflicts leave families and substitute caregivers so emotionally or economically expended that they feel they can no longer care for their children.

'Secondary separation' – when a child loses the foster family that had been caring for him or her – is also a frequent occurrence. These separations take place when refugee or internally displaced populations return home after a protracted conflict, intentionally or unintentionally leaving behind the unaccompanied or separated children who were in their care.

Refugee children separated from their families face specific risks. Their families may have escaped to another country, which makes tracing and reunification much more difficult, especially when the family still resides in a conflict area. Moreover, separated refugee children living with families from the host country face a heightened risk of exploitation and denial of basic rights, including the right to an identity and to a quality education. Monitoring care arrangements is particularly difficult in such circumstances.

Family-based care versus institution-alization. Research and experience clearly show that community-based and family-based care are preferable to orphanages and other forms of residential care. Institutionalization hurts children and communities because it tends to constrain children's cognitive and emotional development, ultimately hindering their social and economic performance as adults. This is true in both emergency and non-emergency settings. The length of stay and a child's age are key factors: The longer children spend in orphanages, the more likely their development will be compromised. The experience of orphanage care is most damaging for children under age five, and especially for children under three, because it is during those tender years that children develop physical, psycho-logical and social skills that will be crucial over the course of their lives.

Growing up in institutions means that children are denied the experience of family life and the acquisition of skills that children develop within a family environment. Children in institutional care are also at a higher risk of violence and abuse from staff, relief workers and other children, especially if they have a disability. But care in a community or family also poses risks. Government and child protection agencies should ensure adequate and regular monitoring and periodic review of all substitute care arrangements.[322]

It is widely believed that many orphanages implicitly encourage separation because they are seen as the only venue capable of offering food, shelter and schooling to children

> **"They made some of us orphans, killed some or all of our relatives, made us homeless and some of us disabled. They denied most of us the love of our parents."** – Young woman, 18, Rwanda

from poor families. Indeed, experience has shown that thousands of families have tried to have their babies and young children accepted into orphanages because they could not properly care for them on their own.[323] Poverty, lack of basic services and poor screening procedures are the overwhelming reasons for children being admitted to orphanages, not lack of family.

The problem is exacerbated by the fact that orphanages often receive support based on the number of children they take in, not the number of children they place out via family reunification or fostering. In the worst cases, unscrupulous orphanage managers profit financially while inexperienced relief organizations blindly support orphanages over more appropriate – and sustainable – family-care options. This is especially unfortunate because studies show that supporting children in orphanages is far more expensive than family-based care.[324]

Emergency residential care will always be required for some children while family tracing and fostering efforts are pursued. For children in temporary arrangements, close monitoring is needed, along with rapid searches for alternative solutions such as safe fostering or small group homes (for adolescents). Longer-term care may be required for a small number of children who cannot be reunited or placed in foster care.

However, if the focus is on keeping children in families – by paying school fees, helping to provide shelter or providing cash transfers – fewer children will need residential care. Humanitarian attention can then give priority to children in families, develop foster-care alternatives, establish community-based monitoring mechanisms and provide essential services in communities, rather than concentrating on children in special institutions.

Orphanages built during conflict, such as those established after the genocide in Rwanda in 1994, may continue to operate long after the conflict has subsided. Such institutions compete for limited humanitarian resources. They also draw attention away from efforts to establish more appropriate alternatives and invest in child protection systems that seek to strengthen family care and prevent family breakdowns.

Care and protection are the most immediate issues facing separated children, particularly those who are unaccompanied. But it is also crucial to trace their families as early as possible in an emergency, as the chances of finding family members diminishes with time. This is especially true for younger children.

The situation of unaccompanied and separated children seeking asylum in industrialized countries poses challenges as well. Although reliable statistics are difficult to obtain, up to 30 per cent of the disappearances in Europe could be linked to human trafficking, according to one 2004 estimate.[325]

WHAT THE MACHEL STUDY SAID

The 1996 Machel study focused on involuntary separation on the scale of what transpired in Rwanda, where more than 100,000 children were separated from their families due to the genocide. The study underscored the importance of alternative family care over institutionalizing children, and it highlighted how inter-agency collaboration led to a remarkably successful family tracing rate during the Rwandan emergency.

CHANGES IN APPROACH AND UNDERSTANDING

The past decade has brought new levels of awareness about the complex issues surrounding separated and unaccompanied children. This growing knowledge base is already being translated globally into more effective emergency responses as well as strategies for prevention.

For example, there is now greater awareness of the need to move quickly to identify and monitor unaccompanied children who are informally fostered by host country nationals in refugee situations and by nationals in situations of internal displacement. This is especially important in the case of unaccompanied and separated girls, who run a higher risk of abuse

SEEING THE EXPERIENCE OF CHILDREN THROUGH THEIR EYES

Between 2005 and 2007, UNHCR launched an innovative experiment to understand the problems faced by refugee and returnee children, some of whom had been separated from their families. These so-called 'participatory assessments', carried out in sites where UNHCR was operating in southern Africa, used artwork as a medium to encourage reflection and discussion. The objective was to understand children's views of their own problems and to give them an opportunity to help solve them.

Although situations differed from site to site, many common issues were identified. Among them was that children living without parents are especially vulnerable due to lack of adult protection and economic resources. In Malawi, children pointed to the particular difficulties faced by those living alone or as foster children. The former are vulnerable to attack, they said, and the latter are badly treated. These children often go hungry, are unable to attend school, are vulnerable to exploitation and are more likely than others to turn to prostitution for survival. In Botswana, unaccompanied children were seen as the most likely to exchange sex with older men for food, cash or other needs. The risk of transactional sex for unaccompanied or separated children was also identified in camps in Namibia and Zimbabwe. In Mozambique, one boy reported that unaccompanied and separated children in foster-care arrangements "are treated like slaves."

These assessments gave children the opportunity to express themselves, which enhanced their confidence and tended to garner respect from adults. Other results included the development of standard operating procedures and child protection committees to ensure early identification and monitoring of unaccompanied children; training on children's rights for UNHCR personnel, NGOs, government officials, refugees and local communities; and the establishment or improvement of facilities for safe participation in recreational and learning activities. Findings from the assessments have been integrated into UNHCR's strategies and programmes and have encouraged the agency and its partners to give children a larger role in shaping their own futures.

Source: United Nations High Commissioner for Refugees, *Through the Eyes of a Child: Refugee children speak about violence – A report on participatory assessments carried out with refugee and returnee children in Southern Africa, 2005–2007*, UNHCR, Geneva, 2007.

and exploitation than boys. There is also increased understanding of the reasons behind intentional separations, which frequently result from destitution and despair induced by conflict, and of the scope of actions possible to protect family unity in the midst of armed conflict. More people now recognize that only a comprehensive response can fully address the consequences of separation – one that engages all sectors to support family unity on economic, educational and judicial levels.

PROGRESS IN POLICY AND PRACTICE

Developing inter-agency guidelines and a coordinated response. Progress has been significant in designing prevention measures and responses to involuntary and voluntary separations. For example, the Inter-agency Guiding Principles on Unaccompanied and Separated Children (2004), which outline the principles enshrined in international standards and reflect good practice, have been widely disseminated and used. UNHCR has developed guidelines for determining the best interests of the child, including children who are unaccompanied and separated.[326] Draft UN Guidelines on the Appropriate Use and Conditions of Alternative Care for Children seek to ensure that children do not find themselves in out-of-home care unnecessarily, and that when they need such care, the type and quality corresponds to the rights and specific needs of the child concerned. The guidelines are designed to promote and facilitate the progressive implementation of the Convention on the Rights of the Child.

In practice, responses have reflected increased coordination among all actors, further clarification of roles and responsibilities within various agencies, and concrete efforts to develop and use context-specific guidelines and tools collaboratively. For example, under humanitarian reform and the cluster approach, stronger lines of accountability have been established among humanitarian actors. These should result in more effective care and protection for children.[327]

Building on successful efforts. Over the years, concerted action has been taken to prevent separation in various contexts. There has been a move away from institutionalized care for separated children in emergencies. And coordinated, multi-stakeholder efforts have resulted in positive tracing and family reunification in shorter periods of time.

When efforts to trace and reunify are timely and sufficient resources are allocated, family tracing has proved extremely successful, even after several years of separation. In Goma, Zaire (now the Democratic Republic of the Congo), the families of all but a few hundred very young children out of a caseload of more than 10,000 children were traced between 1994 and 1996. More recently in that country, 465 unaccompanied children were reunited with their families out of 561 children who were registered with the help of the Red Cross.[328] In Guinea, UNICEF and the International Rescue Committee helped identify and monitor 1,385 refugee children living outside camps; 964 children were reunified with their families, a majority of whom were from Sierra Leone.[329] The Durable Solutions Committee in Guinea, comprised of government officials and members of the UN and NGO communities, has filled a serious gap by finding appropriate solutions for each child left behind after large-scale repatriations. This procedure is expected to become standard practice in refugee situations.

The use of modern technology, including print and broadcast media, is also facilitating rapid unification. In Albania, radio, newspapers and television were all successfully employed for this purpose. And in Rwanda, where tens of thousands of children were reunited with their family after the genocide, radio was used to inform parents how and where to find their missing children.[330]

REMAINING GAPS

Launching a timely, well-funded response. Concerted efforts to reunite war-affected children with their families often start too late, sometimes many months or even years after the onset of the emergency. In other cases, insufficient resources are set aside for family tracing and reunification efforts. The consequence is that thousands of separated children may never see their families again. To make matters worse, tracing family members in conflict and politically sensitive situations may not always be feasible.

Developing and applying the right policies. Significant gaps remain both in the evolving understanding of how best to protect separated children in conflict and post-conflict settings, and in securing the expertise needed to oversee the systematic application of guidelines and policies. For example, there are significant 'pockets' of separated children, particularly in low-intensity conflicts, who are often neglected by humanitarian assistance. This points to the need for new policy and practice. Unsystematic and inadequate monitoring systems for alternative care arrangements must be replaced, especially considering the critical need for data on separated children in informal, unsupervised foster care. This includes adequate identification of separated children, especially girls. Finally, there is still only limited understanding of – and inadequate programme and policy guidance on – the long-term impact of conflict on child separation.[331]

Investing in family-based care. NGOs, UN agencies and others need to institute an inter-agency agreement to invest in family-based care rather than orphanages. Resources are also required to sustain family reunification and reintegration programmes.

RECOMMENDATIONS

The 10-year strategic review presented to the General Assembly in 2007 stressed that the prevention of and response to the separation of children from their families must remain a priority at all stages of a crisis. Specific recommendations towards this end follow:

1. **Channel investment to children in family-based care.** UN agencies and NGOs should channel resources to support and monitor separated and unaccompanied children in substitute family care. New orphanages should not be created, and priority should be given to establishing formal foster care and other safe, community-based care options. Emergency residential care should only be provided for those with no other viable alternatives.

2. **Develop a practical inter-agency protocol.** UN agencies and international NGOs should develop a practical protocol usable by all actors to provide adequate care and protection of separated children. This should include assessments of legal and regulatory frameworks, pre-positioned agreements on alternative care arrangements and prepared statements on orphanages, if necessary.

3. **Ensure more systematic responses and programme application.** Member States, UN agencies, international NGOs and others need to ensure more systematic and early application of relevant policies and guidelines by all actors in conflict and post-conflict settings. This includes working with governments and/or local NGOs to create and strengthen 'focal points' for separated children within child protection networks and child welfare committees.

4. **Organize capacity building at all levels.** UN agencies and NGOs should organize training for relevant actors at the national, regional and community levels on all issues related to the separation of children in armed conflict as part of emergency preparedness. This includes organizing grass-roots awareness campaigns about why orphanages are bad for children.

5. **Continue data collection and monitoring.** UN agencies and NGOs should continue to monitor the situation of separated children over time. Governments and agencies should track the numbers and conditions of children in alternative family care, residential care and child-headed households, and among other high-risk groups. Monitoring should be linked to response, ensuring compliance with internationally accepted policies and practice around reunification, foster care, record-keeping and follow-up. ■

KEY RESOURCES

Save the Children, 'Facing the Crisis: Supporting children through positive care options', Save the Children UK, London, 2005.

United Nations Children's Fund, *The Lost Ones: Emergency care and family tracing for separated children from birth to five years*, UNICEF, New York, April 2007.

'Draft UN Guidelines for the Appropriate Use and Conditions of Alternative Care for Children', Presented by the Government of Brazil, 18 June 2007.

United Nations High Commissioner for Refugees, 'Guidelines on Determination of the Best Interests of the Child', UNHCR, Geneva (provisional release May 2006, final version forthcoming 2008).

International Committee of the Red Cross/International Rescue Committee/Save the Children UK/UNICEF/UNHCR/World Vision, 'Inter-agency Guiding Principles on Unaccompanied and Separated Children', 2004.

8.10 PREVENTING AND RESPONDING TO CHILD RECRUITMENT

During the past decade, children's involvement in armed forces and groups has garnered significant international attention, sparked in part by the 1996 Machel study. The unlawful recruitment of children is a violation of international law and a source of physical, emotional, social and psychological harm.[332] Yet despite widespread initiatives to protect children and young people from recruitment, gain their release and reintegrate them into society, many continue to suffer and die as a direct result of armed conflict.

The term 'children associated with armed forces and groups' refers to persons under 18 years of age who have been recruited or used by an armed force or group in any capacity. This includes but is not limited to fighters, cooks, porters, messengers and spies. It also includes children exploited for sexual purposes.[333]

Children forced into combat or non-combat roles risk being killed, injured or permanently disabled. They may be forced to witness or participate in atrocities. They are deprived of their homes and families and, with that, the opportunity to develop physically and emotionally in familiar and protective environments. In many contexts, girls associated with armed forces or groups are subjected to gender-based violence, including sexual violence, and risk contracting sexually transmitted infections such as HIV. They may become pregnant or give birth during their time with combatants. In such instances, their children are also exposed to the dangers and hardships of military life and face risks to their survival, development and well-being.

As revealed in the Machel study and subsequent reports, the causes of recruitment are many and varied. Children are most vulnerable to recruitment when family and community protection systems are weakened, basic services are lacking and livelihood options are limited. At particular risk are children living and working on the street, child labourers, children in conflict with the law and child victims of sexual exploitation.

Family members can become separated when fleeing from conflict. Yet having escaped the perils of combat zones is no guarantee of a safe and secure environment. Even camps for refugees and the displaced have become targets of parties to conflict. If such camps are not securely guarded, child recruitment is likely to increase.[334] Lack of security in and around camps also increases the vulnerability of children to other rights violations, including sexual violence and abduction.

The types of assistance available for a child's release from armed groups often determine his or her ability to make the transition from military to civilian life and to securely integrate into society. For this reason, the disarmament, demobilization and reintegration (DDR) process involves several long and complicated steps.

The Paris Principles define child reintegration as a "process through which children transition into civil society and assume meaningful roles and identities as civilians who are accepted by their families and communities, for the most part, in a context of local and national reconciliation." They go on to say: "Sustainable reintegration is achieved when the political, legal, economic and social conditions needed for children to maintain life, livelihood, and dignity have been secured. This process aims to ensure that children can benefit from their rights, formal and non-formal education, family unity, dignified livelihoods, and safety from harm."[335]

Thousands of children have been assisted by formal and informal DDR programmes. Since 1994, 34 formal processes have been carried out, 22 of them in Africa.[336] In Liberia alone, more than 11,000 children were registered in formal DDR programmes. Hundreds of millions of dollars are allocated to such programmes each year. They cost an average of $1,565 per person.[337]

Experts caution that the presence of formal DDR programmes should not be a precondition for the release and reintegration of children. In fact, the majority of children who are disarmed, demobilized and reintegrated into society do so through informal processes. Some

Afghanistan © UNICEF/NYHQ2004-0654/Brooks

of these are children who escape a combat situation or are left behind and return directly to their communities. Others are forced into hiding and migrate to urban areas or other countries.

For many children, recognition and participation in DDR processes can play an important protection role. In Uganda, the security clearance and document given to children who were formerly involved with armed groups gives them a sense of confidence that they can return to their communities without suspicion. In an informal demobilization process in eastern Democratic Republic of the Congo, children asked for demobilization papers as protection from re-recruitment and from being charged as deserters.[338]

Experience over the past 10 years has continued to demonstrate that children tend to confront enormous challenges upon returning to their communities. These include social stigma, psychosocial distress, and lack of educational and livelihood options. Successful reintegration, therefore, is one of the most important steps in ensuring a child's well-being.

WHAT THE MACHEL STUDY SAID

The 1996 Machel study described the participation of adolescents and children in armed forces and groups as one of the most alarming trends in contemporary warfare. It also observed that the "children most likely to become soldiers are those from impoverished and marginalized backgrounds and those who have become separated from their families."

By urging that child recruitment become part of the international peace and security agenda, the study provided the impetus for a deeper look at the issue. At the time of the original Machel study, the move away from the term 'child soldiers' was already under way. A consensus developed around a broader and more inclusive definition focused on 'children associated with armed forces and groups' to ensure that it included not only children with guns but also those in a variety of non-combat roles.

PROGRESS IN POLICY AND PRACTICE

The Machel study emphasized that "one of the most urgent priorities is to remove everyone under 18 years of age from armed forces." Since that time, progress in both policy and practice has emerged out of extensive consultations involving multiple stakeholders and experience on the ground.

Key developments at the global level. Among the highlights of international action against child recruitment are the following:

- The 1997 Cape Town Principles,[339] resulting from a symposium coordinated by UNICEF and the NGO Working Group on the Convention on the Rights of the Child, have been indispensable in developing programmes to demobilize children used by armed forces or groups and reintegrate them into society.

- The Optional Protocol to the CRC on the involvement of children in armed conflict, which entered into force in 2002, prohibits the

> **"After I was taken to the front, they gave me blood to drink, which they said was the first test, and will make me more and more brave."** – Young man, age not specified, Liberia

compulsory recruitment of children below age 18 into national armed forces and armed groups. It requires States to take "all feasible measures" to prevent children from participating directly in hostilities. The protocol allows governments to set a minimum voluntary recruitment age of over 15 years but prohibits any recruitment of persons under age 18 by armed groups. While recognizing that States determine their own international legal obligations for voluntary recruitment age, many humanitarian and human rights actors, including UNICEF, have urged States to set a minimum age of 18 in all circumstances.[340]

■ In 2006, standards for the disarmament, demobilization and reintegration of adults and children were presented to the General Assembly and have since become the basis for DDR programmes sponsored by the United Nations. The standards provide a comprehensive set of guidelines, procedures and policies.[341]

■ The 2007 Paris Principles, a commitment made by 66 Member States to date, set legal and operational principles and guidelines to protect children against recruitment and use in armed conflict. This non-binding document aims to help practioners ensure that processes lead to improved care for and protection of children. It provides coherence between governmental commitments, international obligations, and programme principles and best practice.

■ In 2007, the French Ministry of Foreign Affairs partnered with UNICEF to organize a ministerial-level meeting entitled 'Free Children from War' to define ways to honour commitments made through the Millennium Declaration. Through a long consultative process, it also sought to update the Cape Town Principles and other technical guidance.[342] The process is important because of the endorsement of the Paris Commitments by 66 States. This now gives States, UN agencies, NGOs and other partners additional leverage to advocate for preventing unlawful recruitment and supporting the unconditional release and sustainable reintegration of affected children.[343]

A number of lessons and good practices have been useful in promoting reintegration processes, strengthening protection efforts and facilitating the transition of children affected by armed conflict into civil society. They include:

Developing long-term prevention strategies. Efforts by governments, the United Nations, NGOs and civil society have achieved some success in preventing the recruitment and use of children in armed forces and groups. This includes key legislative and policy actions at the national level, such as ratifying and establishing procedures to implement OPAC. But expanded efforts are needed to respond in a more comprehensive way to this multifaceted problem.

For example, while a good deal of attention in recent years was dedicated to reintegrating Guinean children associated with fighting forces in Côte d'Ivoire, Liberia and Sierra Leone, as well as with the Guinean militia Jeunes Volontaires, very few prevention initiatives addressed the risk of ongoing child recruitment. In Liberia, a reintegration programme for children sponsored by UNICEF and local and international NGOs, in collaboration with the Ministry of Social Affairs, included only one component to prevent recruitment. In Sierra Leone, reintegration activities ended in 2005, despite ongoing cross-border and regional risks. The long-term prevention of recruitment has not been given priority. [344]

Success tends to be found where there is collaboration between UN entities, NGOs and communities to mobilize resources and build on existing capacities. This may involve establishing community protection networks and sensitizing community leaders to the issue. Experience in Angola suggests that some re-recruitment was prevented through an

> "Girls also are enrolled in the army, to fight
> or to carry ammunition and other loads." –
> Young people, 15-23, sex not specified, Burundi

SERVICES THAT SUPPORT SUSTAINABLE REINTEGRATION

The activities and/or services that support reintegration efforts include:

- Medical assistance and health care, including general physical examinations, sexual and reproductive health care sensitive to gender-based violence, and HIV prevention and care;

- Mental health and psychosocial support and care, with the degree of support depending on the child's experiences;

- Family tracing, family and community mediation, and family reunification;

- Conflict resolution and peace education, which are particularly important in instances where children of opposing groups return to the same community;

- Education, including vocational training, formal and informal education, health education, life skills and recreational activities;

- Livelihood support based on vocational and skills training, which should include income-generating activities, apprenticeships, micro-loans and other forms of credit, and social entrepreneurship;

- Legal support for issues involving property rights; inheritance, registration and identification; children in conflict with the law; and children's access to justice as victims and witnesses;

- Processes that support truth and reconciliation, including justice and forgiveness for perpetrators and victims.

extensive community-based network whose members accompanied recruited children from demobilization through family reunification. Officials of the UNITA rebel force have acknowledged that the family reunification effort obstructed their recruitment or re-recruitment strategies.[345]

Another essential step in prevention is counterbalancing young people's frustration about the widespread lack of economic opportunities and basic services. As a young woman from Haiti said: "It should be remembered that many of us are involved in crime and in violence to help our families. There are still no alternatives for us."[346] Addressing the underlying causes of recruitment means providing a range of education, skills training and income-generating opportunities as attractive options to a life of violence.

Moreover, reintegration programmes should be closely linked to child protection activities. For example, attention should be drawn through public information and awareness-raising activities to the vulnerabilities of specific groups of children at risk of recruitment or re-recruitment.

Addressing the specific situation of girls. Disarmament, demobilization and reintegration programmes have yet to reach most girls, and formal programmes that include girls do not always reflect their distinct needs. For instance, only about 8 per cent of the demobilized children in Sierra Leone were girls, yet they represented 30 per cent of children involved in the conflict.[347] Girls in Liberia found themselves similarly lacking services. In the Democratic Republic of the Congo, from December 2003 to September 2004 only 23 girls were formally demobilized, compared to 1,718 boys.[348] There are multiple reasons for the frequent exclusion of girls from DDR programmes. Girls may be marginalized or isolated by their families and the community due to their involvement in an armed group. As a consequence, they are often difficult to reach. Many young girls are forced into marriage with combatants, often referred to as 'jungle marriages' or 'bush marriages', and commanders may refuse to release them for demobilization. When these relationships result in pregnancies, girls are often shunned or abused by their families and/or communities. Social and economic opportunities remain extremely limited to them, and they have described themselves as feeling trapped. It has been documented that some girls faced with these problems in Sierra Leone, for instance, have either returned to the bush or have threatened to return.[349]

It is essential to develop broader, more inclusive and comprehensive support for reintegration programmes that include girls who may have indirectly become the victims of conflict. These programmes should be outside of formal DDR processes.

FOLLOW-UP IS KEY TO SUCCESSFUL REINTEGRATION

A reintegration programme that links social workers with children formerly involved with armed forces and groups is proving successful in various parts of Sudan, including Transitional Areas, the east and Khartoum state. The social workers help identify needs, resolve conflicts and make referrals to other social services. The pilot programme, implemented by Save the Children USA, has also established community child protection networks to complement the activities of the social workers. The concept has spread to Gedarif state, where the Children's Development Foundation and the State Ministry of Social Welfare have assigned social workers to every child demobilized from the town of Bentiu.

In the Gula district of northern Uganda, community follow-up is provided by volunteer counsellors or caregivers through a programme sponsored by the Gulu Support the Children Organisation. Volunteers receive a bicycle to facilitate their work. Follow-up, which entails a risk assessment, is usually conducted two weeks after the child's return to the family and/or community, then 3, 6 and 12 months later, as necessary. 'Low risk' children include those having spent only a short period of time (i.e., a few weeks) with an armed force or group, non-involvement in atrocities, lack of serious health problems and having one or both parents still alive. 'High-risk' children include girls who had children while involved with armed groups and abductees with serious health problems.[350]

A major challenge in programme delivery is providing confidential support to girls, so that their associations with combatants are not made known to the community, which could result in discrimination and stigma.[351] In Sierra Leone, for example, recovery programmes have strongly emphasized the social and economic reintegration of girls.

Community-based efforts such as conflict mediation and traditional healing practices have succeeded in reducing tensions and discrimination in some communities, resulting in greater acceptance of returnees. As explained by one young woman from Empowering Hands, a community-based organization in the Gulu district of Uganda, "Because most of us are formerly abducted children, people thought we couldn't do anything. But now they recognize that we have a contribution to make."[352]

"There are many of us who do not have jobs or anything. Some people in my family still fear me because they still believe I have the 'bush trick' in me; we get the evil eye and are discriminated against. There is nowhere to go." –
Young man, 22, Sierra Leone

There is growing recognition that the skills acquired by recruited children, such as organizational and leadership abilities, can be transferred to civilian life. This recognition highlights the potential of these skills for empowerment, peacebuilding, peer support, and individual resilience and autonomy. Specific strategies for girls' protection should ensure that:

- Girls who are excluded or unable to participate in DDR programmes are reached and given a choice to receive assistance. Ideally, they should be contacted through networks of other girls who were associated with armed forces or groups;

- Assistance involves consulting girls on their needs, encouraging active participation and informing girls of their options.

Promoting sustainable reintegration. The long-term success of reintegration depends largely on the availability of social and economic opportunities. Current programmes, however, are often too short in duration and too limited in scope to achieve this end. The process of identifying durable solutions in an unstable and economically deprived post-conflict society should not be underestimated. Moving from demobilization, transitional care and reunification to long-term reintegration poses challenges in terms of operations and resource allocation. It also requires clearly

defined strategies in order to be sustainable. Reintegration should therefore be an overarching priority during all phases of the DDR process (including planning, development and implementation), from the onset of peace negotiations to long-term development strategies.

A decade of programming knowledge has encouraged a turn towards more effective and diverse approaches to reintegration – approaches that are inclusive, flexible, grounded in the community and based on child rights. Follow-up or monitoring activities should be conducted regularly "to monitor the living conditions of the demobilized children, the quality of their relationship with family members and the level of their reintegration into the community, and … allow mediation of disputes when necessary".[353]

REMAINING GAPS

Despite the widespread ratification of related treaties and commitments made by governments, major progress is yet to be seen in preventing the recruitment and use of children in armed conflict. Significant investment is urgently needed in programme assistance for effective reintegration support. Other priorities have been identified in numerous programme evaluations and review processes:

Extending the age limit for interventions. Most child protection agencies and initiatives are specifi-

cally focused on children. Although many young people were recruited and used by armed forces or armed groups when they were children, they may be older than 18 by the time of demobilization. However, they still require assistance in the transition to adulthood. Recently, collaboration has expanded among key UN agencies, including the International Labour Organization (ILO), UNICEF and the United Nations Development Programme (UNDP), along with NGOs, to develop more coherent programmes for young men and women aged 15 to 24. A key area is economic support, which continues to be a major challenge. Recent ILO experience, for example, suggests that bolstering the livelihood skills of youth is not enough. Their parents and guardians also need economic assistance to ensure that older children have access to education as part of the reintegration process.[354]

Providing 'catch-up' programmes in literacy, life skills and vocational training. Young people who have missed out on schooling and training opportunities are likely to be unemployed and marginalized. This increases their vulnerability to recruitment and gender-based violence. Those with a limited ability to read and write require skills that can both lead to a livelihood and confer a measure of protection. In fact, both formal and non-formal education, along with skills training, can make a significant difference in whether a child or young person reintegrates successfully.[355]

In many contexts, it has been useful to combine literacy and non-formal education programmes with activities devoted to income-generation and life skills. For young people with more developed skills, promoting opportunities to secure a livelihood must be a priority. For children who have been released from armed groups – as well as others who have missed out on education because of the conflict – the emphasis needs to be on 'catch-up' programmes in basic literacy and vocational training.

Increasing job opportunities for youths. In many post-conflict societies, young people have little choice but to remain unemployed or accept short-term, hazardous or exploitative work.[356] In Sierra Leone, for example, children formerly associated with armed forces or groups have drifted back to mining areas, working as low-paid diamond diggers because they lack education and safe opportunities to earn income.[357]

Support for livelihood development can only partially succeed if it does not take into account the realities of post-conflict economies or the specific challenges of urban and rural environments. Training programmes often meet only short-term needs, including psychosocial needs, but fail to provide a foundation for long-term employment. For example, young people learn skills that are not really marketable

FARMING AND LIFE SKILLS BOOST CHANCES THAT CHILDREN IN SUDAN WILL REJECT VIOLENCE

In South Kordofan (Sudan) a programme sponsored by the Food and Agriculture Organization of the United Nations is teaching agricultural and life skills to children and young people as an alternative to violence. The Junior Farmer Field and Life Schools, which complement formal education, teach both traditional and modern agricultural practices. Students learn sowing and transplanting, weeding, irrigation, pest control, and the use and conservation of resources. Life skills are also emphasized, such as HIV awareness and prevention, nutrition education and business skills. Participants also receive psychosocial support. Even students who eventually opt out of farming as their primary livelihood are acquiring practical skills, such as gardening for subsistence, and are demonstrating greater confidence and self-esteem.

Source: Food and Agriculture Organization of the United Nations and World Food Programme, *Getting Started! Running a junior farm field and life school*, FAO and WFP, Rome, 2007.

and are streamed into saturated markets in particular vocations, such as carpentry or hairdressing. Typically, the biggest obstacle is the barely functional state of local economies. Employment opportunities are virtually non-existent, people have little income, and costs are high as a result of competition for scarce

resources. Such conditions make effective programming especially challenging, particularly for reintegration programmes.

For all these reasons, vocational preparation programmes need to offer young people competitive and adaptable skills as well as substantially longer-term training in such fields as business development and entrepreneurship. A combination of education, apprenticeships and vocational training in collaboration with the private sector, if possible, can often be effective.

According to a joint UN agency policy paper on the subject, "There is some evidence that youth interventions have so far relied too heavily on the supply side (building up skills) as opposed to increasing job opportunities for trained youth."[358] Policies involving private-public sector partnerships to encourage job placements are recommended.

Moving from targeted to community-based assistance. In the 10-year interval between development of the Cape Town Principles and the Paris Principles, there was a marked shift away from targeted assistance to community-based support for children associated with armed conflict. This occurred partly because assistance to specific groups of children tended to perpetuate stigma. The targeted approach also had the unanticipated consequence of stirring up jealousies and social divisions at a time when unity was desperately needed. Moreover, such an approach may have inadvertently encouraged recruitment and re-recruitment by creating the impression that joining an armed force or group could potentially yield rewards.

Similarly, cash benefits to returning children are also now widely regarded as inappropriate. Stipends or cash benefits can be viewed as rewarding demobilized soldiers, which can divide communities. They can also create incentives for some commanders to re-recruit children to benefit from their demobilization. In the case of Liberia, for example, a 'transitional allowance' of $300 was provided to the parent or guardian of each demobilized child after his or her return to the community. Consequently, the programme quickly drew the attention of children who had not been recruited or taken part in hostilities. Naturally, their families were anxious to join the demobilization

> **"If the organization doesn't provide machines after training, [the training] is as good as useless. It's like teaching someone to hunt without giving them a spear."** – Young men, 18, Uganda

process in order to receive financial remuneration.[359] For these and other reasons, current thinking on the subject emphasizes support to all children affected by armed conflict and their inclusion within strategies for post-conflict recovery.

There will always be, however, circumstances in which specialized agencies will need to deliver services to certain segments of the population. Examples include girls who are mothers or people living with HIV. An inclusive approach essentially means that a programme can provide tailored services to a group of children with special circumstances while also responding to a wider range of vulnerabilities. This poses many programming challenges, including finding ways to balance support to specific groups with the imperative to build a protective environment for all children affected by armed conflict, particularly when funding is scarce.

In Uganda, several humanitarian organizations have attempted to develop programmes centred on the causes of vulnerability rather than focusing on a particular group. This is proving to be effective, although the criteria used to identify vulnerabilities are still being refined.[360]

Ensuring that programming meets the needs of all children is intrinsically linked with funding channels and disbursement. Often, limited funds for DDR processes are earmarked for specific target groups and interventions, which limits the flexibility and inclusivity of programmes.

Providing long-term funding for formal and informal DDR processes. Reintegration is the most expensive component of the disarmament, demobilization and reintegration process, partly because effective programming requires longer-term solutions. It is estimated that 70 per cent of the resources invested in DDR programmes go to reinsertion and reintegration.[361]

Because DDR programmes occur during transitional post-conflict periods, funding mechanisms do not necessarily have a long-term horizon. And it has been difficult to obtain funding and advocacy support for more informal DDR programmes for children, especially while a conflict is ongoing. Fortunately, donors are recognizing the value of release and reintegration programmes for children in advance of formal peace and DDR processes, including the role that such programmes can play in preventing re-recruitment.

As agreed by the agencies and governments that subscribed to the Paris Principles and Paris Commitments, longer-term commitments should last a minimum of three to five years and aim for sustainable integration or reintegration in formal and informal programmes. In addition, there must be better understanding and recognition of post-conflict and transitional environments that experience low-level, chronic conflict.

RECOMMENDATIONS

The 10-year review of the Machel study presented to the General Assembly in 2007 called attention to the fact that the disarmament, demobilization and reintegration of children requires programming outside of formal DDR processes. It emphasized that reintegration has "wide-ranging aims, different for each boy and girl involved, including building emotional trust and reconciling with family and community, providing access to education and developing a means of livelihood." Among other recommendations, the report stressed that reintegration programmes should include all children affected by conflict. It also said that such programmes must be comprehensive and long term if they are to succeed in preventing future recruitment. Additional recommendations follow:

1. **Ensure adequate financial support to prevent child recruitment.** Donors should significantly increase the amount of flexible, long-term funding available for preventing child recruitment and re-recruitment. UN agencies and international NGOs should advocate for funding commitments to last a minimum of three years and to include a biannual review by the follow-up forum established by the Paris Principles. This will ensure that programme targets

"It should be remembered that many of us are involved in crime and in violence to help our families. There are still no alternatives for us." –
Young woman, 17, Haiti

are met and programming gaps funded.

2. **Provide technical assistance to develop appropriate policies and strategies.** Humanitarian agencies should provide States with coordinated assistance to develop policies to prevent recruitment, as well as for the release, demobilization and reintegration of children and young people associated with armed forces or groups. Additionally, States, UN agencies and NGOs should formalize a technical group with a mandate and budget to monitor technical implementation and to share knowledge and experiences on good practice – both globally and nationally.

3. **Develop a stronger base of evidence on which to devise future strategies.** Donors and protection agencies should invest more on research and evaluation to enhance the knowledge base on reintegration support and informal and formal DDR processes. Particular attention should be given to children who do not participate in a formal demobilization process. Multiple lessons and assessments from formal DDR exercises in Africa need to be cross-analysed with those from Asia and other regions and in contexts outside of peace accords and formal mechanisms. Expanded research collaboration with academic institutions could augment the rigour of methodologies.

4. **Ensure that reintegration strategies do not discriminate and do align with international standards.** UN agencies, international organizations and NGOs should ensure that reintegration strategies are consistent with the Paris Principles and the UN Integrated Disarmament, Demobilization and Reintegration Standards. They should cover all children affected by conflict, not only those associated with armed forces or groups. Strategies should adhere to rights-based and inclusive community-based approaches and should involve all sectors. Support should be sensitive to the child's gender and appropriate for his or her age.

5. **Focus on livelihood support.** Member States, UN agencies and NGOs must better integrate reintegration concerns for children into broader national strategies and socio-economic frameworks. They should heavily emphasize links between education, skills training and socio-economic development as an important goal for peace-building and a strategy to prevent recruitment and re-recruitment. They should also promote safe private-sector initiatives to create an economically viable environment for the reintegration of children and youth. ■

KEY RESOURCES

Coalition to Stop the Use of Child Soldiers, <www.child-soldiers.org/home>.

I. McConnan and S. Uppard, 'Children Not Soldiers: Guidelines for working with child soldiers and children associated with fighting forces', Save the Children UK, London, January 2001, <www.reliefweb.int/library/documents/2002/sc-children-dec01.htm>.

'The Paris Principles: The principles and guidelines on children associated with armed forces or armed groups', February 2007, <www.unicef.org/media/files/Paris_Principles__-_English.pdf>.

United Nations Children's Fund, 'Children in Conflict and Emergencies', <www.unicef.org/protection/index_armedconflict.html>.

United Nations Disarmament, Demobilization and Reintegration Resource Centre, <www.unddr.org/index.php>.

8.11 ENDING GENDER-BASED VIOLENCE AND SEXUAL EXPLOITATION

Gender-based violence is a broad term for violence directed at an individual because of his or her gender. It includes domestic physical abuse, sexual violence, harmful traditional practices (such as female genital mutilation/cutting and childhood marriage) and sex trafficking.

Gender-based violence is fundamentally rooted in gender inequality and discrimination, affecting women and girls disproportionately. Nearly one third of adolescent girls worldwide report that their first sexual experience was forced.[362] Almost half of all sexual assaults are against girls 15 years or age of younger.[363] One out of three women has been physically or sexually abused at some point in her lifetime.[364]

But the peacetime reality of gender-based violence pales in comparison with what occurs during war and its aftermath. Although clearly prohibited under international law, systematic violence against women and girls is often employed to achieve military or political objectives. It may include such actions as terrorizing and displacing communities, providing incentives for irregularly paid rebels to bear arms and using torture during interrogations.

Sexual violence has become an increasingly common aspect of contemporary warfare, although its full scope is difficult to quantify because of under-reporting and data-collection challenges. It is well known that boys are victimized by sexual violence as well as girls. However, it is also clear that adolescent girls tend to be the first to be victimized during armed conflict and in conditions of severe economic hardship. The consequences can be grave. Sexual violence can have lifelong implications for a child's well-being and physical and emotional development. Apart from serious psychological effects, sexual violence can cause severe physical harm, including genital lesions, traumatic fistula and other wounds. Additional effects are unwanted pregnancies and the danger of contracting HIV and other sexually transmitted infections.

Rape victims[365] and children born of rape often experience rejection, stigma, fear and increased poverty upon their return home. In Burundi, survivors revealed that "they had been mocked, humiliated and rejected by women relatives, classmates, friends and neighbours because of the abuse they had suffered."[366]

In both emergency and post-conflict contexts, high rates of unemployment, lack of basic services, and the breakdown in community infrastructure and social structure limit economic opportunities and social protection. Poverty and a lack of options for earning a livelihood make young girls especially vulnerable, leading to a high risk of sexual exploitation. Such children may migrate in search of safer environments or to gain access to shelter and basic services. Subsistence income is frequently sought through dangerous and illegal activities such as the sex trade. This is particularly prevalent in capitals and big cities.

In camp settings, girls may engage in sex as a means to obtain food, protection and/or basic necessities such as plastic sheeting for shelter. Exploitation can be exacerbated when assistance to camp populations is decreased, either as a means to encourage repatriation or due to technical or funding difficulties.

Trafficking for sexual exploitation continues to be at the forefront of risks to children – girls as well as boys. Conflict zones are often the point of origin and the transit routes for trafficking as well as destination areas. Warlords and armed forces regularly seek to profit from criminal activities and are in a position to exploit children who may be displaced.

Trafficking that leads to enslavement, prostitution and rape can constitute a war crime. In most countries, it is a violation of domestic penal law. Nevertheless, it appears to be flourishing, with international organized crime gangs and mafias/cartels playing a significant role.

Frequently, trafficked children do not return to their community or country of origin for fear of further human rights violations, such as retribution by traffickers, stigma by their community or the risk of being trafficked again. And they often face difficulties when applying for refugee status because asylum countries are often reluctant to recognize the need for international protection on these grounds alone.

> "[Girls who have been raped] now take care of children born from the killers. It's a trauma on top of trauma." – Young women, 19–29, Rwanda

GETTING TO THE REALITY OF GENDER-BASED VIOLENCE

The Columbia University Program on Forced Migration and Health is developing a novel methodology – the 'neighbourhood' method – to capture incidence rates of gender-based violence in places where reporting mechanisms are suspected to significantly underestimate the magnitude of the problem.

Using this method, a relatively small sample of women is interviewed about domestic and sexual violence experienced by them, their neighbours and other specified 'universes' of women and girls. For example, in four camps for internally displaced persons across one district in northern Uganda in late 2006 and early 2007, 204 respondents reported on the experiences of 268 sisters and 1,206 neighbours. The method revealed alarming rates of domestic violence and rape. An appalling 42 per cent of women had been beaten in family violence during the preceding year alone. The rates are much higher when viewed across multiple years.

The neighbourhood method gathers multiple estimates, rather than relying on a single source of data, to determine the incidence of gender-based violence. It also provides a practical, efficient means of collecting information vital for programming. The method provides information on the magnitude and nature of physical violence against women and girls that is relevant for both programme development and advocacy. It also reveals reporting and disclosure trends and provides a baseline against which to measure change over time.

Source: A. Ager et al., 'From Incidents to Incidence: Measuring GBV amidst war and displacement', United Nations Humanitarian Perspectives Discussion Series, New York, 2007.

WHAT THE MACHEL STUDY SAID

The Machel study raised several issues involving the dangers faced by women and girls in times of war. "Rape poses a continual threat to women and girls during armed conflict, as do other forms of gender-based violence including prostitution, sexual humiliation, mutilation, trafficking and domestic violence," the study said. "While abuses such as murder and torture have long been denounced as war crimes, rape has been downplayed as an unfortunate but inevitable side effect of war."

The study emphasized that acts of violence, particularly rape, committed directly against civilian populations during armed conflicts constitute a violation of international law. It also noted the significant challenges associated in applying international humanitarian law and human rights law. The recommendations called for appropriate legal remedies to reflect the nature of the crime.

The study highlighted the interaction of military and law enforcement personnel and humanitarian aid workers with children, articulating the importance of holding them accountable for their actions as an integral part of preventing gender-based violence.

PROGRESS IN POLICY AND PRACTICE

Taking action at the global level.
The need to increase protection from sexual and gender-based violence has been receiving heightened attention in Member States, non-governmental organizations and the United Nations system itself. However, tangible progress has been incremental.

In 1998, the Rome Statute of the International Criminal Court recognized that acts of sexual violence committed in a situation of armed conflict can constitute a war crime. Wars in the former Yugoslavia and Rwanda led to strong provisions on sexual violence in the International Criminal Court and resulted in important prosecutions. More recently, arrest warrants have been issued against perpetrators of gender-based violence and other crimes in the Democratic Republic of the Congo, the Sudan and Uganda.

In October 2000, Security Council Resolution 1325, a non-binding policy framework, called on parties in armed conflict to implement special measures to protect women and girls from gender-based violence. The Security Council has also begun to examine the issue of systematic violence against women as a threat to international peace and security. This was evidenced by the specific call for reporting on efforts taken to protect women in some mandate renewals. And in July 2005, Security Council

Liberia © UNICEF/NYHQ2007-0664/Pirozzi

Resolution 1612 called for systems to monitor and report certain violations of child rights perpetrated by armed groups or forces in armed-conflict settings. These include rape and sexual violence against children.

In June 2008, the Security Council unanimously adopted Resolution 1820, which recognizes the new role sexual violence has taken on in contemporary conflict and post-

conflict settings. The resolution reiterates that sexual violence is a war crime, a crime against humanity and a constituent act of genocide. It advances efforts to sanction perpetrators and raise the political, military and economic costs of such violence.

Increasingly, stakeholders are working together to ensure systematic and comprehensive responses at the global, regional, national and local

SETTING AN EXAMPLE: CODES OF CONDUCT FOR UN AND NON-UN PERSONNEL

In an effort to put an end to sexual violence by aid workers and others, dozens of United Nations entities and other organizations have signed the Statement of Commitment on Eliminating Sexual Exploitation and Abuse by UN and Non-UN Personnel, issued in December 2006. The principles contained within it are addressed to all those involved in programme delivery, including international and national UN staff as well as employees of national partner organizations. The statement is just one of a series of similar actions, prompted by reports of sexual abuse.

The United Nations Department of Peacekeeping Operations, for example, has instituted specific conduct-related measures for each peacekeeping mission. These measures include designating areas where prostitution is suspected or known to occur as off-limits to mission personnel and requiring personnel to wear their uniforms at all times when outside their barracks. The department is also piloting a comprehensive data tracking and reporting system on misconduct allegations for all categories of personnel in UN peacekeeping missions. Once completed, the system will provide an important means for monitoring misconduct. It will also help ensure that prior offenders are not rehired or deployed.

the General Assembly adopted Resolution 62/214, the United Nations Comprehensive Strategy on Assistance and Support to Victims of Sexual Exploitation and Abuse by United Nations Staff and Related Personnel. The strategy reaffirms the Secretary-General's zero-tolerance policy on sexual exploitation and supports implementation of a comprehensive approach throughout the UN system to assist victims of such abuse by UN staff and related personnel.

Strengthening the United Nations' response. A new inter-agency initiative, UN Action against Sexual Violence in Conflict (UN Action), is committed to scaling up the UN response to sexual violence during and immediately after conflict. UN Action builds upon and reinforces the efforts of 12 UN system entities to protect women from rape during war and respond to the needs of survivors. It aims to align the United Nations' work more effectively behind national efforts (both government and NGO) to address sexual violence.

The need for concerted action is clear: Despite international and national legislation to prevent and redress gender-based violence, enforcement still faces extensive challenges. For one, national and international conflicts undermine legal systems; in some cases, legislation is disregarded or circumvented procedurally.[369]

levels. One of the mechanisms for partnerships has been the cluster approach, which was developed as a way to strengthen the effectiveness of humanitarian assistance.

Establishing rules of conduct for national and international personnel. Much attention has been drawn to the role sometimes played by peacekeepers and humanitarian workers in perpetrating sexual violence and exploitation. At the time of the 1996 Machel study, discussion of the issue was mostly kept behind closed doors. Although evidence of abuse continues, the problem is now openly acknowledged, and measures such as codes of conduct and reporting systems have been put in place. During the past decade, the United Nations and other international organizations have issued standards of conduct to staff, provided training to personnel[367] and promulgated zero-tolerance policies along with terms for impunities and jurisdictions of military and civilian employees.[368]

Most recently, in December 2007

"I lost my father and my mother because of the war. A neighbour took me into his home to look after his children in Bujumbura. He raped me and I found myself pregnant, unwillingly. I came back home pregnant but I was chased away, so I returned to Bujumbura. I provoked an abortion and because of it was put in prison. I had been sentenced to life, but thanks to a presidential pardon my sentence was reduced to 20 years." – Young woman, 20, Burundi

Further complicating matters is that many States deny the existence of sexual violence and use harassment, intimidation and the closing of treatment facilities to prevent humanitarian agencies from treating abused children and young people. In some societies, girls who have reported rape have been charged with adultery. In others, a rape victim may be forced to marry the rapist, or the perpetrator may be required to pay a small fine, often given to the family rather than the survivor. Under some legal systems, proving rape is almost impossible and has traditionally exposed victims to humiliating and traumatic lines of questioning. Consequently, perpetrators are not penalized and survivors are doubly victimized.

It can be especially difficult

ENDING THE ATROCITIES IN THE DEMOCRATIC REPUBLIC OF THE CONGO

'Stop Raping our Greatest Resource: Power to Women and Girls of the Democratic Republic of the Congo' is a global campaign to call attention to systematic rape and other atrocities being committed against women and girls in eastern parts of the Democratic Republic of the Congo. It also demands an end to impunity for perpetrators of such violence. The campaign, initiated by local women, the NGO 'V-Day' and UNICEF (representing UN Action), encourages collaboration with local partners and survivors. It is sponsoring social mobilization activities such as educational workshops, and outreach via a website, music, theatre, radio and print materials.

> **"Young boys faced different types of physical abuse, whereas young women were raped during the war and they were traumatized. Because of the mentality in Kosovo, these women do not talk much about what they have experienced."** – Young men, 16–19, Kosovo

MITIGATING THE RISKS ASSOCIATED WITH FIREWOOD COLLECTION[370]

In many developing countries, gathering firewood is the primary responsibility of women and girls. Wood is often essential for cooking and heating, and its sale can provide income to meet a family's basic needs. But the safety risks associated with firewood collection have been well documented over the past decade, and very few strategies to overcome them have been implemented. Exceptions are those devised by the Women's Commission for Refugee Women and Children, which is working to reduce the vulnerability of girls and women to violence while carrying out this task in and around camps for refugees and displaced persons. The project is assessing alternative fuel options, firewood collection techniques and protection mechanisms. It advocates a multifaceted approach to the problem, including physical protection, alternative sources of cooking fuel and more efficient technologies, as well as the provision of services. Experts caution, however, that alternative income-generating activities are needed if the strategies are to succeed.

for refugees to navigate and understand the judicial and administrative processes of asylum countries. Typically, they have little or no previous experience with justice systems and face language barriers, and they frequently fear discrimination, bias or corruption.

Developing inter-agency guidelines.
During the past decade, a number of manuals, guidelines and training kits have been produced to improve the efficiency and quality of responses to gender-based violence. The development of these tools demonstrates greater inter-agency cooperation and partnership. Some of the most widely consulted guidelines currently include the IASC's Guidelines for Gender-based Violence Interventions in Humanitarian Settings: Focusing on Prevention of and Response to Sexual Violence in Emergencies and UNHCR's 2003 Sexual and Gender-Based Violence against Refugees, Returnees and Internally Displaced Persons: Guidelines for Prevention and Response.

The IASC guidelines were developed so that communities, governments and humanitarian actors could establish and coordinate a set of minimum interventions in each sector to prevent and respond to sexual violence during the early phase of an emergency. Similarly, the UNHCR guidelines provide a framework for preventing and responding to gender-based violence in displacement contexts. They include special considerations for refugee children.

In 2007, an inter-agency task force was created to focus on the specific vulnerabilities of women and children who collect firewood in camps and other emergency settings. The aim is to identify ways to enhance protection and ease burdens for those responsible for this task, while also developing strategies to reduce the harmful environmental impact of energy production.

Forging an integrated, multisectoral approach. While it is critical to improve security in camps and other emergency settings to protect girls from exploitation and abuse, these measures are unlikely to be effective without assistance that meets their real needs, including a viable means of earning a livelihood. Good practice in programming and strategies to end gender-based violence therefore rely increasingly on multi-sectoral, integrated approaches. They include legal support, provision of security, psychosocial and health care, prevention of sexually transmitted infections including HIV, emergency contraception, and educational and livelihood support.

Gender-based violence is deeply rooted in structural and systemic inequality, so initiatives have also been undertaken to advance the overall status of girls. Experience suggests that, whenever possible, interventions should build on existing structures and networks within national ministries or departments to ensure sustainability.

REMAINING GAPS

More than a decade after the 1996 Machel study, abusive and exploitative conditions continue to endanger children and their families. The ultimate goal – ending gender-based

Source: K. Bambrick, *Silent Victims, Young Girls at Risk: An evaluation of post-war rape and the responses to rape in the provinces of Sierra Leone,* Campaign for Good Governance, Freetown, Sierra Leone, 2004, p. 35.

violence against civilians during and in the wake of war – remains elusive. The need for more effective prevention mechanisms and protection strategies is stronger than ever. In addition, greater attention should be paid to the long-term impact of gender-based violence. More effort and resources are also required to address impunity for perpetrators and to assist survivors, particularly through child-specific responses.

Building better prevention mechanisms. Without advances in the status of girls and equal opportunities, eliminating violence against girls will be difficult at best. More effort is required to target discrimination and violent behaviour on the part of men and boys, instil in them a respect for human rights, and enlist them as protectors of women and girls. The emphasis

should be on behaviour change through communication and dissemination of public information on unacceptable behaviours. The aim is to foster attitudes that promote gender equality.

Ending impunity for perpetrators and creating integrated systems of protection. Although a growing number of countries have laws to address gender-based violence, enforcement is generally weak. Additional national legislation and enforcement are required to protect children from the specific criminal nature of sexual violence during conflict. This must be coupled with efforts to ensure that survivors are able to access effective justice mechanisms. At the same time, the need for broader, more holistic systems of child protection must be acknowledged and acted upon.

Sudan © UNICEF/NYHQ2005-0944/Haviv

Bridging the resource and capacity gap. Governments and humanitarian actors are faced with significant resource and operational challenges in mounting an effective response. Typically there are insufficient trained health and social services staff, weak implementation of guidelines, and a lack of minimum standards in programming, particularly with regard to responses specifically directed to children. This was confirmed by a recent rapid assessment in Kenya. It revealed that in virtually all settings, including camps and communities, efforts to address gender-based violence were restricted by lack of resources and inadequate capacity across all service-delivery sectors.

Mobilizing the necessary funds. In 2006, a study of projects addressing sexual violence analysed funding through the Consolidated Appeals Process (the humanitarian sector's main funding body for emergencies). The study showed that these projects received significantly less funding than other thematic areas of humanitarian intervention during complex emergencies. Projects focusing specifically on sexual violence received approximately 21 per cent of funding requested, whereas all other areas of humanitarian work received approximately 59 per cent of emergency funding requested.[371]

RECOMMENDATIONS

The 10-year review of the Machel study presented to the General Assembly in 2007 stressed the protection of children from gender-based conflict as well as the specific needs of child survivors "as distinct from those of women." It called for community awareness campaigns and education initiatives that reach out to boys and men as well as measures to enhance the livelihood options for women and girls. In addition, it urged stronger efforts on the part of Member States and the UN system to investigate and address allegations of abuse. Other, more specific recommendations follow:

1. **Collaborate for comprehensive and direct service provision.** UN agencies, relevant ministries and NGOs should collaborate through the UN Action against Sexual Violence in Conflict initiative to scale up assistance for child survivors. This includes multi-sectoral prevention and response; attention to child-specific, gender-sensitive and age-appropriate approaches; and integration of free services for survivors into existing institutions.

2. **Ensure access to justice for children.** Governments should protect children from gender-based violence, and UN agencies and NGOs should support and encourage governments as they adopt and apply appropriate legislation. Systematic, child-sensitive and timely investigation and prosecution of violations should be ensured while taking into account the well-being and safety of survivors, including those in camps for refugees and internally displaced persons.

3. **Implement non-negotiable and systematic codes of conduct.** UN agencies and international NGOs should implement standardized and systematic codes of conduct regarding sexual violence and exploitation that should include a unified zero-tolerance policy for all humanitarian staff, peacekeepers, and international and national partners. Specifically, this should include training peacekeepers, and law enforcement officers to address the needs of girls and to respond to allegations; providing progress reports to the UN Secretary-General on combating sexual exploitation and abuse from staff of UN agencies and NGOs; and preparing child-friendly complaint mechanisms.

4. **Programme for education and livelihood support.** UN agencies, international partners and NGOs should support accessible education and livelihood measures based on comprehensive analyses that focus on girls and their families for prevention of exploitation and abuse, empowerment of women and girls, and social protection. Specifically, this includes partnerships with the private sector for long-term employment strategies and apprenticeship opportunities; vocational and skills training; participatory market assessments; and micro-loans and credit. In addition, these measures should adhere to international labour standards, such as ILO Conventions 182, which calls for the elimination of the worst forms of child labour, and 138, which establishes a minimum age for employment.

5. **Invest in changing attitudes and behaviours.** To challenge the social, cultural, economic and political determinants of violence, UN agencies and NGOs should ensure adequate resources are invested in public information and education strategies that address men and boys. This implies promotion of gender-equitable attitudes and behaviours in communities, and participation of youth in developing key messages and campaigns.

6. **Provide substantial and long-term funding to develop comprehensive strategies.** Overall, funds are inadequate to address the extent of the problem and meet the needs of survivors. Increased, predictable and sustained funding by donors is a necessity, while diversion of funding from other areas must be avoided. ■

KEY RESOURCES

Office of the UN High Commissioner for Refugees, 'Sexual and Gender-Based Violence against Refugees, Returnees and Internally Displaced Persons: Guidelines for prevention and response', UNHCR, May 2003, <www.rhrc.org/pdf/gl_sgbv03.pdf>.

Stop Rape Now website, 'UN Action against Sexual Violence in Conflict', <www.stoprapenow.org>.

United Nations Children's Fund, 'Child Protection from Violence, Exploitation and Abuse', <www.unicef.org/protection/index.html>.

United Nations Inter-Agency Standing Committee, 'Guidelines on Gender-based Violence Interventions in Humanitarian Settings: Focusing on prevention of and response to sexual violence in emergencies', IASC, Geneva, September 2005, <www.humanitarianinfo.org/iasc/content/products/docs/tfgender_GBVGuidelines2005.pdf>.

WomenWarPeace.org, a portal on women, peace and security, <www.womenwarpeace.org/issues/violence/>.

World Health Organization, 'Sexual and Gender-based Violence in Emergencies', <http://www.who.int/hac/techguidance/pht/SGBV/en/>.

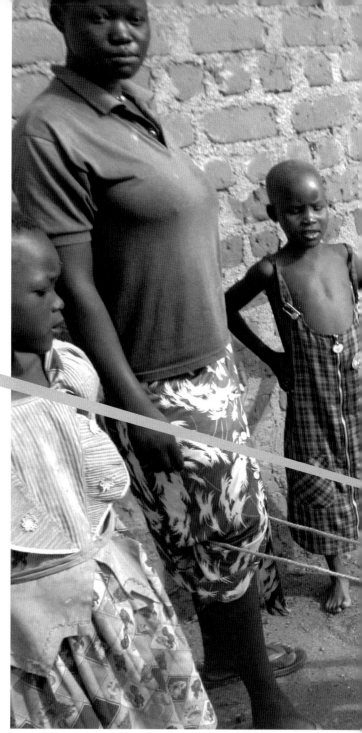

Uganda © UNICEF/NYHQ2004-1176/LeMoyne

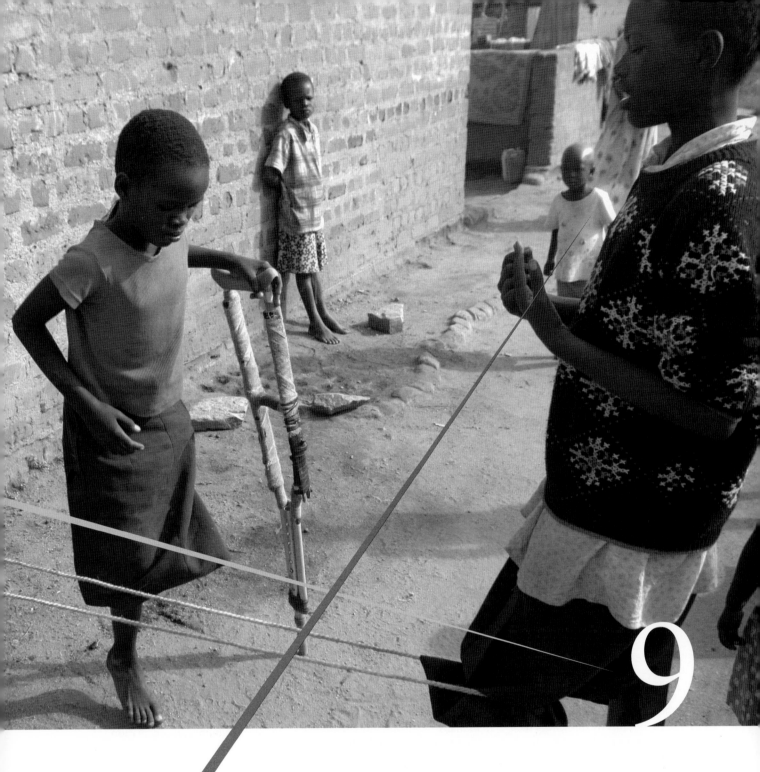

PREVENTING CONFLICT
AND BUILDING PEACE

9

United Nations Headquarters © UNICEF/NYHQ2002-0105/Markisz

GIVING FORM TO CONCEPT

Conflict prevention does not seek to end conflict per se but to replace violence or armed conflict with non-violent responses and resolution. Although conflicts are not always rational, finding ways to avoid them makes good sense. As some analysts argue, it is far less costly to prevent armed conflicts than to respond to them once they have started.[373] It is estimated that every dollar spent on prevention can potentially save the international community more than four dollars.[374]

Conflict prevention has come to mean taking a distinctly proactive stance in response to volatile situations. Since conflicts result from numerous influences at many levels, preventing them requires action at the local, national, regional and inter-regional levels. At the same time, a 'culture of peace' must be promoted, based on the principles of tolerance, rights, responsibilities, reconciliation and coexistence.

In the words of former UN Secretary-General Kofi Annan, preventing conflicts requires that we "understand their origins and seek to make violence a less reasonable option. We must also take care that preventive action does not ignore the underlying injustices or motivations that caused people to take up arms."[375]

In a passage more specific to children, the following statement, adopted at the 2000 International Conference on War-Affected Children in Winnipeg as a follow-up to the

More than a decade ago, Graça Machel challenged us to move forward, not just by mitigating the effects of war on children but by preventing it in the first place.

Preventing conflict and building peace are long-term processes that need to be sustainable. Establishing a foundation for peace means creating the systems and structures that allow for the full functioning of society, and creating the capacities that can help people resolve conflicts non-violently.

Children and young people must play a key role in this process – not only because peace and security are basic ingredients for the full realization of children's rights but

because children are such a large proportion of the world's people. In many countries, more than half the population is under the age of 25, and often under age 18.[372]

All too often, children are seen as victims and youth are belittled as a source of problems. If their energy is channelled creatively, however, children and young people can become powerful forces for peace. All conflict prevention strategies and interventions, both on the ground and at the policy level, should be pursued with the active participation of children and young people – in a way that is inclusive and matches their evolving capacities.

> **"I believe that a change can occur.**
> **War can be stopped."** – Young woman, 15, Pakistan

Machel study, also drew attention to root causes as well as practical measures to prevent conflict:

> States, international and regional organizations, NGOs, community leaders, the private sector and youth must address, in concrete terms, the root causes of conflict, including inequity, poverty, racism, ineffective governance and impunity, which lead to the denial of children's economic, social, cultural, civil and political rights. We commit to practical and comprehensive conflict prevention measures, including conflict prevention initiatives, mediation, child protection networks, early warning and response systems, alternatives for adolescents at risk, and the promotion of conflict resolution skills and education.[376]

Both conflict prevention and peace-building require the willingness and capacity of the population to resolve conflict by non-violent means, which must be sustained through generations. Yet sadly, one of the best predictors of future conflict is having recently emerged from one: About half the countries transitioning from war will likely slip back into conflict within a decade.[377] According to one assessment, all 'new' conflicts in 2005 and 2006 were actually post-conflict relapses.[378]

In response, and in order to draw international attention and resources to the 'transition gap' between humanitarian and develop-ment operations, the United Nations established a Peacebuilding Commis-sion in 2005. It now refers to 'peace-building' as a specific set of activities designed to assist post-accord countries in moving from war to sustainable peace.

However, there are inherent complexities in defining and measuring peace and conflict prevention. Despite the creation of the commission, no clearly articulated peacebuilding paradigm or timeline has emerged. A 2006 United Nations Capacity in Peace-building Inventory highlighted this as one of the greatest challenges in operationalizing peacebuilding and in determining what constitutes a 'successful' peace.[379] The same ambiguity remains today.

That said, two points are clear: First, peacebuilding and conflict prevention involve many of the same actions on the ground because they aim for the same outcome. Second, children and young people need to be an integral part of any peacebuilding or conflict prevention strategy or intervention, in any sector, for the results to be durable. In addition, child-specific indicators should be developed to measure peace.

WHAT THE MACHEL STUDY SAID

Graça Machel was very clear in 1996: We can spend a lot of energy and resources protecting children from the impact of war, but the most effective form of protection is to prevent war in the first place while promoting peace and reconciliation. "The International Community must shatter the political inertia that allows circumstances to escalate into armed conflict and destroy children's lives," the Machel study urged. "This means addressing the root causes of violence and promoting sustainable and equitable patterns of human development."

But the Machel study went beyond this, recognizing the fundamental nature of children's contributions to building a lasting peace in their societies. Mrs. Machel wrote that "part of putting children at the centre means using youth as a resource."

In 2007, the Machel review presented to the General Assembly emphasized the centrality of children to conflict prevention and peace-building by stating that all efforts should be made to integrate and mainstream children's concerns into such processes.

PROGRESS AND GAPS IN POLICY AND PRACTICE

Since the mid-1990s, the international community, including the United Nations, regional organizations and NGOs, has made some progress in building a foundation for peace.

Linking global and local efforts. In 2006, then Secretary-General Kofi Annan noted that a "culture of prevention" was taking root at the United Nations.[380] Policymakers

> **"We the children should raise our voices so more people listen to us. Some kids like me have the passion, but we just don't know how to do it."** –
> Boy, 14, Democratic People's Republic of Korea

and studies, including the World Report on Violence against Children, increasingly cite prevention as the way forward in terms of protecting children and young people and addressing their concerns.[381] The 2007 World Programme of Action for Youth pointed to peace and security as the chief elements necessary to achieve the goals it laid out.[382] And on 12 February 2008, the President of the Security Council said in a written statement: "The Security Council stresses … the need to adopt a broad strategy of conflict prevention, which addresses the root causes of armed conflict in a comprehensive manner, in order to enhance the protection of children on a long-term basis."[383]

Creating a culture of prevention and a culture of peace require building institutions and capacities at all levels. Although some progress has been made at the global level (particularly in policymaking) and at the country level, the links are few and far between. Country-level interventions are still not as strategic, systematized, well documented or supported as they should be. The opposite is also true – global policymaking is often not fully informed by country-level experiences.

Local knowledge and networks, linked internationally, are essential for effective strategies both to protect the rights of children and to enable them to contribute meaningfully. One noteworthy example is the Global Partnership for the Prevention of Armed Conflict, a network of more than 1,000 civil society organizations formed in 2005. As stated in its Global Action Agenda, effective strategies combine 'bottom-up' and 'top-down' action, but local ownership is essential.[384] While few child-focused or youth organizations have yet to become part of the network, the Global Partnership has selected peace education and conflict resolution in schools as the first pilot project for its Knowledge Generation and Sharing Network.[385] The Alliance of Civilizations, created in 2005 under the auspices of the United Nations, also identified youth as a priority for its work. In seeking to integrate a youth perspective into all its projects, including cross-cultural and inter-religious dialogues, the Alliance collaborates with broad networks of youth organizations around the world.[386]

Creating effective early warning systems. Conflict prevention, like any risk management strategy, also requires careful diagnosis and 'upstream' action, well before a crisis breaks out. Towards this end, effective early warning systems are essential. A growing number of institutions, both within and outside the UN system, now regularly monitor and analyse conflicts. A good deal of work has been done to develop indicators. But no systematic approach has yet evolved to bring together the diverse perspectives needed to identify situations in a way that will spark preventive action. The Inter-Agency Standing Committee is working towards this end. Comprised of UN and non-UN humanitarian groups focusing on disasters and conflict, the Committee regularly puts out an Early Warning/Early Action report through one of its working groups. But the influence of such reports on political decision-making is debatable.[387]

In addition, few organizations have integrated the impact on children and children's involvement into their criteria for predicting conflict. Monitoring and reporting mechanisms such as those implemented with Security Council Resolution 1612 can be useful in sounding the alarm to prevent further recruitment of children. But for a response to be truly preventive, action must take place at a much earlier stage.[388]

Early warning constitutes an important area of work only if it leads to early action. Such action remains rare, largely due to lack of political will and consensus. In fact, while a culture of prevention may be taking root conceptually, in many senses a 'culture of reaction' still prevails. Within the UN system there are a number of bodies, some bringing together various parts of the system, that can review situations and make decisions when a conflict is imminent. But making similar decisions earlier in the conflict cycle continues to be a challenge.

The early stage is when prevention can be most effective, and when children and young people have the greatest role to play. To the extent that their participation can involve them in creating stability and positive life options as alternatives to violence, so much the better. In Nepal, for example, schools were frequently caught in the crossfire between the army and non-state combatants. As part of a larger advocacy effort, children and children's clubs declared themselves to be 'zones of peace' and effectively spread the message that no one was allowed to enter school grounds with arms (see box on page 181).[389] In Sri Lanka, mothers came together to force those attempting to recruit children into combat out of their villages. And in Côte d'Ivoire, thousands of children participate in local recreation centres; as a result, few were drawn into the country's recent conflict.[390] Such early action needs to be strengthened, based on additional research and documentation.

The key question is this: Just as children's concerns are increasingly incorporated into peace agreements and negotiations, how can they be built into multilateral processes and national strategies to prevent conflict?

Developing mechanisms for post-conflict peacebuilding. The Peacebuilding Commission could be one entry point for addressing the concerns of children and young people as part of a peacebuilding strategy. Since its inception in 2005, the Commission has helped develop pilot programmes in Burundi, Guinea-Bissau and Sierra Leone. In Burundi and Sierra Leone,[391] youth have been identified as priorities, and relevant programmes have been recommended. This attention to youth is important, but it should not overshadow the rights of younger children. In-country UN leaders should ensure that children's concerns are incorporated and given priority.

At the same time, such efforts as the Peacebuilding Commission are limited in scope. Governments have primary responsibility to ensure integration of children's issues into all national and subnational peace-building strategies and frameworks, and to place these on the Commission's agenda. Donors must support these efforts financially, and the UN system must support them through its mandate, expertise and on-the-ground capacity for implementation.

Adopting conflict-sensitive approaches. Aid as well as development and humanitarian assistance can have unintended consequences on the dynamics of conflict. And all too often they are negative.

The non-neutrality of aid is becoming more widely understood by the international community and aid agencies. As a result, the use of conflict analysis tools and methodologies, such as peace and conflict impact assessments and 'do no harm' analyses, have gained traction in development and humanitarian practice since 1999. They have helped organizations design programmes that, at the very least, do not exacerbate tensions and, at best, contribute to prevention.[392] In March 2007, the UN Development Group's Working Group on Post-Crisis and Transition adopted a guidance tool on integrating prevention into UN country strategies. UN conflict analyses have also informed post-conflict needs assessments in Haiti, Somalia and the Sudan, among other countries, as well as a number of UN country strategies. Their use needs to be more systematic, however, and thus far, issues affecting children have been largely excluded.

Donors are increasingly identifying the need to look at peacebuilding and conflict prevention through this lens. But there has been little synergy in the way that peacebuilding agents engage with sector specialists working in related areas. And few agencies have developed sector-specific or cross-sectoral frameworks geared towards preventing conflict and building peace. In terms of programming focused on children, an early attempt to make these links was a matrix of indicators to identify the relationship between education and conflict, developed by the Canadian International Development Agency in 1999.[393] Organizations such as Save the Children have also begun to look at the impact of education on conflict and peace in their Rewrite the Future Campaign.[394]

EDUCATION AS A ROAD TO PEACE

Research commissioned by the Development Assistance Committee of the Organisation for Economic Co-operation and Development shows that well-managed, high-quality education systems can help prevent civil unrest and encourage conflict resolution, tolerance and reconciliation. They can also reduce both poverty and inequality, and lay the foundations for good governance and effective institutions.[395]

But while education can build bridges, education systems also have the potential to entrench or exacerbate existing inequalities and prejudices. "Schools are almost always complicit in conflict," a World Bank study pointed out. "They can reproduce skills, values, attitudes and social relations of dominant groups in society; accordingly they are usually a contributory factor in conflict."[396] As witnessed in Germany during the 1930s, for example, a government may intentionally manipulate teachers to enhance its power base. The content of both formal and informal educational materials can also be used to instil a logic and culture of violence and an unquestioning hatred of others.

Unhappily, education is still a scarce commodity in many countries, and competition for it can be a source of tension. In Burundi, for example, access to education was unequal along ethnic lines, prompting one scholar to caution, "If access to education remains unequal to Hutu, Tutsi and Twa, and if the glaring disparities in education provision between different provinces persist, the exclusion that is at the root of Burundi's conflict will remain and any peace agreement will be short-lived."[397]

Quality education that is free, safe and accessible to all children and young people is not only a basic right before, during and after conflict but a necessary component of prevention and sustainable peacebuilding. The 2008 global debate initiated by Save the Children on the critical links between education and peace has prompted calls for education to be systematically included in peace agreements. It has also led to recommendations to adopt children's safe access to and completion of quality education as criteria for measuring sustainable peace.

became a flashpoint in an attempt to consolidate a fragile peace.[398] But studies that aim to understand the consequences of aid and humanitarian assistance remain rare. This, in turn, limits the evidence base to inform development of conflict-sensitive approaches. Analysis that examines both the positive and negative impacts of aid on conflict needs to be more consistently conducted, at both the macro level and the project level, and at all stages.

In addition, many people still perceive that conflict sensitivity is only necessary in times of armed conflict, failing to recognize that aid can exacerbate tensions at any time and can also undermine efforts to prevent conflict. Similarly, just because an intervention is labelled as 'peacebuilding' does not necessarily mean it will have a positive impact on conflict.[399]

BUILDING A CULTURE OF PEACE

The Machel study recommended that all sectors of society come together to build 'ethical frameworks'. These should incorporate traditional values of cooperation among religious and community leaders with international legal obligations, such as the Convention on the Rights of the Child. Peace education is an important aspect of this. The Machel study recognized that peace education may not always be successful, nor enough on its own.

Research following the 2004 tsunami in Aceh (Indonesia) and Sri Lanka showed that, despite more use of analytic tools, conflict sensitivity is not yet a systematic component of aid programming. In Sri Lanka, for example, the huge influx of aid favouring populations displaced by the disaster over those who remained displaced by conflict

But the study emphasized that laying such groundwork is "indispensable to rebuilding shattered societies" and to conflict prevention.

Progress can be seen in terms of the global frameworks that have been established and in the burgeoning number of peace education initiatives. In 1998, the United Nations declared 2001–2010 to be the International Decade for a Culture of Peace and Non-Violence for the Children of the World. The designation was described as an attempt to inspire a global movement to foster peace by promoting "the principles of freedom, justice and democracy, all human rights, tolerance and solidarity." [400]

Teaching peace and non-violence. Peace education programmes aim to build capacity by developing knowledge, and cognitive, interpersonal and self-management skills, attitudes and values that prevent conflict and contribute to a culture of peace.[401] Such programmes often seek to reinforce empathy and tolerance and an appreciation of diversity, cooperation and respect. Others take a life-skills approach, emphasizing social and emotional development and HIV prevention as well as peer mediation and dispute resolution. Such programmes target both formal and informal education and take diverse forms, from developing school curricula and material to campaigns for peaceful coexistence using art, theatre or sports.

PROMOTING PEACE EDUCATION AMONG REFUGEES IN AFRICA

Since 1998 the Peace Education Programme has been carried out in camps and refugee settlements in 13 African countries, jointly implemented by INEE and UNHCR. It has now been incorporated into the education curricula of the Democratic Republic of the Congo, Kenya and Liberia – a testament to the programme's effectiveness. It covers both formal and non-formal community education for adults and out-of-school youth, based on the concept that peace is everyone's responsibility.

The programme methodology is rights-based. It centres on children's psychological and ethical development and is designed to promote skills that build positive and constructive behaviour. Many graduates have formed peace committees to minimize conflicts within and among communities; some youth groups have initiated sports and cultural events promoting non-violence. The programme has had a major, though unplanned, benefit on women's empowerment and power sharing within communities. One lesson already learned is that success depends on adults in the community reinforcing the skills and values children learn in school – and vice versa.[402]

Peace education has been applied in a range of contexts. In areas with ongoing conflict, programmes tend to respond to the effects of such conflict on children. In Aceh, for example,

UNICEF collaborated with local education experts to build conflict resolution and non-violence into the curricula of public and private schools. Peace education is offered

"There is an Icelandic word, *frekja*, which has no direct translation in the English language, but applies to pushiness, greed, cheek and nerve. To elbow our way to the front of a line is *frekja*. To snatch a toy from your sibling is *frekja*. To think that you have the right to cause others pain, mental or physical, is *frekja*. I believe that *frekja*, mixed with overbearing behaviour, is the cause of war." – Young woman, 16, Iceland

Central African Republic © UNICEF/ NYHQ2006-2592/Kamber

to refugees and internally displaced persons and in schools in returnee areas so that returning children and those who have remained can learn to live together again.

Other programmes focus on building a culture of peace in post-conflict settings or other contexts that may be at risk of violence. To reduce violence and reliance on arms among children and young people, for example, the Hague Appeal for Peace and the UN Department for Disarmament Affairs have developed initiatives for peace and disarmament in such post-conflict countries as Cambodia and Peru, and in countries such as Albania, where weapons still proliferate. Such programmes have reached out to children, educators, communities and government leaders in formal and informal education settings.

Special peace education projects for regions in transition, for example in Eastern Europe, include components such as human rights and democratic citizenship as well as anti-discrimination programming that promotes inclusion of children from minority groups, including the Roma. 'Citizen education' is included in many curricula around the world, whether there is open conflict or not, as a move towards conflict prevention.

Taking a critical look at peace education. While an impressive array of programmes can be cited, more effort is needed to understand their impact, both short term and long term. Also needed is more attention to monitoring and evaluating the components of these programmes to support an evidence base for their effectiveness.

Peace education for children and young people can sometimes be of questionable value, particularly in the middle of an intractable conflict, when adult role models still base their behaviour around conflict.[403] Entrenched attitudes towards the hostilities may be "deep-seated," according to a recent study, with "unchangeable convictions constituting the backbone of a group's collective narrative."[404]

Research conducted in the Occupied Palestinian Territory and Sri Lanka suggests that entrenched attitudes cannot be altered without taking into account everyday experiences of economic struggle or political unrest.[405] In situations of extreme hardship, peace education programmes may be out of sync with the harsh realities of daily life. Moreover, such programmes may detract from activities that children view as more pressing, such as acquiring food, water and other basic necessities.

Another approach to building a culture of peace is sponsoring exchange programmes for young people on opposite sides of a conflict. This could include, for example, exchanges between Palestinian and Israeli children or Greek and Turkish

Cypriots, in politically neutral locations outside contested areas or areas of hostilities. But caution is necessary. Although they can be valuable, exchange programmes have sometimes resulted in questionable outcomes, especially when children are placed face to face with peers who may not have experienced the same hardships resulting from war. Research has shown this can increase frustration and alienation and, at worst, be counterproductive.[406]

ADDRESSING ROOT CAUSES OF CONFLICT

Since children and young people are integral to successful peacebuilding, they must also be part of any attempt to address the structural and more immediate causes of conflict. Many observers think of political agreements, security, economic development or good governance as key to peacebuilding and prevention. What they often fail to see is the role that children can play in these processes.

There are implications for children under each of these categories, not only in terms of their potentially positive – or negative, if neglected – impact, but also in terms of how 'getting it right' will enhance children's contributions to peacebuilding in their communities for years to come.

A number of sectors require new thinking and holistic approaches to address long-standing problems and prevent future flashpoints. For example, disparities in access to

education can affect future employment opportunities and become the seeds of conflict. Similarly, education without the possibility of employment can also breed dissent.

It is clear that many international organizations and NGOs committed to working for children's rights now see peacebuilding and conflict prevention as important components of their work. The Christian Children's Fund, Save the Children, UNICEF and War Child Holland, for example, all have peacebuilding programmes that actively engage children. But for peace to last, these interventions need to be strategic, systematized, supported, and linked to national and international mechanisms. In addition, improved programming requires assembling and sharing a body of evidence on children and peacebuilding.

As UNICEF's post-crisis strategy points out, it is not about doing more during this time, it is about doing more things differently. Below is a brief discussion of the sectors that should be addressed:

Promoting good governance. The development of good governance is key to addressing equity and accountability. It covers a range of activities, including strengthening public administration, and requires the establishment of government systems that reflect the needs of the whole population, including children and young people.

Post-conflict situations offer a window of opportunity for changing systems of governance: Constitutions can be rewritten or new legislation devised, including laws that relate

---

DRAWING YOUTH INTO PEACEBUILDING IN LIBERIA

It is a widely held view in Liberia that the country's conflict was fuelled by disenfranchised youth. As part of the peacebuilding process, therefore, the country carried out extensive consultations nationwide and hosted a National Youth Conference in 2005, all of which fed into the development of a National Youth Policy.

The policy has been generally well received. It raised the profile of youth issues and empowered youth organizations to take part, actively and formally, in high-level processes, including the Truth and Reconciliation Commission and the National Electoral Commission. However, awareness of the policy still needs to be raised, especially in rural districts. Another positive outcome appears to be improved perceptions of youth by adults, many of whom previously held condescending views of the younger generation's potential.[407]

> **"I volunteer my time because I want the community to know someone cares about them."** – Young man, age not specified, Uganda

specifically to children. Electoral democracy often receives high priority in post-conflict contexts, but it often excludes adolescents at the very point when it is strategically important to give them political alternatives to violence. This, too, needs to be addressed by supporting young people to participate in certain aspects of the political process. The failure to do so in South Africa, for example, led many young people to feel alienated and betrayed – after having fought actively in the struggle against apartheid.[408]

Programming options include youth organizations, youth participation in community decision-making and media made by young people for young people, as well as non-traditional forms of expression, such as music and theatre, that give young people a public voice. 'Golden Kids News', a popular Sierra Leone radio programme 'by kids and for kids', is an example of how young people can get their opinions heard and kick-start debate on issues important to them.[409]

Developing national youth policies is another way to ensure that youth can contribute to democratic governance. These policies should be drafted with the active participation of youth representatives, reflecting their diverse regions, ages, gender and social strata, especially including those who are marginalized. This approach can promote accountability to young people, place them on the

political agenda and ensure they are not excluded from the political process.

Such policies and processes should define the role of youth in society, and the responsibility of society to youth. Their purpose should be threefold: to enable youth to identify major issues that affect them; to promote the establishment of services and structures to meet their needs; and to encourage youth to participate in decision-making processes.[410]

Reforming the security sector. Children and youth routinely talk about the need for safety and security as a primary concern.[411] A secure environment is vital for their development and for accessing basic services. Without it they cannot participate meaningfully in building peace in their communities. Girls, moreover, have specific security requirements.

Security sector reform is now recognized as a core peacebuilding activity. It comprises strengthening government strategic planning, justice systems, accountability mechanisms and civilian oversight of the military. Just as peacekeeping missions have standards and policies specific to children, they must not be overlooked when supporting States in developing or reforming their security sectors. This is true both from a human security standpoint (i.e., ensuring children's safety) and as a measure to prevent conflict. Post-conflict countries such as El Salvador

and Guatemala have high rates of criminality in part because of poor demilitarization and security sector reform. Furthermore, repressive policies that routinely violate the rights of young people have become the norm to combat criminality in a number of countries in the Latin America and Caribbean region.[412]

It is vital to listen to how children themselves perceive their security and to consider their priorities when designing policy and programmes. While this is increasingly recognized, children's ability to play active roles in creating safe spaces in which they can grow and flourish is often overlooked. One arena in which children can have a big impact is at the community level. In Zambia, for example, children were instrumental in creating school councils that are helping curb violence in educational institutions; in Angola, children are reporting on violations of their rights.[413] Such actions can also place children in stronger positions to negotiate with adults to prevent unacceptable behaviour or violence.[414]

Creating well-functioning judicial systems. Well-functioning judicial systems, including those for juvenile justice, are essential to protect children and fulfil their rights. Doing this correctly means respecting human rights: Because children in conflict with the law often suffer from social and economic hardships and are denied their basic rights, good justice systems go hand in hand with equitable development.

In post-conflict countries, achieving a balance between reconciliation and justice is all-important. Research has shown that to restore respect for the rule of law and children's sense of justice it is important that perpetrators be held accountable for their actions. When they are not, a lingering sense of injustice can contribute to the desire for revenge and ongoing social tensions.

Children and young people also need to have a role in reconciliation efforts. Not only have they been victimized by war, many have been perpetrators as well: those children and young people who have been associated with armed groups also need a chance to heal and be accepted back into their communities. Children have contributed to national reconciliation processes in a number of countries, including Guatemala and South Africa. But what stands out most is their role in Sierra Leone's Truth and Reconciliation Commission (see box in chapter 6, 'Children's participation in truth and reconciliation commissions'). The key is to ensure that children's contributions to such processes are not mere tokenism but are truly meaningful and will lead to genuine reform.

A significant challenge to building peace is ensuring that communities receive the attention they deserve. Communities bear the brunt of war but can often feel detached from broader national reconciliation efforts. Effective reconciliation at the community level lies at the heart of converting societies from cultures of war to cultures of peace. It is also at the local level where children and young people often play the most effective and powerful roles.

In Rwanda, children and young people have come together to create

CHILDREN AS ZONES OF PEACE[415]

The idea that a gathering of children should constitute a 'zone of peace' – that is, a place where children are safeguarded and have access to essential services – first emerged during the 1980s. Agreements were negotiated between warring parties to stop the bloodshed during what were called 'days of tranquillity' or 'corridors of peace', the first of which was an immunization campaign in El Salvador.[416] The idea has transformed considerably since the early days. It is now being implemented more systematically to prevent some of the harmful effects of war on children and to promote their participation in peacebuilding.

During the conflict in Nepal, for example, children put the concept into practice in partnership with government officials. They began by cultivating the idea that schools, which had sometimes been used as recruiting grounds for children, should be safe havens. The concept caught on and led to formation of a national coalition as well as public commitment of support by five major political parties. Child protection guidelines for security forces were subsequently circulated by the Office of the Prime Minister. When the Government declared schools to be zones of peace, the edict was respected by both warring parties.[417] Now, in a post-conflict environment, the Children as Zones of Peace initiative supports government efforts to set up comprehensive child protection systems at all levels. Child representatives now attend village protection committees – one clear sign that the programme is on the right track.

Sudan © UNICEF/NYHQ2006-2191/Cranston

a theatre festival that explores an aspect of their history that is yet to be taught in schools. As an informal education programme, the plays offer a new way for audiences to reflect on the theme of reconciliation as it relates to the recent genocide and to build solutions for the future.[418]

Creating employment, supporting livelihoods and delivering basic services. In the post-war context, securing alternative livelihoods for youth going through a disarmament, demobilization and reintegration process often depends on wider economic growth and on creating institutional capacity to support ex-combatants in society.[419] Many

current and former child soldiers express fear of going back to situations where they had no schools, no skills and no prospects. They often cite poverty as a factor driving them to join armed groups in the first place.[420]

"The term reintegration of ex-combatants is somehow a peculiar one," says one expert, reflecting on the situation in Sierra Leone. "It suggests that the ex-combatants need to be supported and equipped to make their re-entry to peaceful society successful, but does not ask if there is still something into which to reintegrate."[421]

For long-term peacebuilding to succeed, sustainable economic development must take root.

Recognizing that employment creation, income generation and reintegration are key to peacebuilding, a new UN system-wide policy paper will present guiding principles to improve coherence and strategy formulation, and to help scale up and coordinate efforts.

Delivery of basic services is equally important, and particular care must be taken to ensure that they are available during post-conflict reconstruction and recovery. This requires adequate levels of education, health care and nutrition, along with construction or reconstruction of infrastructure to allow delivery of services. Special attention must be paid to reaching women, children and young people.

As discussed in depth in earlier chapters, a critical factor in peace-building and conflict prevention is ensuring that people have access to basic services – including but not limited to displaced persons or returning refugees. Inequitable distribution of services can increase geographical and social disparities and reinforce simmering grievances.

RECOMMENDATIONS

The primary recommendation of this strategic review echoes the emphasis of the Machel study in 1996: The best way to protect children and young people from armed conflict is to prevent wars and to build peace. Recommendations that speak specifically to engaging children and young people in peacebuilding and conflict prevention follow:

1. **Invest more heavily in conflict prevention.** Governments have the primary responsibility for preventing structural and more immediate causes of armed conflict. The international community and the United Nations play a supporting role, and they should invest in strengthening national capacities for peace and conflict prevention. This involves both government and civil society, including children and young people.

2. **Promote the links between child rights and conflict prevention/ peacebuilding.** Governments, the United Nations, and local and international civil society must systematically build the links between the rights of children and their involvement in conflict prevention and peacebuilding – both vertically, from the local to the international level, and 'sideways', in on-the-ground operations and peacebuilding processes.

3. **Empower children and young people to be forces for peace and conflict prevention.** Children and young people are an integral part of successful efforts to prevent conflict and build peace. It follows that they must be specifically included in any attempt to address the structural and more immediate

causes of conflict. Programming should be designed to enable their participation and be appropriate to their evolving capacities, and it should reflect their contributions and perspectives. This must not be a token exercise; rather, it should be followed by concrete action.

4. **Ensure that all development and humanitarian programming is sensitive to conflicts.** Humanitarian and development actors, UN Member States, UN agencies and NGOs should assess the impact of their programmes and strategies on conflict and peace. The goal is to better understand potential risk factors, underlying tensions, and the capacities of children and youth to both prevent conflict and build peace. This includes improved integration of issues

affecting children into broader conflict resolution and peacebuilding interventions. All programming for children should be more conflict-sensitive.

5. **Assemble and share a body of evidence on children and peacebuilding and conflict prevention.** All actors, including Member States, UN agencies and civil society, should monitor and evaluate peacebuilding programming to assess the capacities of children and young people in this role. A body of evidence should be established, which could then provide guidance in applying conflict-sensitive approaches to development, post-conflict transition and emergency phases of programming. ■

KEY RESOURCES

'Children and Security Sector Reform', Geneva Centre for the Democratic Control of Armed Forces (DCAF), <www.dcaf.ch/children-security/_publications.cfm>.

Global Campaign for Peace Education, <www.haguepeace.org/index.php?action>.

Global Partnership for the Prevention of Armed Conflict, <www.gppac.net>.

Inter-Agency Network for Education in Emergencies (INEE) Peace Education Programme, <www.ineesite.org/peaceed>.

United Nations Peacebuilding Commission, <www.un.org/peace/peacebuilding/>.

United Nations Headquarters © UNICEF/NYHQ2007-1548/Markisz

10

YOUNG PEOPLE
DEMAND ACTION

> **"Above all, children who have survived conflict must tell their stories, while the rest of us must listen and act upon what we hear." –**
> Young woman, 17, United Kingdom

During preparation of this 10-year review of the Machel study, the views of 1,700 children in 92 countries were sought to help pave the way forward. The material was gathered in a 'Voices of Youth' companion booklet and launched as part of the presentation to the General Assembly in 2007. The booklet highlighted eight specific requests – or 'demands', in the words of the children – that they would like to see implemented in their communities and across the globe:

- We want our rights to be respected.

- We want justice and to be safe from violence.

- We want to learn.

- We want to be healthy.

- We want jobs and a means to survive.

- We want more support and care for the excluded and forgotten.

- We just want to be children.

- We want to participate.

Since the focus of this report is on action, a follow-up survey was subsequently undertaken among youth-led organizations to seek ways to satisfy these demands. Youth organizations are often even better positioned than those headed by adults to understand and connect with other children and young people. And because of their experience, many of these organizations can provide practical suggestions about the resources and support needed to be effective at the grass roots. The energy, insight and creativity with which children responded were strong evidence that they are determined and capable of being positive forces for change in their societies.

Although the time and resources available for the follow-up survey allowed only limited outreach, positive responses came from youth organizations in Afghanistan, Cambodia, the Democratic Republic of the Congo, Haiti, Iraq, Somalia and Timor-Leste. The organizations were asked to review the eight demands listed above, consult with members of their organizations and communities, and answer the following questions:

1. What are the three most urgent demands in your community?

2. What needs to be done to realize those demands?

3. What support do children, young people and their organizations need to contribute to this change?

The participating organizations, which work at the community level on issues ranging from the protection of child rights to media training to conflict resolution, included:

- **Health and Development Centre for Afghan Women (Kabul, Afghanistan):** It implements projects related to women's rights and gender-based violence against girls and women in Afghanistan through work in the areas of health, education, vocational training and capacity building.

- **People's Health Development Association (Phnom Penh, Cambodia):** It offers life skills training and health services, a youth centre and counselling for young people in Phnom Penh.

- **Action des jeunes pour le Développement Communautaire et la Paix (Goma, Democratic Republic of the Congo):** It advocates for human rights and for protection of marginalized children and youth. It also provides training and safe spaces for peaceful dispute resolution.

- **Concelho Nacional Juventude de Timor-Leste (Timor-Leste):** It enhances the capacity of youth organizations through facilitation and bridging with government and donor agencies. It also facilitates community reintegration through dialogue and peace campaigns.

- **Union des Amis Socio Culturels d'Action en Développement (Port-au-Prince, Haiti):** It supports the creation of local youth groups and provides materials and training on education, health care, human rights and the environment.

- **Iraqi Democratic Coalition for Youth Empowerment (Baghdad, Iraq):** It improves opportunities for young people by providing literacy and leadership training, and advocates for children's and women's rights.

- **Youth Development Organization (Bosaso, Somalia):** It offers youth development programmes in sports, education, health and job creation and trains young people in using the media to reach out to their communities.

CALLS FOR ACTION

The most urgent call made by these youth-led organizations is to be free to grow into adulthood safe from violence of any kind. They made it clear that when armed conflict compromises children's security, wholesale violations of child rights follow.

Without security, children and young people are denied the right to attend school, to play and compete with each other, and to learn the skills necessary for future jobs. They are denied the right to participate in decision-making that affects their lives, their communities, their countries and the world.

The role of the community is paramount. In their recommendations, children and young people emphasize the importance of looking for solutions through dialogue with parents and local elders. Families and communities are seen as best equipped to respond to children's educational, health and psychosocial needs, and to foster peace and tolerance.

Most of the recommendations recognize that the State bears principal responsibility for protecting and caring for children, especially those who are abused and exploited. But youth-led organizations also pressed their case for change in their communities, noting the obligation of governments to help foster changes through better implementation and monitoring of policies already in place. Theconcerns raised most frequently follow, along with examples of more specific recommendations:

Security and justice

Young people ask for stronger legislation and better enforcement of the rule of law, especially in rural areas. They see clear links between security and peacebuilding, peace education, and constructive dialogue between youth and authorities. In their responses, they emphasize preventive measures that foster peace and tolerance within their communities. More specifically, they suggest:

- Providing educational opportunities on the topics of peace and tolerance as an alternative to 'hate campaigns' (the Democratic Republic of the Congo);

- Training police forces, judicial officials and those involved in custodial care on issues related to justice for children (Somalia);

- Organizing training courses for parents on peaceful coexistence and non-violent conflict resolution (Iraq).

Access to basic services

Young people see education, health care and nutritious food as vital to their development. They suggest that NGOs and humanitarian organizations focus on reaching areas where governments are unable or unwilling to provide basic services. Where education is not available for all or families cannot afford to send children to school, they want more support for home schooling and financial incentives for parents. Young people also ask for youth-friendly information about health, diseases and nutrition, and they push for youth-friendly services in health centres.

More specifically, youth organizations suggest:

- Offering home schooling as an alternative in communities where schooling for girls remains a challenge (Afghanistan);

- Improving the quality of community health services and protecting the rights of young clients (Cambodia);

- Supporting young people in providing information to their peers on topics that are relevant to their lives, for example, through youth magazines (Somalia).

Cultural and recreational opportunities

Young people ask for safe spaces and community centres where children can play, interact and develop freely.

They suggest that these places be managed in partnership with young people and community leaders. They also ask for more opportunities to engage in cultural and artistic events where they can express themselves. More specifically, they suggest:

- Building playgrounds and recreational facilities in schools, and making safe, child-friendly spaces available at beaches, libraries and museums (Timor-Leste);

- Encouraging schools to organize cultural and artistic activities such as theatre and music (Iraq);

- Creating public places and sponsoring activities that can reduce idleness and stress among children and youth (Haiti).

Employment opportunities

Young people ask for vocational training and skills development programmes matched to the local labour market. They also propose that incentives be provided to encourage young people to become entrepreneurs in a wide variety of areas, including tackling environmental degradation. Governments can use public work schemes to offer employment to young people, but young people also recognize that there are opportunities in war-torn countries where the private sector is often a step ahead in supporting livelihoods. More specifically, they suggest:

- Ensuring that vocational programmes reach out to both female and male students (Afghanistan);

- Cooperating with local youth councils to provide technical and vocational training for young people in their communities (Cambodia);

- Providing microcredit to poor families (especially women) and young people to enable them to earn a living and to fight off hunger (Haiti and Iraq);

- Promoting youth employment and economic opportunities as a mechanism to combat marginalization, neglect and socio-economic violence against children and young people (the Democratic Republic of the Congo).

Engagement and participation

Young people ask for genuine opportunities to participate and to engage in dialogue with communities and governments. The surveys cite the importance of various mechanisms for this engagement, ranging from development of national youth policies, representation in government decision-making bodies and youth structures in schools or local NGOs. In short, young people recognize that there are ample opportunities for their involvement because all of these bodies initiate programmes and activities that affect their lives. However, they would like to see a

more diverse group of youth representing their needs, a group that extends beyond the urban and more fortunate young people who often sit on national youth committees and councils. More specifically, youth organizations suggest:

- Increasing the participation of youth who are socially and economically marginalized and giving them the skills to participate effectively (the Democratic Republic of the Congo);

- Creating youth councils and networks that can develop policies and programmes, with support from and in collaboration with communities, NGOs, the government and donors (Cambodia);

- Facilitating the creation of groups and networks that enable young people to organize themselves and address problems in their communities (Haiti).

WHAT DO YOUNG PEOPLE NEED?

Throughout the consultation process for this review, children and young people expressed a strong desire to participate in decisions that directly and indirectly affect them. Youth organizations – and by extension, young people at large – need support for legitimate and effective participation.

The biggest constraint for many youth organizations is lack of funding.

Although young people can accomplish great things through volunteering and the creative use of their own (often limited) resources, funding is required to build strong organizations and create programmes that reach and involve marginalized youth.

Many young people are well aware of the needs in their communities, but they often lack management experience and the knowledge of how to work within 'the system'. Young people need skills training on such issues as project management and grant writing as well as technical training in advocacy and policy work.

Young people want to work hand in hand with adults to find solutions for problems in their communities and countries. They have the creativity and energy to make a difference, but they benefit from the experience and guidance of adults.

The youth-led organizations consulted also had a clear vision of their potential contributions through children's parliaments, councils and other mechanisms. Although they expect their governments to provide them with the necessary space to operate, they want to maintain their independence, make their own decisions, undertake awareness campaigns on key issues, mobilize their peers, and serve as a link between their communities and governments.

Finally, those consulted want to be supported as they reach out to other youth organizations, young people and children living in similar circumstances. These networks provide them with a sense of solidarity and shared understanding. Together they can identify ideas and activities that have worked and can learn from each other.

MOVING FORWARD

The youth-led organizations that were consulted emphasized that solutions need to be rooted in their communities. Nevertheless, they also recognized that governments and the international community have an important role to play in ensuring that the right policies are in place and are implemented.

In order to move towards full and effective implementation of the demands expressed by children and young people, youth organizations proposed the following priorities:

- Improved security in their communities brought about by child-friendly judicial procedures and a greater focus on prevention and peacebuilding measures;

- Alternative approaches to ensure that they receive basic services, including improved access to health-related information and context-appropriate educational opportunities as well as stronger outreach to rural areas;

- Spaces to engage with their peers and to express themselves through various mediums, including culture, music and sports;

- Opportunities to develop livelihood skills and greater support for employment schemes that reflect the needs of their communities;

- Institutionalized channels for their active and sustained participation so they can help shape the decisions that affect their lives;

- Greater resources and guidance as they organize themselves to work with their peers, adults and others in tackling the challenges in their communities. ■

KEY RESOURCE

Office of the Special Representative of the Secretary-General for Children and Armed Conflict, Global Youth Action Network, UNFPA, UNICEF and Women's Commission for Refugee Women and Children, *"Will You Listen?" Young voices from conflict zones,* companion booklet to the 10-year Machel Strategic Review, UNICEF, New York, October 2007.

Liberia © UNICEF/NYHQ2007-2212/Pirozzi

11

LOOKING AHEAD: A PLATFORM OF RECOMMENDATIONS AND KEY ACTIONS

The following recommendations elaborate upon the findings presented to the United Nations General Assembly in 2007 and are the result of intensive consultation between Member States, UN agencies, non-governmental organizations, development professionals and experts.

As demonstrated throughout this publication, we must re-galvanize our political will, moral resolve and actions in the field to maintain progress and fulfil the vision and recommendations of Graça Machel's 1996 study. In addition to Mrs. Machel's detailed recommendations, the commitments adopted during the past decade by Member States through the General Assembly – especially the principles outlined in A World Fit for Children – the Security Council, regional bodies and other mechanisms provide the benchmarks for our next steps.

RECOMMENDATIONS

A. ACHIEVE UNIVERSAL IMPLEMENTATION OF INTERNATIONAL NORMS AND END IMPUNITY

Recommendation 1: Achieve universal adherence to international standards and norms

(a) Member States must uphold existing international standards and operationalize those obligations through accelerated national legislative reform and systematic implementation and monitoring:

- Member States and UN agencies should establish procedures to ensure that conclusions and recommendations of the Security Council Working Group on Children and Armed Conflict, the Committee on the Rights of the Child, the Human Rights Council and other bodies are strategically disseminated to groups including civil society, children, the public, non-state armed actors and professionals working in related areas, such as members of the police, the judiciary and the military as well as medical, immigration and refugee authorities.

- Civil society actors such as national human rights institutions and NGOs should be supported to elaborate and submit independent reports on the implementation of treaties including the Convention on the Rights of the Child and the Optional Protocol on the Involvement of Children in Armed Conflict to relevant treaty bodies.

- To establish benchmarks by which to measure further implementation, civil society actors should be supported at the national level in providing sustained follow-up to the recommendations of relevant treaty bodies, including monitoring.

(b) Member States and the United Nations system should continue to review the need for further legal instruments and mechanisms for compliance:

- The Human Rights Council should ensure that concluding observations and recommendations by the Committee on the Rights of the Child on reports submitted by States parties on the implementation of the Optional Protocol on Children and Armed Conflict form the basis of the Universal Periodic Review.

- The Universal Periodic Review mechanism of the Human Rights Council should integrate information on grave violations against children in situations of conflict, in accordance with Member States' compliance with their obligations under international human rights and humanitarian institutions.

(c) All Member States and other stakeholders should formally endorse relevant standards and guidelines that enhance the protection of children and ensure their systematic implementation:

- Member States, civil society organizations, UN agencies and international NGOs should further incorporate legal and

"We ARE the future, and people should be aware of that. Right now, we are inheriting a very unstable world." – Young woman, 16, Colombia

programme standards on children and armed conflict in organizational policy and operational documents, such as standard operating procedures, manuals and strategic plans. In this regard, it will be useful for the Committee on the Rights of the Child to consider the implementation of these standards and guidelines in their recommendations on Member States' efforts to translate international law into domestic law.

■ Progress towards harmonization of inter-agency, government and donor standards should be systematically monitored through a standard framework of indicators and benchmarks.

■ The Inter-Agency Standing Committee should ensure that standards pertaining to conflict-affected children are incorporated in new cluster guidelines and assessment tools. In particular, the Common Humanitarian Action Plan guidelines should require clear articulation of child-related strategic objectives.

Recommendation 2: End impunity for violations against children

(a) Member States must ensure systematic and timely investigation and prosecution of crimes against children in the context of armed conflict and provide assistance to victims.

(b) Member States should apply targeted measures, including sanctions where appropriate, against individuals, parties to conflict and other entities within their jurisdiction, including the private sector, that persistently commit or are complicit in the commission of grave violations against children in situations of armed conflict:

■ The Security Council should establish mechanisms that make it possible to take sanction measures in all situations of concern regarding the children and armed conflict agenda, including the exploration of establishing a sanctions committee. The Security Council should give equal priority to all categories of grave violations and all relevant situations of concern.

■ All Member States should adopt specific measures towards ending impunity for violations against children in armed conflict. Such measures may include, inter alia, adopting extraterritorial provisions for relevant crimes; ensuring national provisions are in compliance with rules and provisions of the International

Criminal Court; applying the universality principle where relevant; ensuring that domestic legislation criminalizes arms trade to countries with a record of illegally recruiting and using child soldiers; and adopting provisions that address money laundering and permit freezing the assets of persons or legal entities accused of grave violations against children in armed conflict.

(c) For the purpose of child protection, the United Nations should, when possible, undertake dialogue with parties to conflict, including non-state actors, and develop systems to hold non-state actors accountable:

■ The United Nations should, when possible, engage in dialogue and support the development of concrete and time-bound action plans with all parties to conflict to halt recruitment and use of children in violation of applicable international law, and to address all violations and abuses against children in close cooperation with the Office of the Special Representative of the Secretary-General as well as with UNICEF and the UN country task forces on monitoring and reporting. Continuous monitoring and verification of action plans should be ensured.

Recommendation 3: Prioritize children's security

(a) In all security-related matters, parties to conflict should recall that child rights are non-derogable and should ensure that children are protected from death, injury, harm, arbitrary arrest and detention, torture and other cruel, inhuman and degrading treatment.

(b) All parties to conflict must ensure safe and unhindered access to and delivery of humanitarian assistance to all children in collaboration with humanitarian agencies:

- To address the challenges of responding in insecure environments, Member States, UN agencies and non-governmental organizations should work collaboratively to develop common approaches and specific advocacy efforts for improved humanitarian access.

- Concerned governments and other relevant actors should ensure greater security and safety of refugee and internally displaced communities in and around camps and settlements.

(c) Member States should fulfil commitments under the Programme of Action to Prevent, Combat and Eradicate the Illicit Trade in Small Arms and Light Weapons in All Its Aspects (UN document A/CONF.192/15) at the national, regional and global levels. They

should implement existing legal instruments that address landmines and explosive remnants of war and develop a legally binding instrument on cluster munitions:

- States should review their domestic legislation and practice in order to halt the illicit transfer of small arms and light weapons to countries where grave violations against children are committed. Violations of arms embargoes should be criminalized and prosecuted.

- Member States should include in their national reports under the UN Programme of Action information on measures taken or needed to protect children from small arms and light weapons.

- States are encouraged to ratify the Convention on Cluster Munitions adopted in May 2008 and actively support its implementation.

Recommendation 4: Strengthen monitoring and reporting

(a) Member States, United Nations entities and non-governmental organizations must establish an inclusive system with a common framework, including agreed indicators and provisions for the disaggregation of data and for the timely collection, verification, analysis and reporting of

information on all impacts on children and violations of their rights; human and financial resources must be increased to support these activities:

- All key stakeholders, including Member States, UN entities and non-governmental organizations, are urged to dedicate greater levels of human and financial resources in order to consolidate the monitoring, reporting and response mechanism. Because they are an integral part of the global Monitoring and Reporting Mechanism, donors should continue to fund activities that prevent and respond to grave violations against children and support should be given to building the capacities of partners and systems at national and local levels.

(b) Regarding Security Council Resolution 1612 (2005), the capacities of the UN entities charged with implementation of the mechanism should be enhanced as appropriate, at both the field and the Headquarters level:

- The Security Council Working Group on Children and Armed Conflict established pursuant to Resolution 1612 (2005) should also ensure that it has adequate capacity and support for the timely consideration of reports as well as preparation, delivery

Georgia © UNICEF/NYHQ2008-0689/Volpe

and follow-up to its conclusions and recommendations.

Recommendation 5: Promote justice for children

(a) Member States should uphold international standards, norms and guidelines on juvenile justice and ensure that their national legislation and systems treat all juveniles in a manner that takes into account their particular vulnerability – including ensuring access to legal assistance; focusing on prevention and reintegration; resorting to detention only as a last recourse; and ensuring separation of juveniles from adults when they are detained:

- Member States, in cooperation with donors, UN entities and non-governmental organizations, should establish or sustain a national system that includes a distinct juvenile justice system and promotes diversion, alternatives to deprivation of liberty and restorative approaches.

- The policies and programmes of UN agencies should be aligned with the 'Guidance Note of the Secretary-General: UN Approach to Justice for Children' (September 2008). Both Member States and UN agencies should aim to integrate children's concerns in legislative, judicial and security sector reforms, including those of law enforcement institutions such as the police.

(b) Member States should promote the rule of law by ensuring children's access to justice; obstacles that affect children within legal systems should be identified and addressed:

- To improve children's access to justice, the United Nations and NGOs should support community-based legal and paralegal services for children, families and communities as well as the legal empowerment of children and their communities.

(c) Member States should establish child-friendly mechanisms to promote the participation of children in the decisions that affect them and the protection of children in all justice systems, including transitional justice processes.

- Member States and the international community should support the participation of children in transitional justice processes in line with the child's best interest and draw on good practices with regard to child-protective measures and child-friendly procedures; in addition, they should provide adequate resources to support the transitional justice processes, related programmes for children and their inclusion in reparations programmes.

B. CARE FOR AND PROTECT CHILDREN IN ARMED CONFLICT

Recommendation 6: Ensure access to basic services

(a) Member States must ensure the continuity of an integrated package of such basic services as education, health, nutrition, water and sanitation, HIV and AIDS initiatives, reproductive health, psychological support and social services; the availability of these services should be ensured and all barriers to access removed, including costs:

- Inter-Agency Standing Committee members (UN and non-governmental organizations) should continue to work together to develop and strengthen common tools for integrated rapid assessments and other information management instruments; in addition, they should ensure that data are adequately disaggregated by age group, gender, ethnicity and other key criteria.

(b) United Nations entities, non-governmental organizations and donors should ensure that support for basic services is aligned with government systems, including when delivered by non-state providers, and is sustained through all phases of a conflict:

We must re-galvanize our political will, moral resolve and actions in the field to maintain progress and fulfil the vision and recommendations of Graça Machel's 1996 study.

- UN agencies and international NGOs should support the objective to transfer functions to government and civil society; this requires gradual integration of actions into policies, plans and programmes while building and strengthening national capacities.

- In order to scale up activities and increase benefits for children, the integration of sectors and systems should be emphasized to facilitate the coordination of a response between national governments, members of civil society and international actors. Donors and international partners must take into consideration that this will be a long-term process and must be willing to commit resources to its success.

Recommendation 7: Support inclusive reintegration strategies

(a) Stakeholders should ensure that release and reintegration strategies and activities are in line with the Paris Commitments and Principles, as well as Integrated Disarmament, Demobilization and Reintegration Standards; among other things, they should be inclusive of all conflict-affected girls and boys:

- UN agencies and international organizations and NGOs should ensure that reintegration standards are rights-based and adhere to inclusive community-based approaches and multi-sectoral programming, as well as have a strong emphasis on gender-sensitive and age-appropriate support.

- UN agencies and international NGOs should advocate for a biannual funding review of reintegration support to ensure that funding is long term and flexible, and that programme funding gaps are filled.

(b) Strategies should ensure long-term sustainability and community-based approaches, with emphasis on education and livelihood support, including youth-oriented employment strategies and market analyses; particular attention should be given to girls, including ensuring confidential access to reintegration support to mitigate stigmatization:

- Member States, UN agencies and NGOs must better integrate reintegration concerns for children into broader national strategies and socio-economic frameworks. They should heavily emphasize links between education, skills training and socio-economic development as an important goal for peace-building and a strategy to prevent recruitment and re-recruitment.

- Donors and protection agencies should invest more funding on research and evaluation to enhance the knowledge base on reintegration support, in particular on the well-being of children who do not participate in formal demobilization processes.

Recommendation 8: End gender-based violence

(a) Member States, with support from UN agencies and non-governmental organizations, should give priority to protecting children from gender-based violence by adopting appropriate national legislation and ensuring systematic and timely investigation and prosecution of such crimes, in accordance with the wishes of survivors:

- UN agencies, relevant ministries and NGOs should collaborate through the UN Action against Sexual Violence in Conflict initiative to scale up assistance for child survivors. This includes multi-sectoral prevention and response; attention to child-specific, gender-sensitive and age-appropriate approaches; and integration of free services for survivors into existing institutions.

(b) All stakeholders must give particular attention to the specific needs of child survivors as distinct from those of adults and ensure that adequate resources are invested in community-awareness campaigns and education initiatives that seek to reach boys and men as well as girls and women:

- To challenge the social, cultural, economic and political determinants of violence, UN agencies and NGOs should ensure adequate resources are invested in public information and education strategies that address men and boys. This implies promotion of gender-equitable attitudes and behaviours in communities and participation of youth in developing key messages and campaigns.

(c) In addition to targeting the behaviour of perpetrators in the strategy to prevent sexual exploitation and abuse, all stakeholders should prioritize livelihood support measures that focus on women and girls:

- UN agencies, international partners and NGOs should support accessible education and livelihood measures based on comprehensive analyses that focus on girls and their families. Specifically, this includes partnerships with the private sector for long-term employment strategies and apprenticeship opportunities; vocational and skills training; participatory market assessments; and micro-loans and credit.

(d) Member States, especially troop-contributing countries, and the United Nations system should enhance current efforts and ensure that rigorous systems are in place to promptly investigate and address allegations of sexual exploitation and abuse, including systematic training, specialized investigation capacity, stronger sanctions against perpetrators, mechanisms for referral to child protection actors, and the adoption and implementation of a comprehensive, child-friendly policy on assistance and support for survivors:

- UN agencies and international NGOs should implement standardized and systematic codes of conduct for sexual violence and exploitation, including a unified zero-tolerance policy for all humanitarian staff and peacekeepers, and child-friendly complaint mechanisms.

C. STRENGTHENING CAPACITY, KNOWLEDGE AND PARTNERSHIP

Recommendation 9: Improve capacity and knowledge for quality care and protection of children

To address insufficiencies in the base of expertise and programme learning, Member States and other stakeholders should invest more across all sectors in building, strengthening and expanding international and national capacities for knowledge acquisition and management. Research should be more aligned with needs in the field and should be documented, disseminated and applied.

- Key stakeholders, such as Member States, regional organizations and UN entities, should invest significant resources in building the base of expertise on child protection, including training of local service providers and capacity building of national institutions. Evaluations of the impact of training should be routinely undertaken through such methods as knowledge assessment.

- The United Nations should establish a global information management system. This system should build on existing data collection systems; work with specialized research institutions to develop a collaborative methodology to better gather, collate, analyse and distribute data on conflict-affected children; and establish agreed-upon indicators that are relevant to the programme context.

- As part of humanitarian reform and the cluster approach, expanded cooperation is needed to develop indicators that examine the multifaceted experiences of children and young people in conflict settings.

Recommendation 10: Ensure complementarity among key actors and mainstream children and armed conflict concerns

(a) All stakeholders, including UN entities, donors and non-governmental organizations, must continue to improve complementarity and cooperation across intersecting mandates. Benchmarks should be established to bring the concerns of children affected by armed conflict into the mainstream of the policies, priorities and programmes of UN entities and institutional processes:

- The United Nations, international NGOs and members of civil society should establish partnership mechanisms at the national and subnational levels along the lines of the country-level humanitarian partnership teams agreed upon by the Global Humanitarian Partnership.

- Periodic assessments should be undertaken to gauge progress in mainstreaming against specific criteria: (i) the extent to which issues affecting children in armed conflict are brought to the highest levels of decision-making of Member States and the UN system, including the governing boards of agencies, funds and programmes;

(ii) commitment to and promotion of children and armed conflict concerns by senior management; (iii) integration of these concerns into doctrine and policy frameworks, strategic plans, operational mandates, reports to main bodies, and programmes and activities; (iv) adequacy of in-house knowledge, expertise and training to inform policies, strategies and day-to-day operations; and (v) adequacy of resource support to ensure these recommendations are implemented.

- Protection outcomes for children affected by armed conflict should be a measure of success for the work of all stakeholders, including UN entities, donors and non-governmental organizations.

(b) The work of the Office of the Special Representative of the Secretary-General for Children and Armed Conflict has demonstrated a continuous need for a high-level Special Representative to advocate for children affected by armed conflict. This role should strengthen that of Member States themselves, complementing UN system partners, such as UNICEF, peacekeeping and political missions, field leadership and other child protection actors.

Recommendation 11: Operationalize the engagement of regional bodies

(a) Regional and intergovernmental bodies must more proactively address children and armed conflict concerns, including through the establishment of a high-level mechanism for advocacy, the development of action plans to implement declarations, and capacity building of child rights expertise in their secretariats:

- In order to more specifically translate commitments and declarations into action, regional bodies should: (i) review previous commitments, including through peer review mechanisms; (ii) include an agenda item dedicated to children affected by armed conflict in annual summit meetings; (iii) seize opportunities, such as through regional follow-up to A World Fit for Children; and (iv) establish a high-level advocate and child rights expertise in their peace and security structures.

(b) Regional intergovernmental bodies should ensure that children and armed conflict considerations are built into their peacemaking, peacekeeping and peacebuilding activities, with the support of the United Nations when necessary.

"Teaching others and giving awareness of the importance of sharing and living together in one country, sharing one culture can help. But the adults don't come to our meetings, and we can't tell adults what to do." – Young man, 17, Sri Lanka

Recommendation 12: Ensure that funding matches children's needs and priorities

(a) Donors should individually and collectively ensure early, multi-year, flexible and thematic funding as called for by, inter alia, the principles of the Good Humanitarian Donorship initiative. Donors should prioritize child-focused programming, taking into account the need for a long-term approach:

- Donors and implementing agencies should identify ways in which funding can be better managed to ensure continuity and sustainability of critical programmes from conflict to post-conflict situations and from an emergency to a developmental phase.

(b) In appeals for conflict-related emergencies and post-conflict reconstruction, the UN system, governments and non-governmental organizations should clearly articulate child-focused objectives and disaggregated needs:

- The Inter-Agency Standing Committee should ensure that Common Humanitarian Action Plan guidelines require clear articulation of child-related strategic objectives.

D. PREVENTING CONFLICT AND BUILDING PEACE

Recommendation 13: Consolidate the role of United Nations peacekeeping in child protection:

(a) The Security Council should continue to include child protection provisions in the mandates of peacekeeping operations:

- To facilitate fulfilment of child protection obligations, the UN Secretariat should adopt a mechanism to ensure that peacemaking, peacekeeping and peacebuilding take into account the needs and problems of children affected by armed conflict.

(b) To support effective partnerships with other key actors that have protection mandates, the Secretary-General should ensure that the needs for and roles of child protection advisers are assessed during the preparation of peacekeeping mandates.

Recommendation 14: Increase the participation of and support for children and youth

(a) Member States should make a greater commitment to address obstacles to the participation of young people in decision-making

and should actively promote children's engagement in national- and local-level governance, peace processes, and justice, truth and reconciliation processes:

- Member States, humanitarian actors and communities should promote the safe and meaningful engagement of children and young people in decisions that affect their lives through: (i) institutionalizing mechanisms for participation; (ii) adapting and using global standards and guidelines with careful consideration of the local context; and (iii) building the capacity of adults and staff to work with children and youth in conflict and post-conflict situations.

- Member States, UN entities, and international and local non-governmental organizations should increase support for the development of inclusive child- and youth-led organizations, networks and partnerships by increasing children's access to information, building capacity and sensitizing adults to the importance of children's participation in civil society.

(b) Increased technical and financial investment should include focused support for youth organizations, centres and activities, secondary and tertiary education, livelihood schemes and leadership opportunities:

- Donors, Member States, UN entities, and international and local non-governmental organizations should seek to make participatory processes sustainable, ensuring continuation of donor support and integration into local and national systems.

Recommendation 15: Integrate children's rights in peacemaking, peacebuilding and preventive actions

(a) All peacemaking and peace-building processes should be child-sensitive, including through specific provisions in peace agreements, the participation of children in those processes and the prioritization of resources:

- The international community should ensure that the protection of children and their concerns are systematically and clearly incorporated in all peace processes at the earliest stages, irrespective of the mediating parties and whether the initiative is led by the United Nations, a regional body or a national government.

- Provisions on children in peace agreements should address protection of children from all forms of grave violations; accountability for child rights violations, including through truth and reconciliation initiatives; the establishment of institutional and legal reforms that protect children from exploitation; and implementation of child-friendly disarmament, demobilization and reintegration procedures that ensure their full and successful reintegration in post-conflict structures.

(b) Member States, UN entities and regional intergovernmental bodies are urged to elaborate preventive approaches including, inter alia, early warning systems and community conflict resolution and reconciliation:

- Humanitarian and development actors, Member States, UN agencies and NGOs should assess the impact of their programmes and strategies on conflict and peace. The goal is to better understand potential risk factors, underlying tensions, and the capacities of children and youth to both prevent conflict and build

peace. This includes improved integration of issues affecting children into broader conflict resolution and peacebuilding interventions.

(c) Private sector entities must be cognizant of the impact their activities and investments have on children in countries affected by conflict and take measures that include regulating trade and joining corporate responsibility initiatives.

CONCLUSION

This milestone publication has been prepared to serve as a reference, advocacy and policy tool for Member States, humanitarian actors and civil society groups involved in the issue of children affected by armed conflict. It is also intended to provide the momentum needed to accelerate accountability and operationalize legislation, policy and action at all levels and across all sectors to improve the care and protection of children.

The most important challenge ahead for all actors is translating international standards into national action that can make a tangible difference in the lives of children affected by war. ■

ENDNOTES

1. United Nations, 'Impact of Armed Conflict on Children: Report of the expert of the Secretary-General, Ms. Graça Machel, submitted pursuant to General Assembly Resolution 48/157', UN document A/51/306, New York, 26 August 1996.

2. G. Machel, *The Impact of War on Children*, Hurst & Company, London, 2001.

3. United Nations, 'Report of the Special Representative of the Secretary-General for Children and Armed Conflict', UN document A/62/228, New York, 13 August 2007.

4. United Nations, 'Impact of Armed Conflict on Children: Report of the expert of the Secretary-General, Ms. Graça Machel, submitted pursuant to General Assembly Resolution 48/157', UN document A/51/306, New York, 26 August 1996, para. 32.

5. Program on Humanitarian Policy and Conflict Research, *Transnationality, War and the Law: A report on a round-table on the transformation of warfare, international law, and the role of transnational armed groups*, Program on Humanitarian Policy and Conflict Research, Harvard University, Cambridge, MA, April 2006, p. 6.

6. Stockholm International Peace Research Institute, 'Trends in Armed Conflicts', *SIPRI Yearbook 2008*, SIPRI, Stockholm, 2008, pp. 43, 54.

7. United Nations, 'Report of the Special Representative of the Secretary-General for Children and Armed Conflict', UN document A/62/228, New York, 13 August 2007.

8. Human Security Centre, *Human Security Brief 2006*, University of British Colombia, Canada, 2006, pp. 15-23.

9. A. Mack, 'Global Political Violence: Explaining the post-cold war decline', Coping with Crisis Working Paper Series, International Peace Institute, New York, March 2007, p. 3.

10. United Nations, 'Children and Armed Conflict: Report of the Secretary-General', UN document A/62/609-S/2007/757, New York, 21 December 2007, para. 46.

11. Ibid., para. 48.

12. Ibid., paras. 49-50.

13. This chapter draws from specific inputs to the Machel strategic review and key research initiatives, including: J. Freedman, 'Contemporary Conflict and its Consequences for Children: Input paper on war economies', 17 July 2007; A. Edgerton, 'How Violent Conflicts are Counted', August 2007; the International Peace Institute's series on *Coping with Crisis, Conflict and Change*; and *Human Security Brief 2006*, published by the Human Security Centre.

14. United Nations, 'Statement by the President of the Security Council', UN document S/PRST/2007/24, New York, 29 June 2007.

15. C. Wille with K. Krause , 'Behind the Numbers', Chapter 9, *Small Arms Survey 2005: Weapons of war*, Small Arms Survey, Graduate Institute of International Studies, Geneva, 2005, p. 230.

16. 'International Survey from the Control Arms Campaign', Oxfam International, Amnesty International and International Action Network on Small Arms, June 2006.

17. 'Persistent Instability: Armed violence and insecurity in South Sudan', Chapter 10, *Small Arms Survey 2007: Guns and the city*, Small Arms Survey, Graduate Institute of International Studies, Geneva, 2007. The survey also uncovered high rates of victimization: On average, households were found to have experienced at least one robbery, nearly two fights and close to one armed attack since the signing of the peace agreement. Guns were the predominant weapon used in these acts of violence.

18. Control Arms, *Shattered Lives: The case for tough international arms control*, Amnesty International and Oxfam International, London and Oxford, 2003, p. 4.

19. Coalition to Stop the Use of Child Soldiers, *Child Soldiers: Global Report 2008*, Coalition to Stop the Use of Child Soldiers, London, 2008, p. 41.

20. United Nations, 'Children and Armed Conflict: Report of the Secretary-General', UN document A/62/609-S/2007/757, New York, 21 December 2007; and Global Coalition to Stop the Use of Child Soldiers, *Child Soldiers: Global Report 2008*, Coalition to Stop the Use of Child Soldiers, London, 2008, pp. 305-306.

21. United Nations, 'Children and Armed Conflict: Report of the Secretary-General', UN document A/62/609-S/2007/757, New York, 21 December 2007.

22. United Nations, 'Report of the Secretary-General on Children and Armed Conflict in Somalia', UN document S/2008/352, New York, 30 May 2008, para. 89.

23. Submission to Machel strategic review by the UNICEF country office in Indonesia.

24. United Nations, 'Report of the Secretary-General on Children and Armed Conflict in Nepal', UN document S/2008/259, New York, 18 April 2008.

25. International Crisis Group, 'Colombia's New Armed Groups*'*, *Latin America Report*, no. 20, 10 May 2007, p. 3.

26. V. Thomas, *Overcoming Lost Childhoods: Lessons learned from the rehabilitation and reintegration of former child soldiers in Colombia*, Y CARE International, London, 2008, p. 4.

27. United Nations, 'Children and Armed Conflict: Report of the Secretary-General', UN document A/62/609-S/2007/757, New York, 21 December 2007, para. 116.

28. V. Thomas, *Overcoming Lost Childhoods: Lessons learned from the rehabilitation and reintegration of former child soldiers in Colombia*, Y CARE International, London, 2008.

29. United Nations, 'Children and Armed Conflict: Report of the Secretary-General', UN document A/62/609-S/2007/757, New York, 21 December 2007, paras. 101, 103.

30. United Nations, 'First Periodic Report of the Philippines on the Optional Protocol on the Involvement of Children in Armed Conflict', UN document CRC/C/OPAC/PHL/1, New York, 7 November 2007, para. 202.

31. United Nations Children's Fund and IBON Foundation Inc., *Uncounted Lives: Children, women and conflict in the Philippines*, UNICEF and IBON, December 2007, p. 6.

32. *International Review of the Red Cross*, no. 863, September 2006.

33. United Nations, 'Statement by the President of the Security Council', UN document S/PRST/2007/22, New York, 25 June 2007, para. 5; also see: United Nations Security Council Resolution S/RES/1625 (2005), 14 September 2005.

34. The Kimberley Process is a joint initiative of governments, industry and civil society that imposes extensive requirements enabling members to certify shipments of rough diamonds as 'conflict-free'.

35. United Nations, UN document A/HRC/4/035, New York, 19 February 2007, para 77.

36. A. Mack, 'Global Political Violence: Explaining the post-Cold War decline', Coping with Crisis Working Paper Series, International Peace Institute, New York, March 2007, p. 10.

37. United Nations, 'Report of the Special Representative of the Secretary-General for Children and Armed Conflict', UN document A/62/228, New York, 13 August 2007.

38. United Nations, 'Global Horizontal Note on the Monitoring and Reporting of Grave Child Rights Violations', Security Council Working Group, New York, 6 December 2007, p. 1.

39. United Nations, 'Children and Armed Conflict: Report of the Secretary-General', UN document A/62/609-S/2007/757, New York, 21 December 2007, para. 22.

40. United Nations Assistance Mission to Afghanistan, *Suicide Attacks in Afghanistan (2001–2007)*, UNAMA, Kabul, 1 September 2007, pp. 6, 11, 75-76 and 88.

41. United Nations, 'Children and Armed Conflict: Report of the Secretary-General', UN document A/62/609-S/2007/757, New York, 21 December 2007, para. 53.

42. International Crisis Group, 'Indonesia Backgrounder: Jihad in Central Sulawesi', *ICG Asia Report*, no. 74, 3 February 2004, p. 8.

43. United Nations Office of the Special Representative of the Secretary-General for Children and Armed Conflict, 'Report: Visit of the Special Representative of the Secretary-General for Children and Armed Conflict – Iraq and the region, 13-25 April 2008', UN OSRSG CAAC, New York, August 2008.

44. Amnesty International, *USA: Human dignity denied – Torture and accountability in the 'war on terror'*, Amnesty International, London, 27 October 2004.

45. United Nations, 'Children and Armed Conflict: Report of the Secretary-General', UN document A/62/609-S/2007/757, New York, 21 December 2007, para. 86.

46. Defence for Children International-Palestine Section, 'Palestinian Child Political Prisoners 2006 Report', p. 2.

47. United Nations, 'Children and Armed Conflict: Report of the Secretary-General', UN document A/62/609-S/2007/757, New York, 21 December 2007, para. 87.

48. United Nations Children's Fund, 'Humanitarian Action Update', UNICEF, New York, 21 September 2007, pp. 2-3.

49. Communication with the UNICEF country office in Nepal.

50. United Nations, 'Report of the Special Rapporteur on the Promotion and Protection of Human Rights while Countering Terrorism: Martin Scheinin', UN document A/HRC/6/17, New York, 21 November 2007, para. 70.

51. T. Paffenholz and D. Brede, *Lessons Learnt from the German Anti-Terrorism Package (ATP)*, Deutches Gesellschaft für Technische Zusammenarbeit (GTZ) GmbH, Eschborn, 2004, pp. 40-48.

52. Ibid.

53. World Bank, *World Development Report 2007: Development and the next generation*, World Bank, Washington, D.C., September 2006.

54. Organisation for Economic Co-operation and Development-Development Assistance Committee, 'A Development Co-operation Lens on Terrorism Prevention: Key entry points for action', *Guidelines and Reference Series*, OECD/N92-64-01908-1, OECD-DAC, Paris, 2003, p. 8.

55. United Nations, 'A World Fit for Children', UN document A/RES/S-27/2, New York, 11 October 2002, para 7.

56. Council of Delegates of the International Red Cross and Red Crescent Movement, *30th International Conference of the Red Cross and Red Crescent: Resolutions*, Resolution 3, Geneva, 26-30 November 2007, p. 81.

57. International Committee of the Red Cross, 'International Humanitarian Law and the Challenges of Contemporary Armed Conflicts', ICRC document 301C/07/8.4, Geneva, October 2007.

58. This chapter in particular has benefited from several papers prepared for this report on how violent conflicts are counted (Edgerton 2007); on figures relating to populations of humanitarian concern, including refugees, internally displaced persons and child soldiers (Donahue and Loaiza 2007); and on a preliminary analysis of progress towards the MDGs in countries affected by armed conflict (Donahue and Loaiza 2008).

59. The number of children was calculated based on the set of 33 conflict-affected countries described later in this chapter and data from UNICEF's *State of the World's Children* 2008 report.

60. Figures were calculated by UNICEF based on a combination of data from the Office of the United Nations High Commissioner for Refugees, the United Nations Relief and Works Agency for Palestinian Refugees, the US Committee for Refugees and Immigrants, and the Internal Displacement Monitoring Centre of the Norwegian Refugee Council.

61. United Nations Children's Fund, *The State of the World's Children 1996: Children in war*, Oxford University Press, Oxford, 1996.

62. B. Coghlan et al., 'Mortality in the Democratic Republic of Congo: An ongoing crisis', International Rescue Committee and Burnet Institute, New York and Melbourne, 2008, p. ii.

63. Republic of Uganda Ministry of Health, 'Health and Mortality Survey among Internally Displaced Persons in Gulu, Kitgum and Pader Districts, Northern Uganda', World Health Organization, UNICEF, World Food Programme, United Nations Population Fund and International Rescue Committee, July 2005, p. ii.

64. J. Barenbaum, R. Vladislav and M. Schwab-Stone, 'The Psychosocial Aspects of Children Exposed to War: Practice and policy initiatives', *Journal of Child Psychology and Psychiatry*, vol. 45, no. 1, 2004, pp. 42-44.

65. United Nations, 'Children and Armed Conflict: Report of the Secretary-General', UN document A/62/609-S/2007/757, New York, 21 December 2007.

66. International Campaign to Ban Landmines, *Landmine Monitor Report 2007: Toward a mine-free world*, Human Rights Watch, New York, 2007.

67. United Nations Children's Fund, 'Landmines and Explosive Remnants of War: Machel review thematic paper', UNICEF, New York, June 2007 (unpublished).

68. The reference to countries or territories is intended to indicate the location in which offending parties have committed the violations in question and does not imply the involvement of States parties.

69. The 16 are: *Burundi* – the Wing of Agaton Rwasaa; *Democratic Republic of the Congo* – Forces armées congolaises, Front nationaliste et intégrationaliste (Lendu) and Mai-Mai; *Colombia* – Ejercito de Liberación Nacional and Fuerzas Armada Revolucionarias de Colombia-Ejército del Pueblo; *Myanmar* – Tatmadaw Kyi (government army) and Karen National Liberation Army; *Nepal* – Communist Party of Nepal; *Philippines* – Moro Islamic Liberation Front and the New People's Army; *Sri Lanka* – Liberation Tigers of Tamil Eelam; *Sudan* – Sudan People's Liberation Movement/Army; *Uganda* – Local Defence Units (allied to Uganda People's Defence Forces), Lord's Resistance Army and Uganda People's Defence Forces.

70. Coalition to Stop the Use of Child Soldiers, *Child Soldiers Global Report 2008*, Coalition to Stop the Use of Child Soldiers, London, 2008.

71. B. O'Malley, *Education Under Attack: A global study on targeted political and military violence against education staff, students, teachers, union and government officials, and institutions,* UNESCO, Paris, 2007.

72. United Nations, 'Children and Armed Conflict: Report of the Secretary-General', UN document A/62/609-S/2007/757, New York, 21 December 2007.

73. Watchlist on Children and Armed Conflict, 'Sudan's Children at a Crossroads: An urgent need for protection', Women's Commission for Refugee Women and Children, New York, April 2007, p. 5.

74. United Nations, 'Children and Armed Conflict: Report of the Secretary-General', UN document A/62/609-S/2007/757, New York, 21 December 2007.

75. Ibid.

76. United Nations, 'Report of the Secretary-General on Children and Armed Conflict in Uganda', UN document S/2007/260, New York, 7 May 2007.

77. J. Annan, C. Blattman and R. Horton, *The State of Youth and Youth Protection in Northern Uganda: Findings from the survey for war affected youth,* UNICEF Uganda, 2006.

78. Women's Commission for Refugee Women and Children, *Listening to Youth: The experiences of young people in northern Uganda,* WCRWC, New York, 2007.

79. United Nations, 'Children and Armed Conflict: Report of the Secretary-General', UN document A/62/609-S/2007/757, New York, 21 December 2007.

80. United Nations, 'Report of the Secretary-General on the Protection of Civilians in Armed Conflict', UN document S/2007/643, New York, 28 October 2007, para. 34.

81. A. Harmer et al., *Providing Aid in Insecure Environments: Trends in policy and operations,* Humanitarian Policy Group, Overseas Development Institute, London, 23 September 2006.

82. United Nations, 'Report of the Secretary-General on the Situation in Afghanistan and its Implications for International Peace and Security', UN document S/2008/159, New York, 6 March 2008.

83. Watchlist on Children and Armed Conflict, 'Caught in the Middle: Mounting violations against children in Nepal's armed conflict', Women's Commission for Refugee Women and Children, New York, January 2005, p. 31.

84. The analysis is based on 2008 UNICEF research (by A. Donahue and E. Loaiza) undertaken for this report. It represents an initial attempt to review data drawn from Demographic and Health Surveys and Multiple Indicator Cluster Surveys and organize it by MDG indicator. It is expected that further review and refinement of the process will deepen the results.

85. Armed conflict databases used to identify countries included: (1) the Uppsala Conflict Database, maintained by the Uppsala Conflict Data Program at Uppsala University; (2) the Conflict Barometer of the Heidelberg Institute for International Conflict Research; and (3) Project Ploughshares' Armed Conflict Report. For each database, a list was compiled of countries engaged in armed conflict on their own soil during the period 2002-2006. The three lists were then compared, and any country that appeared on two of the three lists was included in the final list of conflict-affected countries used for this research.

86. Of the 60 million children out of school in conflict-affected countries, 19 million are in India. A substantial portion of this number may not be included in the count if further analysis is able to determine whether certain regions/states/provinces of a country are affected by conflict and whether the data available are similarly broken down. Source: A. Donahue and E. Loaiza, 'Millennium Development Goals (MDGs) in Conflict Affected Countries', UNICEF Strategic Information Section, Department of Policy & Planning, February 2008 (unpublished).

87. UNICEF, *Progress for Children: A World Fit for Children statistical review, Number 6,* UNICEF, New York, December 2007.

88. The gender parity index (GPI) is obtained by dividing the net enrolment/attendance rates for girls by the rates for boys. GPI of 0.96 to 1.04 means that the percentages of boys and girls in school are roughly equal. GPI of more than 1.04 means that the percentage of girls in school is higher than the percentage of boys. GPI of less than 0.96 means that the percentage of boys is higher than the percentage of girls in school.

89. The under-five mortality rate is the probability (expressed as a rate per 1,000 live births) of a child born in a specified year dying before reaching the age of five if subject to current age-specific mortality rates.

90. For further analysis, it would be helpful to determine whether certain regions/states/provinces of a country are affected by conflict and use data from those areas specifically.

91. Debt service is expressed as a percentage of exported goods and services, not including workers' remittances. The debt referred to here includes only long-term public and publicly guaranteed debt and repayments to the International Monetary Fund.

92. See, for example: J. Hart and B. Tyrer, 'RCS Working Paper No. 30: Research with Children Living in Situations of Armed Conflict – Concept, ethics and methods', Refugee Studies Centre, University of Oxford, Oxford, May 2006; Y. Kemper, 'Youth in War-to-Peace Transitions', *Berghof Handbook for Conflict Transformation,* Berghof Research Center for Constructive Conflict Management, Berlin, 2005, <www.berghof-center.org/std_page.php?LANG=e&id=177>; Women's Commission for Refugee Women and Children, *Untapped Potential: Adolescents affected by armed conflict,* WCRWC, New York, 2002; and C. O'Kane, *Children and Young People as Citizens: Partners for social change,* Save the Children South and Central Asia, Kathmandu, 2003.

93. Article 12 of the CRC reads as follows: "1. States Parties shall assure to the child who is capable of forming his or her own views the right to express those views freely in all matters affecting the child, the views of the child being given due weight in accordance with the age and maturity of the child. 2. For this purpose, the child shall in particular be provided the opportunity to be heard in any judicial and administrative proceedings affecting the child, either directly, or through a representative or an appropriate body, in a manner consistent with the procedural rules of national law."

94. See: J. Hart, *Children's Participation in Humanitarian Action: Learning from zones of armed conflict,* Refugee Studies Centre, University of Oxford, Oxford, 2004, p. 4; Women's Commission for Refugee Women and Children, *Untapped Potential: Adolescents affected by armed conflict,* WCRWC, New York, 2002, p. 1; Save the Children Norway, *Building Peace Out of War: Children and young people as agents of peace – The young generation's challenge,* Workshop Study, 2005; Concerned Parents' Association, *Accountability & Reconciliation. Perspectives from children and youth in northern & eastern Uganda,* Concerned Parents' Association with Trans-cultural Psycho-social Organisation, Save the Children in Uganda and UNICEF, 2007; C. O'Kane and C. Feinstein, *Participation is a Virtue that Must be Cultivated: An analysis of children's participation working methods and materials within Save the Children Sweden,* Save the Children Sweden, Stockholm, 2007, p. 6; 'Child Centred Programs', Plan USA website, <www.planusa.org/who/programs.php>; Christian Children's Fund, *Annual Report 2007,* CCF, Richmond, VA, p. 9.

95. See: J. Hart, *Children's Participation in Humanitarian Action: Learning from zones of armed conflict,* Refugee Studies Centre, University of Oxford, Oxford, 2004, p. 7; and E. Delap, 'Fighting Back: Child and community-led strategies to avoid children's recruitment into armed forces and groups in West Africa', Save the Children UK, London, 2004, p. 26.

96. The Women's Commission for Refugee Women and Children titles are: *Listening to Youth: The experience of young people in northern Uganda* (2007, p. 2); *Precious Resources: Adolescents in the reconstruction of Sierra Leone* (2002, p. 6); and *Making the Choice for a Better Life: Promoting the protection and capacity of Kosovo's youth* (2000, p. 4).

97. Save the Children Norway, 'Material and Resources: Children's memorandum', 2007, <www.reddbarna.no/default.asp?V_ITEM_ID=11749>.

98. J. Hart, *Children's Participation in Humanitarian Action: Learning from zones of armed conflict,* Refugee Studies Centre, University of Oxford, Oxford, February 2004, pp. 29-31.

99. Human Rights Watch, *Trapped by Inequality: Bhutanese refugee women in Nepal,* vol. 15, no. 8 (C), HRW, New York, September 2003, p. 9; and A. Naik, 'Protecting Children from the Protectors: Lessons from West Africa', *Forced Migration Review*, vol. 15, October 2002, pp. 16-19.

100. United Nations Children's Fund, *Adolescent Programming Experiences during Conflict and Post-Conflict: Case studies,* UNICEF, New York, June 2004, p. 8; C. O'Kane, C. Feinstein and A. Giertsen, 'Children and Young People in Post Conflict Peace-Building', *Children in an Insecure World,* edited by D. Nosworthy, Geneva Centre for the Democratic Control of Armed Forces, Geneva, 2008; Women's Commission for Refugee Women and Children, *Youth Speak Out: New voices on the protection and participation of young people affected by armed conflict,* WCRWC, New York, 2005, p. 33.

101. K. Peters, 'From Weapons to Wheels: Young Sierra Leonean ex-combatants become motorbike taxi-riders', *Journal of Peace, Conflict and Development,* no. 10, 2007, p. 5; A. Dawes, 'Political Transition and Youth Violence in Post-Apartheid South Africa: In search of understanding', *Years of Conflict: Adolescence, Political Violence and Displacement,* edited by J. Hart, Berghahn Books, Oxford, 2008, p. 2.

102. Save the Children Norway, 'Armed Conflict and Peace-Building', *Information and Advocacy Newsletter,* vol. 1, September 2007, p. 4.

103. J. Hart, 'Children as Participants in Settings of Armed Conflict', draft summary of an e-discussion for UNICEF's Adolescent Development and Participation Unit, 2007, p. 2.

104. Ibid.

105. J. Hart, *Children's Participation in Humanitarian Action: Learning from zones of armed conflict,* Refugee Studies Centre, University of Oxford, Oxford, February 2004, p. 26.

106. J. de Berry, 'The Challenges of Programming with Youth in Afghanistan', Chapter 9, *Years of Conflict: Adolescence, political violence and displacement,* edited by J. Hart, Berghahn Books, Oxford, 2008.

107. L. Ackermann et al., *Understanding and Evaluating Children's Participation: A review of contemporary literature,* Plan International (UK), London, 2003, p. 16.

108. United Nations, '2005 World Summit Outcome', UN document A/RES/60/1, New York, 25 October 2005, paras. 117 and 118.

109. United Nations, 'United Nations Millennium Declaration', UN document A/RES/55/2, New York, 8 September 2000, para. 26.

110. United Nations, 'A World Fit for Children', UN document A/RES/S-27/2, New York, 11 October 2002, paras. 43 and 44, actions 20-32.

111. These resolutions have consistently urged: fulfilment and implementation of the Convention on the Rights of the Child, its Optional Protocol on children and armed conflict, and international humanitarian and human rights law; ensuring humanitarian access; ending impunity and bringing perpetrators to justice; ending the recruitment and use of children and securing their release, demobilization and effective reintegration; that rape in armed conflict is a war crime and that particular attention is needed to the vulnerability of girls during conflict; addressing the proliferation of small arms and need for landmine action and education; that United Nations agencies ensure that concerns relating to children affected by armed conflict are fully reflected in UN field operations for the promotion of peace, prevention and resolution of conflicts and implementation of peace agreements; and, most recently, recognizing the UN Monitoring and Reporting Mechanism (MRM) established by the Security Council.

112. United Nations, 'Resolution 1780 (2007)', UN document S/RES/1780 (2007), New York, para. 17.

113. The 11 countries are Burundi, Chad, Côte D'Ivoire, Democratic Republic of the Congo, Myanmar, Nepal, Philippines, Somalia, Sri Lanka, Sudan and Uganda.

114. Watchlist on Children and Armed Conflict, <www.watchlist.org/advocacy/policystatements/>; and United Nations, 'Comprehensive Assessment of the United Nations System Response to Children Affected by Armed Conflict', UN document A/59/331, New York, 3 September 2004.

115. United Nations, 'Children and Armed Conflict', *Security Council Report: Cross-cutting report,* no. 1, 4 February 2008, p. 7.

116. Ibid., p. 8.

117. Save the Children, 'Can the Powerful Protect? How the UN Security Council needs to shape up to protect children', Save the Children UK, London, July 2007, p. 14.

118. Based on communication with Kendra Dupuy of the International Peace Research Institute (PRIO) on research carried out for 'Education for Peace: Building peace and transforming armed conflict through education systems', PRIO and Save the Children Norway, Oslo.

119. African Union, *Call for Accelerated Action on the Implementation of the Plan of Action Towards Africa Fit for Children 2008-2012,* Second Pan-African Forum on Children: Mid-Term Review, 29 October–2 November 2007, African Union, Addis Ababa, pp. 4, 7 (e), 8.

120. Inter-Parliamentary Union and United Nations Children's Fund, *Child Protection: A handbook for parliamentarians*, Handbook for Parliamentarians No. 7, IPU and UNICEF, Geneva, 2004.

121. Although not addressed in this chapter, international criminal law is also a relevant body of law. It is occasionally referred to in regard to the (international) criminalization of certain violations of children's rights.

122. The four guiding principles underpinning the Convention on the Rights of the Child are: non-discrimination (article 2); the best interests of the child (article 3); the right to be heard, often referred to as the right to participation (article 12); and the right to life, survival and development (article 6).

123. Article 1 of the CRC further specifies that a child is anyone under 18 years of age, "unless under the law applicable to the child, the majority is attained earlier."

124. A General Comment is an interpretation by a treaty body of the content of human rights provisions, either related to a specific article or to a broader thematic issue. General Comments often seek to clarify the reporting duties of States parties with respect to certain provisions and suggest approaches to implementing treaty provisions. They are also referred to as 'general recommendations'.

125. See, respectively, the following Committee on the Rights of the Child General Comments: No. 1 – 'The Aims of Education', UN document CRC/GC/2001/1, New York, 17 April 2001, para. 16; No. 3 – 'HIV/AIDS and the Rights of the Child', UN document CRC/GC/2003/3, New York, 17 March 2003, para. 38; and No. 9 – 'The Rights of Children with Disabilities', UN document CRC/C/GC/9, New York, 29 September 2006, para. 55.

126. United Nations Children's Fund, *Implementation Handbook for the Convention on the Rights of the Child,* third edition, UNICEF, New York, September 2007, p. 660.

127. According to article 39, States parties are to take all appropriate measures to promote the "physical and psychological recovery and social reintegration of a child victim of: any form of neglect, exploitation, or abuse; torture or any other form of cruel, inhuman or degrading treatment or punishment; or armed conflicts." Moreover, the recovery and reintegration process is to take place in an environment that promotes the child's health, self-respect and dignity.

128. Revised guidelines regarding initial reports to be submitted by States parties under article 8, para. 1, of the Optional Protocol to the Convention on the Rights of the Child on Involvement of Children in Armed Conflict, September 2007 (United Nations, 'Revised Guidelines Regarding Initial Reports to be Submitted by States Parties …', UN document CRC/C/OPAC/2, New York, 19 October 2007).

129. Once this initial reporting round is completed, further reporting on the implementation of Optional Protocol on the Involvement of Children in Armed Conflict (OPAC) by the State party is done by incorporating it into its reporting obligation under the CRC (every five years). As such, the first report under OPAC is a key opportunity for States and civil society more broadly (including national human rights institutions and NGOs) to take stock of the implementation process and existing gaps in meeting obligations. Civil society actors can, for example, provide independent reports on national implementation as well as additional information to the Committee on the Rights of the Child so that their views are taken into account during consideration of the reports. States and civil society must also follow up on the recommendations of the Committee at the national level, since these constitute the benchmarks by which to measure future progress in implementation. See: J. Connors, 'How the International Community has Responded to Children and Armed Conflict: What still needs to be done?', OHCHR, Geneva, 28 March 2006, p. 7.

130. The Paris Commitments to protect children from unlawful recruitment or use by armed forces or armed groups had been endorsed by 58 governments as of February 2007. See also: United Nations Children's Fund, *The Paris Principles: Principles and guidelines on children associated with armed forces or armed groups*, UNICEF, February 2007.

131. Further complementing this legal framework, the related issue of trafficking was addressed by the Palermo Protocol to Prevent, Suppress and Punish Trafficking in Persons, Especially Women and Children, which entered into force December 2003.

132. Security Council resolutions related to children and armed conflict include: Resolutions 1261 (1999), 1314 (2000), 1379 (2001), 1460 (2003), 1539 (2004) and 1612 (2005).

133. See, for example: Committee on the Elimination of Discrimination against Women, with regard to the Democratic Republic of the Congo, CEDAW/C/COD/CO/5, 2006, and the Committee against Torture, with regard to its conclusions on Sri Lanka (CAT/C/LKA/CO/2) and Nepal (CAT/C/NPL/CO/20), both adopted in 2005.

134. See: Convention I for the Amelioration of the Condition of the Wounded and Sick in Armed Forces in the Field, 1949; Convention II for the Amelioration of the Condition of Wounded, Sick and Shipwrecked Members of Armed Forces at Sea, 1949; Convention III relative to the Treatment of Prisoners of War, 1949; Convention IV relative to the Protection of Civilian Persons in Time of War, 1949; Protocol I relating to the Protection of Victims of International Armed Conflicts, 1977; Protocol II relating to the Protection of Victims of Non-International Armed Conflicts, 1977; Protocol III relating to the adoption of an Additional Distinctive Emblem, 2005.

135. International Committee of the Red Cross, *Customary International Humanitarian Law*, edited by Jean-Marie Henckaerts and Louise Doswald-Beck, ICRC and Cambridge University Press, Geneva, 2005.

136. International refugee protection includes some fundamental rights and principles, including granting of access to the territory to seek asylum, the principle of *non-refoulement* (no forced return) and access to fair and efficient refugee status determination procedures or prima facie status.

137. In addition to these, other Executive Committee Conclusions relating to refugee children include: No. 47 (1987) and No. 59 (1989) on Refugee Children; No. 84 on Children and Adolescents (1999); and No. 88 on Protection of the Refugee's Family (1999).

138. In particular, see the UNHCR *Guidelines on Policies and Procedure in Dealing with Unaccompanied Children Seeking Asylum* (1997). Other guidelines on this topic include: UNHCR, *Procedural Standards for Refugee Status Determination under UNHCR's Mandate*, November 2003; and UNHCR Social Services Section, *Guidelines for Interviewing Unaccompanied Minors and Preparing Social Histories*, October 1985. In addition to the right to seek asylum and international protection based on their own claims under the 1951 Convention, children may also be granted derivative refugee status as dependants if they are accompanied by a parent or guardian, based on the principle of family unity.

139. Although the Guiding Principles are not technically binding as such, they have been drawn from existing norms in international human rights and humanitarian law and are gaining increasing international recognition.

140. The Convention had 156 ratifications and two signatories as of 1 March 2008.

141. United Nations Children's Fund, with inputs from other UN agencies, 'Landmines & Explosive Remnants of War: Machel review thematic paper', UNICEF, New York, 14 June 2007, p. 3. The 'Deed of Commitment' is an instrument designed specifically for non-state actors to enable them to comply with the spirit and intentions of the Mine Ban Treaty and other international instruments. The full document is available online at Geneva Call, <www.geneva-call.org/home.htm>.

142. As of end 2007, 38 countries had ceased production of anti-personnel mines, including four States not party to the Mine Ban Convention (Egypt, Finland, Israel and Poland). The international trade of this weapon has virtually ceased, with a significant number of non-States parties having export moratoriums in place. See: International Campaign to Ban Landmines, *Landmine Monitor Report 2007*.

143. China (estimated 110 million), Russian Federation (26.5 million), United States of America (10.4 million), Pakistan (estimated 6 million) and India (estimated 4-5 million). See: United Nations Children's Fund, with inputs from other UN agencies, 'Landmines & Explosive Remnants of War: Machel review thematic paper', UNICEF, New York, 14 June, 2007, p. 5.

144. Ibid.

145. As of 1 March 2008, 40 countries had ratified the protocol.

146. Records show that between 12 July and 14 August 2006, Lebanon was littered with an estimated 1 million unexploded submunitions and unexploded ordnance, aggravating an already serious problem of anti-personnel landmines and explosive remnants of war. See: International Campaign to Ban Landmines, *Landmine Monitor Report 2006*, and Cambodia Mine/UXO Victims Information System, *Casualty Reports*, 2000 and December 2006.

147. More specifically, the Committee has requested States parties to abolish arms trade to countries where persons who have not reached the age of 18 may take a direct part in hostilities as members of their State armed forces or non-state armed groups. For example, the Committee on the Rights of the Child considers state practices and legislation with regard to arms trade, whether arms are sold to countries using child soldiers (in contravention of the Optional Protocol on the Involvement of Children in Armed Conflict) and their response more generally to the proliferation of small calibre weapons, in the following: Switzerland CRC/C/OPAC/CHE/CO/1, para. 5; Bangladesh CRC/C/OPAC/BGD/CO/1, paras. 20, 21; Canada CRC/C/OPAC/CAN/CO/1, paras. 14, 15.

148. United Nations Economic and Social Council, 'Rights of the Child: Report of the Special Representative of the Secretary-General for Children and Armed Conflict, Olara A. Otunnu', UN document E/CN.4/2005/77, New York, 15 February 2005, paras. 15, 55.

149. See: article 47 of the First Geneva Convention; article 48 of the Second Geneva Convention; article 127 of the Third Geneva Convention; article 144 of the Fourth Geneva Convention; article 83 of the 1977 Additional Protocol I; article 19 of the 1977 Additional Protocol II; and article 6 of the 2000 Optional Protocol.

150. For example, Norway has recently amended its General Civil Penal Code, incorporating a provision stipulating that a person who, in connection with an armed conflict, conscripts or enlists children under the age of 18 into armed forces or uses them to participate actively in hostilities may be punished for war crimes. This provision applies to acts committed abroad if the act is considered a war crime under international law. The provision entered into force 7 March 2008.

151. No Peace Without Justice and UNICEF Innocenti Research Centre, *International Criminal Justice and Children*, NPWJ and UNICEF Innocenti Research Centre, New York and Florence, September 2002, p. 104.

152. In addition to the Committee on the Rights of the Child, other treaty body procedures can also promote national implementation, including the Optional Protocol to the Convention against Torture, which establishes international and national mechanisms for visits to places of detention, including where children affected by armed conflict may be held. The universal periodic review mechanisms of the Human Rights Council (and its special procedures mandate holders) can play an important role as well by highlighting issues of particular concern to children affected by armed conflict and mainstreaming child rights. See: J. Connors, 'How the International Community has Responded to Children and Armed Conflict: What still needs to be done?', Office of the United Nations High Commissioner for Human Rights, Geneva, 28 March 2006, p. 7.

153. European Union, 'EU Guidelines on Children and Armed Conflict', Ref. no. 15634/03, COHOM 47/PESC 762/CIVCOM 201/COSDP 731, Council of the European Union, Brussels, approved by the European Union General Affairs Council, Brussels, 8 December 2003, para. 6.

154. J. Connors, 'How the International Community has Responded to Children and Armed Conflict: What still needs to be done?', Office of the United Nations High Commissioner for Human Rights, Geneva, 28 March 2006, p. 5.

155. A detailed analysis of this issue is provided in: UNICEF Innocenti Research Centre, *Innocenti Insight: Birth registration and armed conflict*, United Nations Children's Fund, Florence, 2007.

156. UN Security Council, 'The Rule of Law and Transitional Justice in Conflict and Post-conflict Societies: Report of the Secretary-General', UN document S/2004/616, New York, 23 August 2004, para. 8.

157. UNICEF Innocenti Research Centre, 'Background Paper of the Expert Discussion on Transitional Justice and Children', Florence, 10-12 November 2005, p. 5.

158. Ad hoc international criminal tribunals were established by the Security Council as subsidiary organs of the United Nations.

159. The nature and structure of mixed tribunals vary, and they can be established as a treaty-based court, e.g., Sierra Leone, a court that complies with a treaty but is established under national law, e.g., Cambodia, or as a special chamber within a State Court, e.g., Bosnia and Herzegovina.

160. UN Security Council, 'The Rule of Law and Transitional Justice in Conflict and Post-conflict Societies: Report of the Secretary-General', UN document S/2004/616, New York, 23 August 2004, para. 38.

161. Ibid., para. 41.

162. I. Cohn, 'The Protection of Children and the Quest for Truth and Justice in Sierra Leone', *Journal of International Affairs*, vol. 55, no. 1, Fall 2001, p. 2. Referred to in UNICEF Innocenti Research Centre, 'Background Paper of the Expert Discussion on Transitional Justice and Children', Florence, 10-12 November 2005, p. 7.

163. The decisions issued on 20 June 2007 convicted three former soldiers – Alex Tamba Brima, Brima Bazzy Kamara and Santigie Borbor Kanu – of murder, rape and enlisting child soldiers. In August 2007, the Special Court for Sierra Leone also convicted Allieu Kondewa of the Civil Defense Forces militia.

164. In June 2006, Charles Ghankay Taylor was transferred from the Special Court of Sierra Leone to The Hague and now faces 11 counts of war crimes and crimes against humanity. These include conscription or enlisting children under the age of 15 years into armed forces or groups and using them to participate actively in hostilities.

165. 'A UN Approach on Justice for Children' was endorsed by the Rule of Law Coordination and Resource Group, chaired by the Deputy Secretary-General in March 2008.

166. International Criminal Tribunal for the former Yugoslavia (ICTY) ruling on the rapes at Celibici on sexual violence as a war crime and the International Criminal Tribunal for Rwanda (ICTR) ruling on the Akayesu case (The Prosecutor versus Jean Paul Akayesu, Case No. ICTR-96-4-T).

167. Nonetheless, these non-state justice systems must conform with human rights standards.

168. United Nations, 'Prevention and Punishment of the Crime of Genocide', General Assembly Resolution, UN document A/RES/260 (III), New York, 9 December 1948.

169. 'Rome Statute of the International Criminal Court', UN document A/CONF.183.9, adopted 17 July 1998, entered into force on 1 July 2002. For details on the Statute see: <www.un.org/law/icc>.

170. UN Security Council, 'The Rule of Law and Transitional Justice in Conflict and Post-conflict Societies: Report of the Secretary-General', UN document S/2004/616, New York, 23 August 2004, para. 49.

171. Radhika Coomaraswamy, Under-Secretary-General and Special Representative of the Secretary-General for Children and Armed Conflict, 'The Protection of Women and Children during Armed Conflict: Whose responsibility?' presented at the 2007 Chancellor's Human Rights Lecture, University of Melbourne, 13 December 2007, pp. 10-11. In October 2005, the ICC issued arrest warrants for five senior members of the Lord's Resistance Army, including leader Joseph Kony, who was charged with 33 counts of war crime and crimes against humanity, including the forcible enlistment and active use of children under 15 years of age in hostilities. In March 2006, Thomas Lubanga Dyilo, founder and leader of the Union of Congolese Patriots in Ituri, Democratic Republic of the Congo, was indicted by the ICC for war crimes, conscription and enlistment of children under 15 and having them participate actively in hostilities. Germain Katanga, commander of the Patriotic Resistance Force in Ituri, was transferred to the ICC in October 2007 and charged with three counts of crimes against humanity as well as six counts of war crime, which include the illegal recruitment and use of children in active hostilities.

172. Ibid., pp. 9-10.

173. UN Security Council, 'The Rule of Law and Transitional Justice in Conflict and Post-conflict Societies: Report of the Secretary-General', UN document S/2004/616, 23 August 2004, para. 34.

174. The Committee on the Rights of the Child has expressed these concerns in several instances. With regard to the failure to provide compensation to children, it did so in the cases of Croatia and Israel (CRC/C/15/Add. 243, paras. 64, 84-85, and CRC/C/15/Add.195, paras. 58, 59, respectively); on the need to prosecute those who have violated children's rights during conflict, in the case of Indonesia (CRC/C/15/Add. 223, paras. 67, 243); and on the long pretrial detentions in poor conditions and the lack of proper rehabilitation services, in the case of Rwanda (CRC/C15/Add. 234, paras. 70, 71). See: United Nations Children's Fund, *Implementation Handbook for the Convention on the Rights of the Child*, revised third edition, UNICEF, Geneva, September 2007, p. 585.

175. With regard to informal traditions of justice and national human rights commissions, see: UN Security Council, 'The Rule of Law and Transitional Justice in Conflict and Post-conflict Societies: Report of the Secretary-General', UN document S/2004/616, New York, 23 August 2004, para. 36; and 'Principles Relating to the Status of National Institutions', endorsed by GA Resolution 48/134, specifically, the section on 'Additional Principles Concerning the Status of Commissions with Quasi Jurisdictional Competence'.

176. For example, in the General Assembly Report of the Committee on the Rights of the Child A/61/41 of 2006, the Committee encourages States parties to consider assuming extraterritorial jurisdiction (para. 22) and undertakes to develop its own position with regard to whether the obligation to take all measures to implement OPAC – article 6(1) – requires the application of universal jurisdiction (para. 23).

177. The universality principle is an element of international law holding that some crimes are so grave that all countries have an interest in prosecuting them. It is rooted in international law and codified in United Nations instruments. It is only used when the justice system of the country where the violations occurred is unable or unwilling to prosecute. See: UN Security Council, 'The Rule of Law and Transitional Justice in Conflict and Post-conflict Societies: Report of the Secretary-General', UN document S/2004/616, 23 August 2004, para. 48.

178. UN Security Council, 'The Rule of Law and Transitional Justice in Conflict and Post-conflict Societies: Report of the Secretary-General', UN document S/2004/616, 23 August 2004, para. 46.

179. Ibid.

180. Ibid., paras. 46, 47.

181. Ibid., para. 47.

182. Ibid., para. 26.

183. UNICEF Innocenti Research Centre and the International Center for Transitional Justice, *Children and Truth Commissions* (forthcoming 2008).

184. A detailed analysis of participation by adolescents in various processes in conflict and post-conflict situations is provided in: United Nations Children's Fund, *Adolescent Participation in Programme Activities during Situations of Conflict and Post-Conflict: Case Studies*, UNICEF, New York, June 2004.

185. For example, truth commissions in Argentina, El Salvador, Guatemala and Peru each dedicated a chapter to children in their final reports. UNICEF Innocenti Research Centre and the International Center for Transitional Justice, *Children and Truth Commissions* (forthcoming 2008).

186. UNICEF Executive Director Carol Bellamy, press release issued 26 February 1999.

187. UNICEF Innocenti Research Centre and the International Center for Transitional Justice, *Children and Truth Commissions* (forthcoming 2008).

188. For a detailed account of relevant challenges and measures developed to encourage child and adolescent participation in this process, see, for example: UNICEF, *Adolescent Participation in Programme Activities During Situations of Conflict and Post-Conflict: Case Studies*, UNICEF, New York, June 2004; and UNICEF Innocenti Research Centre, Outcome Document (p. 11) and Background Documents (published electronically, pp. 50-64), of the 'Expert Discussion on Transitional Justice and Children', 10-12 November 2005.

189. For example, as part of their 'Children and Transitional Justice Series', the UNICEF Innocenti Research Centre is initiating documentation on children and transitional justice processes in Colombia, Liberia, Peru, Rwanda, Sierra Leone, South Africa and Uganda

(forthcoming publication expected 2008). The International Center for Transitional Justice has also undertaken a research project (report forthcoming) on transitional justice, and disarmament, demobilization and reintegration (DDR) that analyses the relationship between transitional justice mechanisms (e.g., truth and reconciliation commissions) and DDR for children, including both the positive and negative effects.

190. International Center for Transitional Justice, 'Draft Report of the Expert Discussion on Transitional Justice and Children', 10-12 November 2005, pp. 9-10, and in particular its reference to: A. Veale and A. Stavrou, *Violence, Reconciliation and Identity: The reintegration of the Lord's Resistance Army child abductees in Northern Uganda*, Monograph No. 92, Institute for Security Studies, Pretoria, November 2003, p. 47.

191. Women's Commission for Refugee Women and Children, 'Children and Adolescents in Transitional Justice Processes in Sierra Leone', WCRWC, New York, June 2007, pp. 9-10.

192. Information on the International Criminal Court Victims Trust Fund, which is now operational, is available at <www.icc-cpi.int/vtf.html>.

193. General Assembly Resolution 60/147 of 16 December 2005, adopting the Basic Principles and Guidelines on the Right to a Remedy and Reparation for Victims of Gross Violations of International Human Rights Law and Serious Violations of International Humanitarian Law. The Principles adopt a victim-oriented perspective, clarify the scope of the right to a remedy, and in their guidelines, outline what can be done to realize it. They do not limit the concept of reparation to monetary compensation but provide as well for other forms of redress, such as restitution, rehabilitation, satisfaction and guarantees of non-repetition. GA Resolution 60/147 recommended that "States take the Basic Principles and Guidelines into account, promote respect thereof and bring them to the attention of members of the executive bodies of the government, in particular law enforcement officials and military and security forces, legislative bodies, the judiciary, victims and their representatives, human rights defenders and lawyers, the media and the public in general."

194. Principle 4 and 15 of the 'Basic Principles and Guidelines on the Right to a Remedy and Reparation for Victims of Gross Violations of International Human Rights Law and Serious Violations of International Humanitarian Law', General Assembly Resolution 60/147, 16 December 2005.

195. United Nations, 'Concluding Observations on OPAC by the Committee on the Rights of the Child with regard to Guatemala', UN document CRC/C/OPAC/GTM/CO/1, New York, 8 June 2007, paras. 20-21.

196. Another key challenge is ensuring that implementation of reparations programmes is guided by the best interests of the child as well as a rights-based and community-based approach.

197. UN Security Council, 'The Rule of Law and Transitional Justice in Conflict and Post-conflict Societies: Report of the Secretary-General', UN document S/2004/616, New York, 23 August 2004, paras. 54-55.

198. Ibid., para. 54.

199. United Nations, 'UN Guidelines on Justice in Matters Involving Child Victims and Witnesses of Crime', adopted by ECOSOC Resolution 2005/20 of 22 July 2005, UN document E/2005/INF/2/Add.1 of 10 August 2005, Part III – Principles, para 8.

200. For example, article 37 of the CRC bars the death penalty and life imprisonment without possibility of release.

201. These include, among others: the United Nations Standard Minimum Rule for the Administration of Juvenile Justice ('Beijing Rules'), 1985; the United Nations Guidelines for the Prevention of Juvenile Delinquency (Riyadh Guidelines), 1990; and the United Nations Rules for the Protection of Juveniles Deprived of their Liberty, 1990. Other guidelines specifically referred to by the Committee on the Rights of the Child have included the 'Guidelines for Action on Children in the Criminal Justice System' (Economic and Social Council Resolution 1997/30, Annex).

202. For example, the Committee has expressed concern that national practices are not compatible with articles 37, 39 and 40 of the Convention on the Rights of the Child and international guidelines, that there is no adequate and distinct juvenile justice system in place and that training focused on children's rights is needed. See: United Nations Children's Fund, *Implementation Handbook for the Convention on the Rights of the Child*, third edition, UNICEF, New York, September 2007, p. 606.

203. UNICEF Innocenti Research Centre and the International Center for Transitional Justice, *Children and Truth Commissions* (forthcoming 2008).

204. Sierra Leone Special Court, press release, 2 November 2002.

205. United Nations, 'Rome Statute of the International Criminal Court', UN document A/CONF.183.9, adopted 17 July 1998, article 26: Exclusion of jurisdiction over persons under 18. Children under 18 may still be prosecuted under domestic law.

206. Amnesty International, 'United States of America: The threat of a bad example – Undermining international standards as "war on terror" detentions continue', Amnesty International Report 51/114/2003, 19 August 2003.

207. United Nations, 'Concluding Observations of the Committee on the Rights of the Child: Nepal', UN document CRC/C/15/ADD.261, New York, 21 September 2005.

208. United Nations, 'General Comment No. 10 of the Committee on the Rights of the Child: Children's Rights in Juvenile Justice', UN document CRC/C/GC/10, New York, 9 February 2007.

209. United Nations, 'A World Fit for Children', UN document A/RES/S-27/2, New York, 11 October 2002.

210. Ibid., para. 43(b).

211. United Nations, UN document A/51/77, New York, 12 December 1996, para. 36.

212. United Nations, 'Impact of Armed Conflict on Children: Report of the expert of the Secretary-General, Ms. Graça Machel, submitted pursuant to General Assembly Resolution 48/157', UN document A/51/306, New York, 26 August 1996, para. 284.

213. United Nations, 'Report of the Secretary-General: Comprehensive assessment of the United Nations system response to children affected by armed conflict', UN document A/59/331, New York, 3 September 2004.

214. Child protection advisers are currently deployed in the United Nations Integrated Office in Burundi (BINUB); UN Mission for Stabilization in Haiti (MINUSTAH); African Union/United Nations Hybrid operation in Darfur (UNAMID); UN Missions in the Democratic Republic of the Congo (MONUC), Liberia (UNMIL), Nepal (UNMIN) and Sudan (UNMIS); and the UN Operation in Côte d'Ivoire (UNOCI).

215. Peacekeeping Best Practices Section, UN Department of Peacekeeping Operations, 'Lessons Learned Study: Child Protection – The impact of child protection advisers in peacekeeping operations', DPKO, May 2007.

216. United Nations, 'Children and Armed Conflict: Report of the Secretary-General', UN document A/59/695-S/2005-72, New York, 9 February 2005, para. 68.

217. Security Council Presidential Statement on Children and armed conflict, 12 February 2008 PRST/2008/6.

218. Machel 1996, paras. 281 and 303.

219. ECHA and ECPS, which aim to enhance coordination between UN agencies, are two of four committees created by the Secretary-General in the framework of the current UN reform process. Chaired by the Emergency Relief Coordinator, ECHA in particular ensures that political, peacekeeping and security issues are part of humanitarian consultations and the work of the Inter-Agency Standing Committee.

220. The IASC includes such UN humanitarian agencies as the Food and Agriculture Organization of the United Nations (FAO), UNDP, UNFPA, UNHCR, UNICEF, World Food Programme (WFP) and World Health Organization (WHO); the International Committee of the Red Cross (ICRC); the International Federation of Red Cross and Red Crescent Societies (IFRC); the World Bank; the International Organization for Migration (IOM) and the Secretary-General's Representative on the Human Rights of Internally Displaced Persons; as well as representatives of three NGO consortia: International Council of Voluntary Agencies (ICVA), InterAction and the Steering Committee for Humanitarian Response (SCHR).

221. Inter-Agency Standing Committee, 'IASC Work Plan 2007', document PR/0612/1956/0, <www.humanitarianinfo.org/iasc/_tools/download.asp?docID=1956&type=any>.

222. Machel 1996, para. 305.

223. United Nations, 'Report of the Special Representative of the Secretary-General for Children and Armed Conflict', UN document A/62/228, New York, 13 August 2007, para. 66.

224. For information on the cluster approach see <www.humanitarianreform.org> and Inter-Agency Standing Committee, 'Guidance Note on Using the Cluster Approach to Strengthen Humanitarian Response', IASC, Geneva, 24 November 2006.

225. United Nations, 'Report of the Special Representative of the Secretary-General for Children and Armed Conflict', UN document A/62/228, New York, 13 August 2007, para. 68.

226. J. Freedman, 'Contemporary Conflict and its Consequences for Children: Input paper on war economies', Contribution to the Machel study 10-year strategic review, 17 July 2007.

227. B. Verhey, 'What Are Child Protection Networks?', UNICEF Innocenti Research Centre, Florence, February 2006.

228. R. Mountain, 'Humanitarian Reform: Saving and protecting lives in DRC', Forced Migration Review, no. 29, 2008, pp. 28-30.

229. United Nations, 'Impact of Armed Conflict on Children: Report of the expert of the Secretary-General, Ms. Graça Machel, submitted pursuant to General Assembly Resolution 48/157', UN document A/51/306, New York, 26 August 1996, para. 288.

230. See original document 'The Paris Principles: Principles and guidelines on children associated with armed forces or armed groups', February 2007, <www.unicef.org/media/files/Paris_Principles__-_English.pdf>.

231. United Nations, 'Special Measures for Protection from Sexual Exploitation and Sexual Abuse', UN document ST/SGB/2003/13, New York, October 2003.

232. Inter-Agency Network for Education in Emergencies, Measuring the Implementation and Impact of the INEE Minimum Standards, INEE, New York, August 2007, pp. 21-23.

233. Inter-Agency Network for Education in Emergencies, 'Monitoring Systems for Emergency Education', <www.ineesite.org/page.asp?pid=1132>.

234. Christian Children's Fund, International Committee of the Red Cross, International Rescue Committee, Save the Children, Terre des Hommes, United Nations High Commissioner for Refugees.

235. United Nations, 'Report of the Special Representative of the Secretary-General for Children and Armed Conflict', UN document A/62/228, New York, 13 August 2007, para. 79.

236. J. Thompson, Humanitarian Financing Trends: Child programming and protection, Consultant report for Machel 10-year strategic review, July 2007, pp. 7-8.

237. United Nations Central Emergency Response Fund, 'CERF Figures', <ochaonline.un.org/cerf/CERFFigures/tabid/1924/Default.aspx>.

238. United Nations Office for the Coordination of Humanitarian Affairs, 'Humanitarian/Emergency Response Fund', <ochaonline.un.org/FundingFinance/ResponseFunds/tabid/4404/Default.aspx>.

239. Ibid.

240. OCHA Sudan, 'United Nations and Partners Work Plan for Sudan', <www.unsudanig.org/workplan/chf/>.

241. B. Willits-King, T. Mowjee and J. Barham, 'Evaluation of Common/Pooled Humanitarian Funds in DRC and Sudan', OCHA ESS, December 2007, pp. 5, 18, 19, 52. <ochaonline.un.org/OchaLinkClick.aspx?link=ocha&docId=1088368>.

242. Paris Declaration on Aid Effectiveness, an initiative of the Organisation for Economic Co-operation and Development, <www.oecd.org/document/18/0,2340,en_2649_3236398_35401554_1_1_1_1,00.html>.

243. United Nations Development Programme, 'UNDP-Administered Multi-Donor Trust Funds and Joint Programmes', UNDP, New York, <www.undp.org/mdtf/overview.shtml>.

244. For an overview of recent developments in humanitarian funding, see: P. Walker and K. Pepper, 'The State of Humanitarian Funding', Forced Migration Review, no. 29, 2007, pp. 33-35.

245. B. Willitts-King, Practical Approaches to Needs-based Allocation of Humanitarian Aid: A review for Irish Aid on donor practices, July 2006, p. 20.

246. P. Walker and K. Pepper, 'The State of Humanitarian Funding', Forced Migration Review, no. 29, 2007.

247. Good Humanitarian Donorship, <www.goodhumanitariandonorship.org>.

248. A. Stoddard, K. Haver and A. Harmer, Operational Consequences of Reform Project Working Paper: Humanitarian financing reform, Humanitarian Policy Group, Overseas Development Institute, June 2007.

249. P. Walker and K. Pepper, Follow the Money: A review and analysis of the state of humanitarian funding, Feinstein International Center, Tufts University, 2007.

250. The material on the CHAP is from J. Thompson, 'Humanitarian Financing Trends: Child programming and protection', consultant report for Machel 10-year strategic review, July 2007, pp. 7-8.

251. UN document A/55/749, 26 January 2001, pp. 6-7.

252. See Reports by the Secretary-General on the follow-up to the special session of the General Assembly on children, A/59/274, 17 August 2004; A/60/207, 8 August 2005; and A/61/270, 17 August 2007.

253. Ban Ki-Moon, *Children and the Millennium Development Goals: Progress towards A World Fit for Children*, United Nations Children's Fund, New York, December 2007, pp. 55-56.

254. See pages 58 to 60 of chapter 6 of this document on international legal standards and norms for a detailed description of the Convention on the Rights of the Child mechanisms.

255. Organisation for Economic Co-operation and Development, 'Principles for Good International Engagement in Fragile States and Situations', OECD, Paris, April 2007, <www.oecd.org/dataoecd/61/45/38368714.pdf >.

256. S. Grantham-McGregor et al., 'Early Child Development in Developing Countries', *The Lancet*, vol. 369, no. 9564, 10 March 2007.

257. K. Kostelny, *Psychosocial and Protection Outcomes of CCSs: Research on young children in Northern Uganda*, Christian Children's Fund, Richmond, VA, 2008, pp. 4, 8-9, 11, 13, 33.

258. M. Vijayaraghavan et al., 'Economic Evaluation of Measles Catch-up and Follow-up Campaigns in a Country Affected by a Complex Emergency: Afghanistan, 2002 and 2003', *Disasters* (in press), pp. 256-458.

259. A. Anderson et al., 'Standards Put to the Test: Implementing the INEE Minimum Standards for Education in Emergencies, Chronic Crisis and Early Reconstruction', Humanitarian Practice Network Paper, no. 57, HPN, London, December 2006, p. 2.

260. A. Donahue and E. Loaiza, 'Millennium Development Goals (MDGs) in Conflict-Affected Countries', UNICEF Strategic Information Section, New York, January 2008 (unpublished); and United Nations Children's Fund, *Progress for Children: A World Fit for Children statistical review, Number 6*, UNICEF, New York, December 2007. Note: Statistics from conflict-affected states are largely absent from the UNESCO EFA Global Monitoring Reports, because in many cases, figures are unavailable or inaccurate due to poor record-keeping and population movements that complicate already weak demographic data. For an alternative analysis based on a different methodology, see Save the Children, *Last in Line, Last in School: How donors are failing children in conflict-affected fragile states*, Save the Children, London, 2007.

261. A. Anderson et al., 'Standards Put to the Test: Implementing the INEE Minimum Standards for Education in Emergencies, Chronic Crisis and Early Reconstruction', Humanitarian Practice Network Paper, no. 57, HPN, London, December 2006, p. 8.

262. UN News Centre, 'UNESCO Says the World Faces an 18 Million Teacher Shortfall in Coming Decade', 5 October 2006, <www.un.org/apps/news/story.asp?NewsID=20147&Cr=educat&Cr1=>.

263. B. O'Malley, *Education Under Attack: A global study on targeted political and military violence against education staff, students, teachers, union and government officials, and institutions*, United Nations Educational, Scientific and Cultural Organization, Paris, 2007, p. 6.

264. Differences in the estimated number of children out of school in conflict-affected countries are due to the alternative methodologies used by UNICEF and Save the Children.

265. Save the Children, *Last in Line, Last in School: How donors are failing children in conflict-affected fragile states, 2007*, Save the Children, London, p. 20.

266. Ibid., p. 15.

267. Ibid., p. 22.

268. A. Donahue and E. Loaiza, *Millennium Development Goals (MDGs) in Conflict-Affected Countries*, UNICEF Strategic Information Section, New York, January 2008 (unpublished).

269. D. Guha-Sapir and W. Panhuis, 'Conflict Related Mortality: An analysis of 37 datasets', *Disasters*, vol. 28, 2004, pp. 418-428; and W. Moss et al., 'Child Health in Complex Emergencies', *Bulletin of the World Health Organization*, vol. 84, no. 1, 2006, p. 59. Another source noted that pneumonia, diarrhoea and malaria together caused 80 per cent of deaths among Congolese refugee children in the United Republic of Tanzania in 1999 (L. Talley, P. Spiegel and M. Girgis, 'An Investigation of Increasing Mortality among Congolese Refugees in Lugufu Camp, Tanzania, May-June 1999', *Journal of Refugee Studies*, vol. 14, 2001, pp. 417-427).

270. R. Garfield, 'Measuring Humanitarian Emergencies', *Disaster Medicine and Public Health Preparedness*, vol. 1, no. 2, 2007, p. 111.

271. R. Black, S. Morris and J. Bryce, 'Where and Why are Ten Million Children Dying Every Year?' *The Lancet*, vol. 361, 2003, pp. 2226-2234.

272. A. Zwi et al., 'Child Health in Armed Conflict: Time to rethink', *The Lancet*, vol. 367, 2006, pp. 1886-1888.

273. N. Dadgar et al., 'Implementation of a Mass Measles Campaign in Central Afghanistan, December 2001 to May 2002', *Journal of Infectious Diseases*, vol. 187, supplement 1, 2003, pp. S186-S190.

274. B. Loevinsohn and A. Harding, 'Buying Results? Contracting for health service delivery in developing countries', *The Lancet*, vol. 366, 2005, pp. 676-681.

275. M. Vijayaraghavan et al., 'Economic Evaluation of Measles Catch-up and Follow-up Campaigns in a Country Affected by a Complex Emergency: Afghanistan, 2002 and 2003', *Disasters, the Journal of Disaster Studies, Policy and Management*, vol. 30, no. 2, 2006, pp. 256-269.

276. US Centers for Disease Control and Prevention, 'Emergency Measles Control Activities: Darfur, Sudan, 2004', *Morbidity and Mortality Weekly Report*, vol. 53, no. 38, 1 October 2004, pp. 897-899.

277. United Nations High Commissioner for Refugees, *Reproductive Health in Refugee Situations: An interagency field manual*, UNHCR, Geneva, 1999, pp. 2, 11-18.

278. M. Toole and R. Waldman, 'Prevention of Excess Mortality in Refugee and Displaced Populations in Developing Countries', *JAMA*, vol. 263, 1990, pp. 3296-3302.

279. P. Salama et al., 'Lessons Learned from Complex Emergencies over the Past Decade', *The Lancet*, vol. 364, 2004, pp. 1801-1813.

280. H. Young et al., 'Public Nutrition in Complex Emergencies', *The Lancet*, vol. 364, 2004, p. 1899.

281. A. Donahue and E. Loaiza, 'Millennium Development Goals in Conflict-Affected Countries', UNICEF Strategic Information Section, New York, p. 7 (unpublished); and UNICEF, *Progress for Children: A World Fit for Children statistical review, Number 6*, UNICEF, New York, December 2007, p. 4.

282. Ibid.

283. D. Paul, 'Heading Home? Protection and return in northern Uganda', *Humanitarian Exchange Magazine*, no. 36, Humanitarian Practice Network, Overseas Development Institute, London, 2006.

284. R. Brennan, M. Despines and L. Roberts, 'Mortality Surveys in the Democratic Republic of Congo: Humanitarian impact and lessons learned', *Humanitarian Exchange Magazine*, no. 35, Humanitarian Practice Network, Overseas Development Institute, London, 2006; B. Coghlan et al., 'Mortality in the Democratic Republic of Congo: A nationwide survey', *The Lancet*, vol. 367, 2006, p. 50.

285. F. Mason and A. Taylor, *A Review of the Advances and Challenges in Nutrition in Conflicts and Crises over the Last 20 Years*, Food and Nutrition Technical Assistance Project, Academy for Educational Development, Washington, D.C., 2003.

286. G. Hogley Cotes, 'Delivering Supplementary and Therapeutic Feeding in Darfur: Coping with insecurity', *Field Exchange, Emergency Nutrition Network*, vol. 28, 2006, p. 2; and S. Roughneen and S. Fox, 'Integrated Community Health in Darfur: Interacting with culture, dealing with insecurity', *Humanitarian Exchange Magazine*, no. 36, Humanitarian Practice Network, Overseas Development Institute, London, 2006, p. 27.

287. P. Salama et al., 'Lessons Learned from Complex Emergencies over the Past Decade', *The Lancet,* vol. 364, 2004, pp. 1902, 1904.

288. Valid International, *Community-based Therapeutic Care (CTC): A field manual,* first edition, Valid International, Oxford, 2006, p. 2.

289. Ibid., p.150.

290. Ibid., p. 3.

291. WHO/WFP/UNICEF, 'Joint Statement on Preventing and Controlling Micronutrient Deficiencies in Populations Affected by Emergencies', World Health Organization, Geneva, 2007.

292. Inter-Agency Standing Committee, 'Women, Girls, Boys and Men: Different needs – equal opportunities', *Gender Handbook in Humanitarian Action*, IASC, December 2006.

293. World Food Programme, *Gender Mainstreaming in WFP: An integrated assessment,* WFP, Rome, 1998, pp. 3, 6.

294. C. Reis, 'Addressing Sexual Violence in Emergencies', *Humanitarian Exchange Magazine*, no. 32, Humanitarian Practice Network, Overseas Development Institute, London, 2005, p. 33.

295. H. Young et al., 'Public Nutrition in Complex Emergencies', *The Lancet,* vol. 364, 2004, p. 1900.

296. World Health Organization, *Management of Severe Malnutrition: A manual for physicians and other senior health workers*, WHO, Geneva, 1999, <http://whqlibdoc.who.int/hq/1999/a57361.pdf>.

297. Infant and Young Child Feeding in Emergencies Core Group, *Operational Guidance for Emergency Relief Staff and Programme Managers on Infant and Young Child Feeding in Emergencies,* Emergency Nutrition Network, Oxford, 2006.

298. F. Grünewald, 'Darfur and the Dynamics of Crisis Management', *Humanitarian Exchange Magazine*, no. 30, Humanitarian Practice Network, Overseas Development Institute, London, 2005.

299. H. Young et al., 'Public Nutrition in Complex Emergencies', *The Lancet,* vol. 364, 2004, p. 1900.

300. L. Fewtrell et al., *Water, Sanitation and Hygiene: Quantifying the health impact at national and local levels in countries with incomplete water supply and sanitation coverage*, WHO Environmental Burden of Disease Series, no. 15, World Health Organization, Geneva, 2007, pp. 43, 45.

301. World Health Organization, *Frequently Asked Questions in Case of Emergencies: Health risks – Drinking-water and sanitation*, 2008.

302. Intergovernmental Panel on Climate Change, *Climate Change 2007: Impacts, adaptation and vulnerability,* contribution of Working Group II to the Fourth Assessment Report of the Intergovernmental Panel on Climate Change, Cambridge University Press, Cambridge, 2007, pp. 42, 44, 48-49.

303. V. Curtis and S. Cairncross, 'Effect of Washing Hands with Soap on Diarrhoea Risk in the Community: A systematic review', *The Lancet*, vol. 3, 2003, p. 232.

304. World Health Organization, *Guidelines for Drinking-Water Quality,* third edition, incorporating first addendum, vol. 1, recommendations, 2006, WHO, Geneva, pp. 50-51.

305. Office of the United Nations High Commissioner for Refugees, *Statistical Yearbook 2005*, UNHCR, Geneva, 2007, p. 67.

306. United Nations, 'UNICEF Water, Sanitation and Hygiene Strategies for 2006-2015', UN document E/ICEF/2006/6, New York, 15 November 2005.

307. World Health Organization, *Guidelines for Drinking-Water Quality*, third edition incorporating first addendum, vol. 1, recommendations, WHO, Geneva, 2006, p. 78.

308. J. Barenbaum, R. Vladislav and M. Schwab-Stone, 'The Psychosocial Aspects of Children Exposed to War: Practice and policy initiatives', *Journal of Child Psychology and Psychiatry*, vol. 45, no. 1, 2004, p. 42.

309. Inter-Agency Standing Committee, *Guidelines on Mental Health and Psychosocial Support in Emergency Settings*, IASC, Geneva, 2007, p. 2.

310. J. Duncan and L. Arntson, *Children in Crisis: Good practices in evaluating psychosocial programming*, Save the Children Federation, Washington, D.C., 2003, p. 10.

311. Ibid.

312. R. Dybdahl, 'Children and Mothers in War: An outcome study of a psychosocial intervention program', *Child Development*, vol. 72, no. 4, 2001, pp. 1-2.

313. Women's Commission for Refugee Women and Children, *Untapped Potential: Adolescents affected by armed conflict – A review of programs and policies,* WCRWC, New York, 2000, pp. 9, 37.

314. United Nations Children's Fund, *Working with Children in Unstable Situations: Principles and concepts to guide psychosocial responses*, UNICEF, New York, 2003, pp. 22-23.

315. K. Ehntholt and W. Yule, 'Practitioner Review: Assessment and treatment of adolescents who have experienced war-related trauma', *Journal of Child Psychology and Psychiatry*, vol. 47, 2006, p. 1197.

316. Such networks include the Grupo de Acción Comunitaria (GAC), Regional Psychosocial Support Initiative (REPSSI), Regional Emergency Psychosocial Support Initiative, The International Federation Reference Centre for Psychosocial Support, and the International Federation of Red Cross and Red Crescent Societies.

317. M. Lowicki-Zucca et al., 'Estimates of HIV Burden in Emergencies', *Sexually Transmitted Infections*, 2008 (in press).

318. UNICEF Canada, 'HIV/AIDS, Conflict and Displacement', report on the XVI International AIDS Conference affiliated event, Toronto, 12 August 2006, hosted by UNICEF and UNHCR, pp. 26-27, <http://data.unaids.org/pub/Report/2006/hiv_aids_conflict_displacement.pdf >.

319. United Nations Development Programme, 'United Nations System-wide Work Programme on Scaling up HIV/AIDS Services for Populations of Humanitarian Concern: Analysis of PRSPs of countries of concern to establish baseline indicators for output 1', UNDP, New York, April 2007 (unpublished).

320. United Nations Development Programme, 'Analysis and Indicators for Countries of Concern: Baseline and OVIs for populations of humanitarian concern', UNDP, New York, October 2007 (unpublished).

321. This section draws from UNICEF's latest Child Protection Strategy, endorsed by the UNICEF Executive Board on 5 June 2008 (UN document E/ICEF/2008/5/Rev.1). Other calls for child protection systems are made in Save the Children's 'Protecting Children in Emergencies', <www.savethechildren.org/publications/advocacy/policy_brief_final.pdf>, and the United Nations Secretary-General's study on violence against children.

322. Research suggests that some foster parents clearly provide excellent care. At the other end of the spectrum, fostering can involve overt exploitation and abuse, and widespread discrimination. Source: D. Tolfree, 'Children in Residential Care', a paper delivered at the Second International Conference on Children and Residential Care, Stockholm, 12-15 May 2003, p. 5.

323. M. de la Soudiere, J. Williamson and J. Botte, *The Lost Ones: Emergency care and family tracing for separated children from birth to five years,* UNICEF, New York, April 2007, p. 14.

324. D. Tolfree, *Facing the Crisis: Supporting children through positive care options,* Save the Children Fund, London, 2005, p. 2.

325. 'Freedom, Security and Justice for Separated Children?', European Conference, Brussels, 3 November 2004 (sponsored by Defence for Children International, Save the Children and the Separated Children in Europe Programme).

326. United Nations High Commissioner for Refugees, 'UNHCR Guidelines on Determining the Best Interests of the Child', UNHCR Geneva, May 2008.

327. Under the UNHCR-led protection cluster, UNICEF is the designated focal point agency and 'provider of last resort' for child protection.

328. International Committee of the Red Cross, *Annual Report 2007*, ICRC, Geneva, pp. 95-97.

329. United Nations Children's Fund, 'Humanitarian Action: Donor update', UNICEF, New York, 8 March 2004.

330. A. Hepburn, J. Williamson and T. Wolfram, 'Separated Children: Care and protection of children in emergencies – A field guide', Save the Children Federation, Westport, CT, 2004, p. 34.

331. Anecdotal evidence has shown that many separated children are inclined to migrate to urban centres or engage in hazardous work. More comprehensive data collection is required, however, to understand these links.

332. The Paris Principles refer to the term 'recruitment' as the compulsory, forced and voluntary conscription or enlistment of children into any kind of armed force or armed group. 'Unlawful recruitment or use' is recruitment or use of children under the age stipulated in the international treaties applicable to the armed force or armed group in question or under applicable national law. Source: The Paris Principles: Principles and guidelines on children associated with armed forces or armed groups, February 2007, p. 7.

333. Ibid.

334. V. Achvarina and S. Reich, 'No Place to Hide: Refugees, displaced persons, and the recruitment of child soldiers', International Security, vol. 31, no. 1, Summer 2006, pp. 127-164.

335. The Paris Principles: The principles and guidelines on children associated with armed forces or armed groups, February 2007, p. 8.

336. Sweden's Ministry for Foreign Affairs, Stockholm Initiative on Disarmament, Demobilisation, Reintegration: Final report, 2006, p. 9.

337. School for Peace Culture of Autonomous University of Barcelona, Analysis of the Disarmament, Demobilisation and Reintegration (DDR) Programs Existing in the World during 2006, Bellaterra, Spain, March 2007, pp. 21-23.

338. World Bank, 'Child Soldiers: Prevention, demobilization and reintegration', no. 3, Conflict Prevention and Reconstruction Unit, Washington, D.C., May 2002, p. 2.

339. Formally called the 'Cape Town Principles and Best Practices on the Prevention of Recruitment of Children into the Armed Forces and on Demobilization and Social Reintegration of Child Soldiers in Africa'.

340. See also: United Nations Children's Fund and the Coalition to Stop the Use of Child Soldiers, Guide to the Optional Protocol on the Involvement of Children in Armed Conflict, December 2003, <www.unddr.org/tool_docs/option_protocol_conflict[1].pdf>.

341. For further details on the United Nations Integrated Disarmament, Demobilization and Reintegration (IDDR) standards, see <www.unddr.org/index.php>; to download the operational guide, see <www.unddr.org/iddrs/iddrs_guide.php>.

342. Two outcome documents resulted from this process. The first, a short document entitled 'The Paris Commitments', reaffirms international standards relating to the protection of children associated with armed forces and groups and good practice to support their release and reintegration. It is addressed to States. The second document, 'The Paris Principles', provides detailed programme guidance to practitioners to ensure that all disarmament, demobilization and reintegration processes are designed to improve the quality of care for and protection of children. For copies of these documents, see <www.un.org/children/conflict/english/parisprinciples.html>.

343. The Paris Principles: The principles and guidelines on children associated with armed forces or armed groups, February 2007, <www.unicef.org/protection/files/ParisPrinciples_EN.pdf>; and the Operational Guide to the Integrated DDR Standards, <www.unddr.org/iddrs/iddrs_guide.php>.

344. G. Landry, Study on Reintegration of Children in Armed Conflict, Canadian International Development Agency, Gatineau, Quebec, December 2007, p. 7.

345. World Bank, 'Child Soldiers: Prevention, demobilization and reintegration', no. 3, Conflict Prevention and Reconstruction Unit, Washington, D.C., May 2002, p. 1.

346. Office of the Special Representative of the Secretary-General for Children and Armed Conflict, UNICEF, Global Youth Action Network, UNFPA, Women's Commission for Refugee Women, "Will You Listen?" Young voices from conflict zones, companion booklet to the Machel 10-year strategic review, UNICEF, New York, 2007, p. 5.

347. G. Landry, Study on Reintegration of Children in Armed Conflict, Canadian International Development Agency, Gatineau, Quebec, December 2007, p. 10.

348. B. Verhey, Reaching the Girls: Study on girls associated with armed forces and groups in the Democratic Republic of Congo, Save the Children UK, Care, International Foundation for Education & Self-Help (IFESH), IRC, November 2004, p. 2.

349. Women's Commission for Refugee Women and Children, 'Participatory Research Study with Adolescents and Youth in Sierra Leone', WCRWC, New York, April-July 2002, p. 6.

350. A. Veale and A. Stavrou, Violence, Reconciliation and Identity: The reintegration of Lord's Resistance Army child abductees in northern Uganda, Institute for Security Studies, December 2003, pp. 36-38.

351. This approach is now strongly emphasized in the Paris Principles and other guiding principles.

352. Female member of a focus group interviewed by Jenny Pearlman Robinson and Juliet Young, Gulu district (Uganda), 12 May 2007, from Women's Commission for Refugee Women and Children, Listening to Youth: The experiences of young people in northern Uganda, Contribution to the Machel 10-year strategic review with support from UNICEF, June 2007, p. 16.

353. United Nations, 'Children and DDR', section 5.30, Operational Guide to the Integrated Disarmament, Demobilization and Reintegration Standards (IDDRS), UN DDR Resource Centre, New York, p. 221, PDF available at <www.unddr.org/iddrs/iddrs_guide.php>.

354. International Labour Organization, Prevention of Child Recruitment and Reintegration of Children Associated with Armed Forces and Groups: Strategic framework for addressing the economic gap, ILO, Geneva, 2007.

355. J. MacVeigh, S. Maguire and J. Wedge, Stolen Futures: The reintegration of children affected by armed conflict, submission to the 10-year review of the 1996 Machel study on the impact of armed conflict on children, Save the Children UK, London, 2007, p. viii.

356. 'UN System-wide Policy Paper for Employment Creation, Income-Generation and Reintegration in Post-Conflict Settings', May 2008, p. 29.

357. K. Peters, 'From Weapons to Wheels: Young Sierra Leonean ex-combatants become motorbike taxi-riders', Journal of Peace, Conflict & Development, March 2007, p. 2.

358. 'UN System-wide Policy Paper for Employment Creation, Income-Generation and Reintegration in Post-Conflict Settings', May 2008, p. 30.

359. G. Landry, Study on Reintegration of Children in Armed Conflict, Canadian International Development Agency, Gatineau, Quebec, December 2007, pp. 13-14.

360. Women's Commission for Refugee Women and Children, Listening to Youth: The experiences of young people in northern Uganda, contribution to Machel 10-year strategic review with support from UNICEF, June 2007, p. 16.

361. School for Peace Culture of Autonomous University of Barcelona, Analysis of the Disarmament, Demobilization and Reintegration (DDR) Programs Existing in the World during 2006, Bellaterra, Spain, March 2007, p. 7.

362. United Nations Inter-Agency Standing Committee, Guidelines for Gender-based Violence Interventions in Humanitarian Settings: Focusing on prevention of and response to sexual violence in emergencies, IASC, Geneva, 2005, p. 3.

363. United Nations Population Fund, 'UNFPA & Young People: Imagine the largest generation of adolescents in history', UNFPA, New York, 2003, p. 3.

364. United Nations Inter-Agency Standing Committee, Guidelines for Gender-based Violence Interventions in Humanitarian Settings: Focusing on prevention of and response to sexual violence in emergencies, IASC, Geneva, 2005, p. 3.

365. The 2005 IASC guidelines indicate (p. 8) that the terms 'victim' and 'survivor' can be used interchangeably. Most often, 'victim' is used in the legal and medical sectors. 'Survivor' is generally preferred in the psychological and social support sectors because it implies resiliency.

366. Women's accounts from 2003 extracted from Amnesty International, *Lives Blown Apart: Crimes against women in times of conflict,* Amnesty International, London, 2004.

367. United Nations Institute for Training and Research, 'Training for Civilian Personnel in Peacekeeping Operations on the Special Needs of Women and Children in Conflict', UNITAR, Geneva, November 2006, <www.unitar.org/wcc/flyer.pdf>; Save the Children, *The State of the World's Mothers 2003,* Save the Children, 2003, pp. 24-26.

368. Among the codes of conduct, UNHCR adopted one in 2002, and the United Nations Secretary-General's Bulletin 'Special Measures for Protection from Sexual Exploitation and Sexual Abuse' (ST/SGB/2003/13) was issued in October 2003. Also see: UN Department of Peacekeeping Operations (DPKO), *Ten Rules: Code of personal conduct for blue helmets,* 1998, and *We are United Nations Peacekeepers,* 1998.

369. For details of an example in Indonesia, see: Amnesty International, 'Indonesia: The impact of impunity on women in Aceh', AI Index: ASA 21/60/00, Amnesty International, London, 23 November 2000, p. 13.

370. Women's Commission for Refugee Women and Children, *Beyond Firewood: Fuel alternatives and protection strategies for displaced women and girls,* WCRWC, New York, March 2006, pp. 1-5.

371. J. Schipper, *Study on Funding for Sexual Violence in Conflict,* UN Action against Sexual Violence in Conflict (unpublished), May 2007.

372. The implications of the growing proportion of young people in the world's population has been the focus of a number of recent global reports, in particular UNDP's *Youth in Conflict* (2006) and the UN's *World Youth* reports in 2005 and 2007. Data drawn from population statistics in: United Nations Children's Fund, *The State of the World's Children 2008: Child survival,* UNICEF, New York, December 2007.

373. Collier et al. argue that if the true costs associated with political violence, such as disease, prolonged poverty, economic damage and increased likelihood of trafficking and criminality are factored in, a conflict can cost from $60 billion to $250 billion, depending on how these costs are calculated. P. Collier, L. Chauvet and H. Hegre, 'The Security Challenge in Conflict-Prone Countries', *Copenhagen Consensus 2008 Conflicts Challenge Paper,* Copenhagen Consensus Center, Frederiksberg, Denmark, April 2008, pp. 8-12.

374. M. Chalmers, *Spending to Save? An analysis of the cost effectiveness of conflict prevention,* Centre for International Cooperation and Security, Department of Peace Studies, University of Bradford, Bradford, UK, 12 June 2004, p. 2.

375. United Nations, 'Progress Report on the Prevention of Armed Conflict: Report of the Secretary-General', UN document A/60/891, New York, 18 July 2006.

376. 'From Words to Action, Final Conference Report', International Conference on War-Affected Children, Winnipeg, Canada, 10-17 September 2000, pp. 62-63.

377. P. Collier, *Development and Conflict,* Oxford University, Oxford, 1 October 2004, p. 1, <www.un.org/esa/documents/Development.and.Conflict2.pdf>.

378. As noted by Collier et al. 2008: "Nine of the 32 conflicts active in 2005 had been inactive in the previous year, and in 2006 there were a further four new active conflicts. All of these new conflicts in 2005 and 2006 were conflict relapses, further emphasizing the importance of our focus on post-conflict situations."

379. Executive Office of the Secretary-General, *Inventory: United Nations capacity in peacebuilding,* United Nations, New York, September 2006, p. 6.

380. United Nations, 'Progress Report on the Prevention of Armed Conflict: Report of the Secretary-General', UN document A/60/891, New York, 18 July 2006.

381. Paulo Sérgio Pinheiro, *World Report on Violence Against Children,* United Nations, Geneva, 2006, p. 6.

382. United Nations Department of Economic and Social Affairs, *World Youth Report: Young people's transition to adulthood – Progress and challenges,* UNDESA, New York, 2007.

383. United Nations, 'Statement by the President of the Security Council', UN document S/PRST/2008/6, New York, 12 February 2008.

384. Global Partnership for the Prevention of Armed Conflict, 'People Building Peace: A global action agenda for the prevention of armed conflict', Global Partnership for the Prevention of Armed Conflict, The Hague, 2007, pp. 3, 6.

385. Global Partnership for the Prevention of Armed Conflict website, <www.gppac.org/page.php?id=1513>.

386. Alliance of Civilizations, <www.unaoc.org/content/view/92/127/lang,english/>.

387. IASC Sub-Working Group on Preparedness and Contingency Planning, <www.humanitarianinfo.org/iasc/content/subsidi/swg_preparedness/default.asp?bodyID=14&&publish=0&publish=0>.

388. For more details on Security Council Resolution 1612 as an option for prevention, see 'Preventive Strategies for Children and Armed Conflict: Implementation of Security Council Resolution 1612 and other policies', Forum on Children and Armed Conflict, Peacebuilding – The Canadian Peacebuilding Network, March 2008.

389. Save the Children Sweden, *Child Protection in Emergencies: Priorities, principles and practices,* Save the Children, Stockholm, 2007, p. 48.

390. Ibid., p. 19.

391. The peacebuilding framework for Guinea-Bissau had not yet been finalized during the writing of this report.

392. A. Barbolet et al., *The Utility and Dilemmas of Conflict Sensitivity,* Berghof Research Center for Constructive Conflict Management, Berlin, April 2005.

393. Canadian International Development Agency, '*Education and Peacebuilding: A preliminary operational framework*', CIDA, Gatineau, Quebec, 1999.

394. Save the Children, *Rewrite the Future: One year on,* Save the Children, London, September 2007, p. 4.

395. P. Rose and M. Greeley, *Education in Fragile States: Capturing lessons and identifying good practices,* paper prepared for the DAC Fragile States Working Group, May 2006, pp. 2, 3, 4, 7, 22.

396. P. Buckland, *Reshaping the Future: Education and post-conflict reconstruction,* World Bank, Washington, D.C., 2005.

397. T. Jackson, *Equal Access to Education: A peace imperative for Burundi,* International Alert, London, 2000, p. 5.

398. P. Bauman, P. Gazala and M. Ayalew, *Comparative Analysis of the Impact of Tsunami and Tsunami Interventions on Conflicts in Sri Lanka and Aceh/Indonesia,* 2006; executive summary available at <http://web.mit.edu/cis/www/migration/pubs/rrwp/34_tsunami.htm>.

399. A. Barbolet et al., *The Utility and Dilemmas of Conflict Sensitivity,* Berghof Research Center for Constructive Conflict Management, Berlin, April 2005, p. 8.

400. United Nations, 'Resolution 53/25: International Decade for a Culture of Peace and Non-Violence for the Children of the World, 2001-2010', New York, 10 November 1998.

401. M. Sinclair, *Learning to Live Together: Building skills, values and attitudes for the twenty-first century,* UNESCO, Paris, 2004, pp. 21-22; and UNESCO, UNHCR and INEE, *Inter-Agency Peace Education Programme: Skills for constructive living – Overview of the programme,* UNESCO, Paris, November 2005, pp. 8, 14-15.

402. P. Baxter and V. Ikobwa, 'Peace Education: Why and how?', *Forced Migration Review,* vol. 1, no. 22, pp. 22-28; and UNESCO, UNHCR and INEE, *Inter-Agency Peace Education Programme: Skills for constructive living – Overview of the programme,* UNESCO, Paris, November 2005, pp. 11-13.

403. J. Hart, *Children's Participation in Humanitarian Action: Learning from zones of armed conflict,* Refugee Studies Centre, University of Oxford, Oxford, February 2004.

404. G. Salomon, 'Does Peace Education *Really* Make A Difference?', *Peace and Conflict: Journal of Peace Psychology,* vol. 12, no. 1, 2006.

405. J. Hart, *Children's Participation in Humanitarian Action: Learning from zones of armed conflict,* Refugee Studies Centre, University of Oxford, Oxford, February 2004, pp. 26-27.

406. Ibid. p. 26.

407. R. Johnston, 'Developing a National Youth Policy: A programme review', United Nations Development Programme, New York, November 2007.

408. United Nations Development Programme, *Youth and Violent Conflict: Society and development in crisis?* UNDP, New York, 2006, p. 26.

409. See, for example: Search for Common Ground website, <www.sfcg.org/ programmes/sierra/sierra_talking.html>; and R. Taouti-Cherif, *Evaluation of Search for Common Ground-Talking Drum Studio: Sierra Leone election strategy 2007*, Search for Common Ground, Washington, D.C. and Brussels, January 2008, pp. 15-16, 20.

410. R. Johnston, *Youth and Violent Conflict Programme Review: Developing a national youth policy in Liberia*, United Nations Development Programme, New York, 2006.

411. Office of the Special Representative of the Secretary-General for Children and Armed Conflict, Global Youth Action Network, UNICEF, UNFPA and Women's Commission for Refugee Women and Children, "*Will You Listen?" Young voices from conflict zones*, UNICEF, New York, October 2007.

412. UNICEF submission to the Machel strategic review from the Latin America and Caribbean region.

413. C. O'Kane, C. Feinstein and A. Giertsen, 'Children and Young People in Post-conflict Peace-Building', *Seen, but not Heard! Placing Children and Youth on the Security Governance Agenda*, edited by D. Nosworthy, Geneva Centre for the Democratic Control of Armed Forces, (forthcoming 2008).

414. Ibid.

415. Ibid.

416. United Nations Children's Fund, *The State of the World's Children 1996*, p. 34, 'Children as Zones of Peace', <www.unicef.org/sowc96/14zones.htm>.

417. Ibid., p. 11.

418. 'Never Again Rwanda's First Youth Theatre Festival', <www.neveragain rwanda.org/index.php?mod=article& cat=news&article=24>.

419. K. Peters, 'From Weapons to Wheels: Young Sierra Leonean ex-combatants become motorbike taxi-riders', *Journal of Peace, Conflict and Development 10*, March 2007, p. 21.

420. K. Emmons, *Adult Wars, Child Soldiers: Voices of children involved in armed conflict in the East Asia and Pacific Region*, UNICEF East Asia and Pacific Region Office report, 2002, pp. 57, 74-75.

421. K. Peters, 'From Weapons to Wheels: Young Sierra Leonean ex-combatants become motorbike taxi-riders', *Journal of Peace, Conflict and Development 10*, March 2007, p. 3.

INDEX

E

Early warning systems, creating effective, 174–175

Education
achieving universal primary, 9, 28
addressing holistically, 117–118
in Afghanistan, 117
in camp environments, 118
catch-up programmes (life skills, literacy), 156–157
checkpoint closures, effect of, on access to, 14
children's access to, 14
expanding opportunities for older children and out-of-school youth, 119–120
financing, in emergencies, 119
global standards in raising quality of, in emergencies, 114
incident reporting on attacks on schools, 22
in Iraq, 116
jump-starting, through back-to-school campaigns, 117–118
peace, 176–179
providing safe place for, in emergencies, 118
as road to peace, 176
in Sudan, 115, 117
in Uganda, 117

Education for All
commitments, 112
Dakar Conference, 114

Education rights
changes in approach and understanding, 114–115
global standard in raising quality in emergencies, 114
Machel study on, 113–114
progress in policy and practice, 115–118
protecting, 112–121

El Salvador
immunization campaign in, 181
security sector reform in, 180

Emergencies
financing education in, 119
global standards in raising quality of education in, 114
health interventions in, 109
mainstreaming hygiene promotion in, 135

Emergency Nutrition Network, development of, 130

Emergency response funds, 96

Emergency spaces for children, 108

Emotional distress, during and after armed conflict, 20

Empowering Hands, 155

Enforced disappearance as conflict-related violations against children, 25

Enforced displacement, 18

Enslavement, definition of, as crime against humanity, 68

Environmental sustainability, ensuring, 29

Ethiopia
armed conflict and, 10
emergency response funds in, 96
Enhanced Outreach Strategy of, 123
identification as conflict-affected country, 26, 27
lowest MDGs achievers, 28

European Union Guidelines on Children in Armed Conflict, 64

Executive Committee on Humanitarian Affairs (ECHA), 88

Extractive Industries Transparency Initiative, 90

F

Families, separation from, 4

Family-based care
channelling investment to children in, 150
institutionalization versus, 146–147
investing in, 149

Family separation, 146

Field workers, preparing practical guidelines for, 87

Financial resources, increasing, 95–97

Firewood Collection, mitigating risks associated with, 166

Forced displacement as grave violation against children, 25

Fourth Geneva Convention, 13, 61

Fragmented violence, problems in measuring and categorizing, 8

France, leadership of, chair of Working Group, 48–49

Free Children from War, 92–93, 153

Funding continuity, 97–98

G

GAVI Alliance, 123

Gender
becoming more sensitive, 115–116
in defining experience of childhood, 105
education and, 113
nutrition and, 130
in promoting equality, 28
water and sanitation and, 135

Gender-based violence, 151
ending, 161–169, 196–197
Machel study on, 162
progress in policy and practice, 163–167
remaining gaps, 167–169
getting to reality of, 162
HIV associated with, 143
sensitizing police to, 167
unlawful, 4

General Assembly
Resolution 46/182 of, 88
Resolution 62/214 of, 164
work of, on political and diplomatic engagement, 44–45

Geneva Call, 21

Geneva Convention, 61, 82, 105

Geneva 'Deed of Commitment', 21, 53, 63

Genocide
in Rwanda (1994), 117, 147, 149
International Criminal Court (ICC)
and crimes against humanity, 76
jurisdiction on, 68
Security Council Resolution 1820 on, 163
tribunals for the former Yugoslavia and Rwanda on, 67

Geographical disparities, armed conflicts and, 30

German anti-terrorism programme, 14

Global developments in children's participation, 34–35

Global framework, building for justice, 58
peace education initiatives on, 177

Global Fund to Fight AIDS, Tuberculosis and Malaria, 143

Global Partnership, Knowledge Generation and Sharing Network, 174

Global partnership for development, developing, 29

Global Partnership for the Prevention of Armed Conflict, 174

Global standards, setting, 92–94
education quality in emergencies raised by, 114

Global warming, effects of, 134

GOAL, 129

Good Humanitarian Donorship, 97, 199

Grave violations against children, 21–26, 49, 55, 192–194
the Human Rights Council on, 52
Machel strategic review on, 48
Security Council's framework for engagement on Children and Armed Conflict, 54
Security Council monitoring on six, 46
Secretary-General monitoring mechanism on, 47
Security Council Resolution 1612 focus on, 118
Security Council Resolution 1780 condemnation of, in Haiti, 46
Security Council Resolution 1769 on , in Darfur, 51
in Somalia, 90
System-wide Monitoring and Reporting Mechanism, 82
2005 UN Secretary-General's report on children and armed conflict, 18
World Fit For Children agenda on ending, 100

Grenada, back-to-school campaigns in, 117

Guantánamo Bay, 77

Guatemala
arms in, 9
child participation in peacebuilding in, 35
security sector reform in, 180

Guiding Principles on Internal Displacement, 62

Guinea, 153
Durable Solutions Committee in, 149
refugee children in, 149

Guinea-Bissau, peacebuilding in, 175

Guinea worm disease (dracunculiasis), 124

H

Hague Appeal for Peace, 178

Haiti, 186, 188
abduction in, 24
armed conflicts in, 8–9
children in armed conflict in, 8–9
grave violations of children's rights in, 46
identification as conflict-affected country, 26, 27
post-conflict needs assessments in, 175
sexual violence in, 23

recommendations on, 54–55
work of General Assembly in, 44–45

Political processes, facilitating in children's participation, 41

Political violence, children's involvement in, 37–39

Popular Movement for the Liberation of Angola (MPLA), struggle between National Union for Total Independence of Angola (UNITA) and, 12

Populations, estimates of affected, 19–20

Pornography, recruitment of children for, 26

Poverty
as by-product of armed conflict, 23
eradication of extreme, 28

Prematurity, guidelines for managing, 126

Private sector, 90

Private security companies, 10
allegations of misconduct by, 11
outsourcing of military and police functions to, 11

ProCap, 95

Programme of Action to Prevent, Combat and Eradicate the Illicit Trade in Small Arms and Light Weapons in All Its Aspects, 194

Prostitution, 161, 164
as gender-based violence, 162
recruitment of children for, 26

Proxy forces
increased use of, 10
use of, 11

Psychosocial disorders, preventing and treating range of, 125

Psychosocial recovery. *See* Mental health and psychosocial recovery

Psychotherapeutic approaches, 138

Pul-i-Khomri district, 2007 suicide bomb attack against, 13

Q

al-Qaida, 13
links of, 10

R

Rape, 18
in Central African Republic, 68–69
in Haiti, 46
sexual violence and victims of, 161, 163
as war crimes, 67
as weapon of war, 11, 23

Reconciliation
in Angola, 72
culturally sensitive approaches to, 73
in Mozambique, 72
in Rwanda, 72
in Sierra Leone, 35, 38, 72, 73, 181
in Timor-Leste, 72
in Uganda, 72

Recruitment
of children by armed forces, 11, 21–22, 37
unlawful, 4, 10

Red Crescent Movement, 95, 97, 136

Red Cross, 15, 61, 97, 105, 149

Refugees, 25
children as, 146
protecting rights of, and those internally displaced, 62

Regional bodies
engagement by, in political and diplomatic engagement, 52–54
operationalizing engagement of, 198
promoting wider engagement on issue of children and armed conflict in, 54–55

Rehabilitation efforts following emergency, 113

Reintegration
need for follow-up in successful, 155
need for roots in family and community, 107
Paris Principles on, 151
promoting sustainable, 156
recommendation for supporting inclusive strategies, 196
services that support sustainable, 154
in Sierra Leone, 73

Religious leaders and organizations, 89–90

Reparations to children, 68, 72, 74

Reproductive health, making integral part of the emergency response, 124

Reproductive Health in Refugee Situations, 124

Republic of the Congo
Youth Voice radio project in, 90
identification as conflict-affected country, 26, 27

Research initiatives, developing, 41

Resolutions. *See* General Assembly *and* Security Council

Resource wars, emergence of, 11–12

Respiratory infections, 122

Response systems, 81–101
bolstering system in, 100–101
ensuring capacity for response in, 94–98
evolution of efforts to strengthen child protection, 82–86
global response system in, 87
improving programme response, monitoring and knowledge sharing, 98–100
inter-agency collaboration and humanitarian reform in, 88–91
monitoring and reporting mechanism in, 87–88
setting global standards in, 92–94

Revenue sources for armed conflicts, 11–12

Revolutionary United Front, 23

Rheumatic heart disease, 125

Rome Statute of International Criminal Court, 25, 60–61, 76, 163
establishment of, 67–68, 82

Rotavirus, vaccines for, 125

Russian Federation, identification as conflict-affected country, 26, 27

Rwanda
ad hoc tribunals in, 76
approaches to justice and reconciliation in, 72
back-to-school initiatives in, 117
child mortality indicators in, 31
identification as conflict-affected country, 26, 27
sexual violence in, 23, 163
theatre festival in, 181–182
unaccompanied children in, 147

S

Safe spaces, 108, 117, 187–188
in Democratic Republic of the Congo, 186

Sanitation
intervention package, 122
water, sanitation, and hygiene (WASH), 134–137

Save the Children, 35, 176, 179
Alliance, 100, 115, 117
in Norway, 35
on nutrition, 130
Rewrite the Future Campaign, 175

Schools
armed conflict attacks on, 18, 22–23
attacks against, 18
preventing targeting of, 118–119

School shelters, 118

Search for Common Ground, 90

Secondary separation, 146

Security Council
action on recruitment of children and other rights violations, 46–47
advances made by Working Group, 48–49
on armed conflicts, 11
Monitoring and Reporting Mechanism, 82, 83, 86
'name and shame' initiative of, 46
reach of, in political and diplomatic engagement, 45–46
recommendations on, 54–55
Resolution 1261 of, 45–46, 48
Resolution 1308 of, 142
Resolution 1325 of, 142, 163
Resolution 1379 of, 46
Resolution 1539 of, 46, 49, 82, 86
Resolution 1612 of, 47, 48, 49, 82, 86, 88, 100, 118–119, 121, 163, 174
Resolution 1769 of, 51
Resolution 1780 of, 46
Resolution 1820 of, 163
Working Group on Children and Armed Conflict, 55, 65, 192

Security sector reform, 74–75, 180

Senegal, identification as conflict-affected country, 26, 27

Sexual and Gender-Based Violence against Refugees, Returnees, and Internally Displaced Persons: Guidelines for Prevention and Response, 166

Sexual exploitation, 18
as conflict-related violations against children, 25–26
ending, 161–169
Machel study on, 162
progress in policy and practice, 163–167
remaining gaps, 167–169
trafficking for, 161

Sexual humiliation as gender-based violence, 162

Sexually transmitted infections
risk of contracting, 151, 161
sexual violence and, 151, 161

Sexual violence, 9, 18, 67–68, 130, 151, 161
risk of, for girls, 105, 161
as war tactic, 23

Sierra Leone, 51
abduction in, 23, 24
child protection advisers in, 84

child recruitment in, 153
criminal tribunals in, 66
gender-based violence in, 167
girls in, 155
'Golden Kids News', 180
lack of job opportunities in, 157
participatory research with adolescents in, 35
peacebuilding in, 175
Peace Diamond Alliance in, 90
progress for children in, 49
reconciliation and social justice in, 35, 38, 72, 73, 182
recovery programmes in, 155
refugee children in, 149
reintegration of ex-combatants, 153, 182
sexual violence in, 23, 167
Truth and Reconciliation Commission in, 35, 38, 71, 181
United Nations investigations in, 90
Youth Voice radio project in, 90

Small arms
deadly and destabilizing effects of, 9
light weapons and, 62–63

Social justice
in Angola, 72
building global framework for, 58
culturally sensitive approaches to, 73
improving children's access to, 68, 79, 168, 195
in Mozambique, 72
in Sierra Leone, 73
special protections for children involved in, 75–76
in Uganda, 72
upholding, 57–79

Social support structures, reinforcing, 89–90

Socio-economic situation, before a conflict, 30–31

Somalia
armed conflicts in, 10
emergency response funds in, 96
grave violations of children's rights in, 47, 90
identification as conflict-affected country, 26, 27
killing or maiming in, 21
lowest MDGs achievers, 28
listening to youth in, 5
post-conflict needs assessments in, 175
restrictions on humanitarian access in, 24
role of military forces in response to humanitarian emergencies, 110
sexual violence in, 23

Special Court in Sierra Leone, 67

Special Rapporteur of the Commission on Human Rights (2000), 25

Special Representative for Children and Armed Conflict, 51–52

Special Representative of the Secretary-General on human rights and transnational corporations, 12

Sphere Humanitarian Charter and Minimum Standards in Disaster Response, 93

Sphere Project, 136
minimum standards for health services, 124

Sprinkles, 133

Sri Lanka
abduction in, 24
aid programming in, 176

child-friendly spaces in, 108
child recruitment and, 175
grave violations of children's rights in, 47
identification as conflict-affected country, 26, 27
innovative job programmes in, 158
killing or maiming in, 21
malnutrition in, 128
monitoring programmes in, 47, 99
peace education in, 178
tsunami in, 176

Sudan. See also Darfur
abduction in, 24
arms in, 9
back-to-school campaigns in, 117
common humanitarian fund/pooled funds in, 96
Comprehensive Peace Agreement between north and south in, 9
education in, 115, 117
farming and life skills in, 157
GOAL in, 129
grave violations of children's rights in, 47
health services in, 124
identification as conflict-affected country, 26, 27
killing or maiming in, 21
lowest MDGs achievers, 28
malnutrition in, 128, 129
measles immunization status, surveys in, 132
post-conflict needs assessments in, 175
restrictions on humanitarian access in, 24
sexual violence in, 23, 163
small arms and light weapons in, 9

Suicide attacks
in Iraq, 13
rise in, 21

Sulawesi (Indonesia), recruitment of children in, 13

Sustainable reintegration, services that support, 154

Sweden, humanitarian policy of, 119

T

Taliban, 10

Task Force on Children Affected by Armed Conflict, 83

Taylor, Charles Ghankay, 67

Teachers, ensuring of adequate compensation for, 116–117

Terrorism
challenges posed by, 4
internationalization of, 10, 12–14
number of incidents of, 12

Thailand
armed conflict in, 30
identification as conflict-affected country, 26, 27
school attacks in, 22

Timor-Leste
back-to-school campaigns in, 117
child-friendly spaces in, 108
justice and reconciliation in, 72

Torture, 18
as conflict-related violations against children, 24–25

Trade, prohibiting in small arms and light weapons, 63

Trafficking
on gender-based violence, 162
separation from, 4
for sexual exploitation, 23, 26, 161

Transactional sex, risk of, for unaccompanied or separated children, 148

Transitional Federal Government, in Somalia, 10

Transitional justice, 38, 60, 66
mechanisms of, 70–72, 74–75

Transition gap between humanitarian and development operations, 173

Traumatized mothers, counselling, 131

Truth and reconciliation commissions
children's participation in, 35, 38, 71
mechanisms of, 70–71
in Sierra Leone, 35, 38, 181

Tuberculosis (TB), 124, 125

Turkey
armed conflict in, 30
identification as conflict-affected country, 26, 27

Tutu, Desmond, 89–90

U

Uganda
abduction in, 24
armed conflict in, 30
births in, 30
child participation in peacebuilding in, 35, 36
child recruitment in, 152
Christian Children's Fund in, 107
crimes against children in, 68
development in war-torn areas of, 30
early childhood development pro-grammes in, 109
'Empowering Hands' in, 155
grave violations against children in, 47, 84
health services in, 124, 125
HIV in, 143
identification as conflict-affected country, 26, 27
justice and reconciliation in, 72
malnutrition in, 30
mortality rate of children in, 20, 30
participatory research with adolescents in, 35
poverty in, 30
psychosocial support programmes in, 139
reviving education in, 117–118
school attendance in, 30
sexual violence in, 23, 163
vulnerability in, 159

Under-Secretary-General for Peacekeeping Operations, 26

UNESCO, 117

UNHCR, 117

UNICEF, 45, 54, 60, 65, 83–84, 112, 135
in Aceh, 177
Back-to-School Campaign in Afghanistan, 117
Cape Town Principles, 152
Core Commitments for Children in Emergencies, 93, 136, 142–143